THE SPENSERIAN POETS

To *KATHLEEN* and *GEOFFREY TILLOTSON*

Heere could I write what you deserve of praise
Others might weare but I should win the bayes

THE SPENSERIAN POETS

A study in Elizabethan and Jacobean poetry by

JOAN GRUNDY

EDWARD ARNOLD

© Joan Grundy 1969

First published 1969 by
Edward Arnold (Publishers) Ltd
41 Maddox Street, London W1

SBN: 7131 5457 8

Printed in Great Britain by
C. Tinling & Co. Ltd., Prescot, Lancs

Preface

This book grew out of my work in preparation for an edition of the poems of William Browne, begun several years ago in collaboration with Professor Geoffrey Tillotson. It was Professor Tillotson who first suggested that I should write it, and my debt to him, both for many stimulating conversations, and for the generous loan of his unpublished B.Litt. thesis on Browne, and other papers, is great indeed. My debt to Professor Kathleen Tillotson is evident on many of the pages that follow. Everyone who works on Drayton feels gratitude to the editors of the noble Shakespeare Head edition, and Professor Tillotson's acute and sensitive commentary and impeccable scholarship have been a constant inspiration and delight to me.

I should like also to record an earlier debt, to my former teacher, the late F. P. Wilson, who supervised my work for a master's degree on the poetry of Giles Fletcher. What I owe to his original guidance, on this subject, and on all things Elizabethan, is quite incalculable.

My thanks are likewise due to my friend Miss Elizabeth Corney, who read some of this book at an early stage and made helpful comments, and to my friend and colleague, Dr. Katharine Worth, who read the completed manuscript, and who has given generous advice on the many occasions when I have sought it. My nephew, Mr. Stephen Satterthwaite, helped in the correction of my manuscript and in the preparation of the Index. I should like to express my thanks to him; to Miss Margaret Burton, of the Department of English of the University of Liverpool, who typed some of the early drafts; and to Mrs. P. Barry, of the Department of English, Royal Holloway College, University of London, who coped so cheerfully with the final version.

Textual note

Quotations from Drayton are from the Shakespeare Head edition: *The Works of Michael Drayton*, ed. J. William Hebel, 5 vols., B. H. Blackwell, Ltd., 1931–41 (Vol. V, Introduction, Notes, and Variant Readings, by Kathleen Tillotson and Bernard H. Newdigate); from Wither, from the 1622 edition of *Juvenilia* (British Museum copy: 1076. c. 20), and, for works later than 1622, from the Spenser Society reprint, 20 vols., 1871–82; from Giles and Phineas Fletcher, from their *Poetical Works*, ed. Frederick S. Boas, in Cambridge English Classics, 2 vols., 1908–9, except for Phineas Fletcher's 'Epithalamion', which is quoted from Ethel Seaton's edition of *Venus and Anchises*, Royal Society of Literature, 1926. Browne's *Britannia's Pastorals* is quoted from the 1616 edition (Bodleian copy: Douce B 780), *The Shepheards Pipe* from the 1614 edition (British Museum copy: 11623.a.4) and his other poems from the original manuscripts.

Quotations from Spenser are from *The Poetical Works of Edmund Spenser*, ed. J. C. Smith and E. de Selincourt, Oxford University Press.

'When I saw that Clumsy Crow' is reprinted from *Words for the Wind* by Theodore Roethke, The Macmillan Company, New York (1958).

In all quotations I have silently altered 'u' to 'v' and have printed contractions in full with the exception of ampersand.

vi

Contents

Abbreviations

Ap.	*The Locusts, or Apollyonists*
B.P.	*Britannia's Pastorals*
B.R.	*Britain's Remembrancer*
C.V.T.	*Christs Victorie, and Triumph*
D.W.W.	*Du Bartas his Devine Weekes and Workes*
E.H.E.	*Englands Heroicall Epistles*
F.Q.	*The Faerie Queene*
F.V.	*Faire-Virtue, the Mistress of Phil 'Arete*
Hebel	*The Works of Michael Drayton*, edited by J. William Hebel
Lans. 777	British Museum manuscript Lansdowne 777
M.E.	*The Muses Elizium*
P.E.	*Piscatorie Eclogs*
P.I.	*The Purple Island*
P.L.	*Paradise Lost*
P.O.	*Poly-Olbion*
Sarum	Salisbury Cathedral Library manuscript T.2.45 (*Britannia's Pastorals*, Book III)
S.C.	*The Shepheardes Calender*
S.G.	*The Shepheards Garland*
S.H.	*The Shepheards Hunting*
S.P.	*The Shepheards Pipe*
S.S.	*The Shepheards Sirena*
S.Purg.	*The Schollers Purgatory*
Sp. Soc.	*The Works of George Wither*, Spenser Society edition
W.M.	*Wither's Motto*

.

Introduction

Writers on Donne in this century have often sought to bring out
his quality by comparing him with Spenser, in terms unfavour-
able to the latter. There is not room in English literature, they seem to
feel, for both a prince of poets and a monarch of wit. Spenser accordingly has become a hoary Hyperion, swept from the throne by Donne,
the young Apollo. When zeal runs high, the contrast may even be,
rather, that of Hyperion to a satyr, with Donne, of course, as the dazzling Hyperion. Thus Spenser is linked with Du Bartas as, along
with him, the chief exemplar of a poetry that before Donne ('Enfin
Malherbe vint!')

had become either emptily decorative or crudely vehicular of 'messages' regarded
as being more important than the poems themselves.[1]

In this statement even the word 'become' is derogatory, suggesting a
degeneration: one wonders what the character of Elizabethan poetry
was *before* it thus degenerated in Spenser. Or *The Faerie Queene* is
referred to contemptuously as 'the thing': 'No-one has yet interpreted
the thing satisfactorily.'[2] Mr. Alvarez, the author of this last statement,
goes on to explain that the obscurity of which he is complaining is not
the result of any profound or original thought; on the contrary,
Spenser may be being obscure for precisely the opposite reason:
'because it [the poem] is so muddled that he could hardly be considered
to be thinking at all.'[3] Dr. Johnson's famous pronouncement on the
Metaphysicals may, he suggests, be re-written as

[1] Robin Skelton, 'The Poetry of John Donne', *Elizabethan Poetry*, Stratford-Upon-Avon
Studies II (1960), 204.
[2] A. Alvarez, *The School of Donne* (1961), 23.
[3] *ibid.*, 23.

To write on Donne's plan it was at least necessary to live and think; to write on Spenser's, to read and to write.[4]

Judgements so crude and ill-founded are scarcely worth refuting. Apart from the injustice to Spenser, today's increasing emphasis on Donne's traditionalism is already making them look silly. I quote them merely as extreme examples of the kind of prejudice the critical partisanships of the twentieth century have produced. The lyrics of Donne, as F. P. Wilson says, have 'gone to the head of the twentieth century',[5] and to the unsteady vision of the intoxicated the solid corpus of Spenser's work has appeared to dwindle and dissolve. As for that of his followers, it has disappeared altogether. 'Nobody worries about *them*,' says Mr. Alvarez, of Giles Fletcher, Southwell, and Quarles. For Mr. Patrick Cruttwell they exist only as a faceless, indistinguishable collection of nonentities – 'the Daniels and Draytons and Fulke Grevilles', even 'the Spensers and the Draytons'.[6] (Literary prejudice is evidently a great leveller.) The Pelican Guide to English Literature, which relegates Spenser to the Age of Chaucer, gives a page to Drayton, but the merest passing reference to the other poets who are my concern. If not quite sunk without trace, they are, at best, buried in literary history, and covered over with those two narrow words, *Hic iacet*.

I want to take them out of literary history and to look at what is still vital and distinctive in them. This study is accordingly not concerned to trace the course of Spenser's influence through the seventeenth century; 'influence' is, in fact, not my main consideration at all. Many writers, from Barnfield to Yeats, have felt the influence of the poets' poet; but that is another story. The writers I am concerned with both admired and imitated Spenser and shared his values. They sought consciously to maintain and extend into the seventeenth century his methods and values, and in doing so they became the chief bridge between him and Milton. This is an important side to their work, but it is not the only side, nor even the most interesting. Rather, Spenser's was for them the kind of service in which they found perfect freedom: by giving them the security of a tradition, he gave them also liberty to

---

[4] *ibid.*, 44.
[5] F. P. Wilson, *Elizabethans and Jacobeans* (1945), 54.
[6] Patrick Cruttwell, *The Shakespearian Moment* (1954), 62, 67.

be themselves, and it is, finally, as themselves that they have value for us.

The poets I refer to comprise two groups: on the one hand, Michael Drayton, William Browne, and George Wither, with whom were also associated the lesser writers Christopher Brooke and John Davies of Hereford, and, on the other, the brothers Giles and Phineas Fletcher. The grouping is in each case a matter of fact, not simply of critical convenience, an alliance based on shared tastes and aims, as well as on friendship and consanguinity. And although the two groups wrote independently of each other (except for some rather doubtful suggestion of 'borrowings' between Phineas Fletcher's fisher-play, *Sicelides*, and parts of Browne's *Britannia's Pastorals*), they have many affinities, including but not limited to their common devotion to Spenser, which allow them often to be treated as one.

Our present-day neglect of these writers is easily understood. Like Spenser, they wrote long poems, all of them such as to provide strong support for Coleridge's dictum that a long poem will not be all poetry. They wrote many other kinds of poem besides, and, with the exception of Giles Fletcher, they wrote voluminously. Their work is often bad: careless, turgid, long-winded, derivative and dull. To a modern reader intent upon an Arnoldian pursuit of 'the best, the very best', they must appear deserving of one fate only: oblivion. Even readers of less exacting standards must shrink from facing them in bulk. To enjoy them thoroughly one must, perhaps, have a genuine taste for minor poetry, and a capacity, certainly not for indulgence, but at any rate for patience, where their faults are concerned.

I think also that it would be true to say that their bulk, which is the most daunting, is also in a sense the most saving thing about them. They wrote so much, that is, that there was room for them to be often very good, as well as often very bad. If excellence was a hit or miss affair with them, they at least managed to hit as often as they missed. The result is that they really are, despite their faults, considerable poets. Other periods have found them so: leaving aside their own century for the time being, they were greatly admired in the late eighteenth century and in the Romantic period. The Romantic poets seem to have assumed a knowledge of and pleasure in the work of Drayton, Browne, and Wither to be quite natural. Wordsworth was sufficiently familiar with Browne's *Pastorals* to be reminded of a passage from it by Dorothy's comments on a fine scene, during their tour of the Highlands.[7] Keats used some lines from the same poem for a motto before his 'Epistle to George Felton Mathew,' and has many echoes and imitations of Browne in his poetry.[8] Lamb's devotion to Wither and his 'darling rhyme' (the septasyllabic couplet of *Faire-Virtue*) is well known. Clare praises Browne for a very Clare-like passage, and regrets that Johnson's *Lives* did not start with such poets as Spenser and Drayton.[9] It could be argued that our understanding of the Romantic period's Elizabethan revival is distorted, if we limit it to the major authors – Shakespeare, Spenser, Milton – and forget these lesser writers.

Equally, it could be argued that our modern neglect of them, combined with our emphasis upon the Metaphysical 'line,' has distorted our view of their own period. Our map of the period is curiously empty: one gets the impression that the only choice for readers of the day was between Donne and Jonson and their respective followers. In fact, the field was far richer. Literary schools are in part the creation of literary historians: we tend to see in the seventeenth century a few severely parallel lines, whereas what actually existed was a tissue of interconnecting relationships. The Spenserians were evidently well thought of in their own day, respected by many, and enthusiastically admired by some. They had a public, even if, as they were well aware, it was not a courtly one. Wither was for a time a best-seller; his works were aimed, quite frankly, at 'vulgar capacities', and their very success earned him scorn among those who considered themselves above the vulgar, including, most notably, Ben Jonson. Jonson, on the other hand, wrote commendatory verses for Browne's *Britannia's Pastorals*, Book II. Abraham Holland, son of Philemon, the translator of Pliny's *Natural History*, addressed enthusiastic verses to Browne and Drayton jointly.

---

[7] *Journals of Dorothy Wordsworth*, ed. William Knight (1930), 278. Dorothy, describing 'one of the most splendid moonlight prospects that can be conceived', writes 'I should have liked to have seen a bevy of Scottish ladies sailing, with music, in a gay barge.' She continues, 'William, to whom I have read this, tells me that I have used the very words of Browne of Ottery, Coleridge's fellow-townsman.' She then quotes B.P.II.2. (sig. F2r) beginning 'As I have seen when on the breast of Thames . . .'.
[8] See my article, 'Keats and William Browne', in *Review of English Studies*, n.s.VI, (1955), 44–52.
[9] *Letters of John Clare*, ed. J. W. and Anne Tibble (1951), 255. In a letter to John Taylor, 24 July, 1831, Clare writes 'In the Vol of old Poets I very much admire those of William Brown. There is a freshness & beauty about them that supprised me & with which I was not acquainted – there is much english landscape about them & the second song of Britannia's Pastorals commences with one of these'. He adds, 'after all what dissapointment to see Wither in little.' His allusion to Spenser and Drayton occurs in his Journal, 10th Oct., 1824 (*The Prose of John Clare*, ed. Tibble (1951), 113).

The popular writer, Richard Brathwait, did the same for Browne and Wither in his *Strappado for the Divell* (1615). Apart from Wither (and, if we consider only his pastoral poems, not even excluding him), the audience these poets sought and achieved was an educated, cultured one, composed principally perhaps of people like themselves, students and university men, but including women also – not the intellectual élite, but an audience nevertheless of wit and sense and refinement. The first group – Drayton, Browne, and Wither – addressed themselves principally to a London audience; the second – Giles and Phineas Fletcher – had their centre in Cambridge, where they could almost be said to have formed a school of their own. (H. E. Cory has, in fact, written of 'the School of the Fletchers'.)[10] Their work was published at Cambridge; most of Phineas' has its setting and was probably actually written there. (Whenever his name appears – as it does not always – on the title-page, he adds 'Of King's College, Cambridge'.) A. B. Langdale has shown that the Fletchers had their own literary circle at Cambridge during the first decade of the century; it included John Tomkins, organist of King's College, and such friends of Phineas as William Woodford, Anthony Cook, and Samuel Collins.[11] Later Phineas became the friend of the strange and fascinating Edward Benlowes and, through him, of Quarles. Benlowes's poem *Theophila*, of which Douglas Bush rightly says that it 'represents metaphysical religious poetry *in excelsis* and *in extremis*',[12] has clear links with, as well as echoes of, the work of the Fletchers. Cory includes in the 'School of the Fletchers' 'most of the Cantabrigians, Crashaw, Joseph Beaumont, Thomas Robinson, and others'.[13] Of these, the most interesting as an example of faithful discipleship is Robinson's *Legend of Mary Magdalene* (*c.* 1620), written in imitation of Giles Fletcher's *Christs Victorie, and Triumph* (1610). But Crashaw is, of course, the most noteworthy. Giles Fletcher is often named in studies of Crashaw as the chief exemplar before him of 'the Baroque sensibility' in English, but the existence of a direct connection between their work has been strangely ignored.[14]

[10] Herbert E. Cory, *Spenser, the School of the Fletchers, and Milton*, (*University of California Publications in Modern Philology*, II, 5, 1912).
[11] A. B. Langdale, *Phineas Fletcher, Man of Letters, Science and Divinity* (Columbia, 1937), 46.
[12] Bush, *English Literature in the Earlier Seventeenth Century* (1945), 150.
[13] Cory, *op. cit.*, 314.
[14] Joan Bennett, *Five Metaphysical Poets* (1964), 96, referring to the Spanish and Italian influences upon Crashaw, speaks of his style's 'deviation from any of the dominant schools of poetry in the England of his day'. But at Cambridge, when Crashaw was there, the Fletchers were a 'dominant school'.

And, to return to the other group, there are slight but unmistakable signs in their verse that both Vaughan and Marvell knew the work of Browne. Clearly both have read him with pleasure – pleasure above all, no doubt, in his natural descriptions. However finely and (almost) inperceptibly, something from him has sifted down on to their work, making its own small contribution to that modulation from the Metaphysical to something at any rate vaguely suggestive of the Romantic that we notice in both, though especially in Vaughan.

The Spenserians, then, offered to contemporary readers an acceptable alternative to the poetry of Jonson and Donne; a fashionable person could have been caught reading them without necessarily feeling an impulse to hide the book. Nor was it only an alternative they provided: they could, on occasion, write in the modern way too. Twentieth-century criticism, when it has noticed these poets at all, has tended to see them as hopeless stick-in-the-muds. 'But the Daniels and Draytons and Fulke Grevilles survived and wrote on, unchanged,' writes Mr. Cruttwell, 'worthy and honourable writers, but irredeemably limited – and outside their limits was the capacity to change their tune with the changing age.'[15] Drayton, mentioned here, is the Grand Old Man of these poets. Forty years old when James I's reign began, he lived to the age of sixty-eight, writing all the time. To describe him as incapable of changing his tune betrays great ignorance, for not only was Drayton as inveterate a reviser of his work as Yeats, but his revisions, particularly in his sonnet-sequence *Idea*, were all designed to reduce the Elizabethan character of his work and to make it more contemporary in tone. A man who in 1619 at the age of fifty-six could produce 'Since ther's no helpe, Come let us kisse and part' was not hopelessly wedded to the *Amoretti*, even if in 1627 he demonstrated his still-continuing love of the old order by publishing *The Miseries of Queene Margarite*. Lyrics like 'The Cryer' and 'The Heart', also published in 1619, have felt the breath of the new age upon them as surely as have the songs of the Cavaliers. As for the younger poets, Wither's

> Shall I wasting in despair
> Die because a woman's fair?

has probably often been mistaken for Suckling's. Certainly it was not produced under the influence of Spenser. Browne's epitaph on the

[15] Cruttwell, *op.cit.*, 62.

Countess of Pembroke has repeatedly been attributed to Jonson, solely, it seems, because it was considered too good to be by anyone else. A fine elegy of his, 'Is Death so great a gamester?', was originally attributed to Donne, and was printed as his by Waldron in 1802, and again by Grosart. Donne's influence, chiefly that of the 'Epicedes and Obsequies' and the 'Letters to Several Personages', is in fact traceable in several of Browne's elegies and lyrics. Phineas Fletcher has religious lyrics that anticipate (or, it may even be, copy) Herbert's (and occasionally Vaughan's) in manner; in his longer poems, as in his brother Giles's, the patristic wit gives him almost as much common ground with Donne as the allegory does with Spenser. Wither too, in his *Hymnes and Songs of the Church* (1623) and his *Haleluiah* (1641), shows that he shares the ideals and something of the form and manner of Herbert. Religious feeling, at any rate when lyrically expressed, seems in the seventeenth century to reduce literary as well as doctrinal differences: the lyrics of Wither and the Fletchers, like those of Donne and Herbert, can be fruitfully related to the meditative mode expounded by Professor Martz.

While, therefore, it would be a mistake to claim these poets as unacknowledged Metaphysicals, it should at least be clear that, as Brooks and Hardy have said, their poetry and that of the Metaphysicals did not present itself to Milton and his contemporaries in clear-cut opposition.[16] To press their Metaphysical qualities further than this would be to do them a disservice, for it is not here, in my opinion, that their positive achievement lies. The Spenserians were deeply and positively conservative: they looked back to the past with a conscious and aggressive nostalgia. Without rejecting everything in their own period, they disliked a good deal both in its literature and its society, and were aware of themselves as, in part at least, outsiders. A relevant comparison, up to a point, is with the Georgians of the present century. Like the Georgians, the Spenserians cling to old traditions while a new one is fashioning. They are even, in part, the same traditions, or at any rate the same values: patriotism, the English countryside, and the cult of pure beauty matter greatly to both groups. This comparison with the Georgians is, however, probably more damaging than I intend it to be; there is a bankruptcy in the worst of the Georgians that is certainly not characteristic of the Spenserians. But the Georgians are themselves now undergoing a reappraisal, in which, it is to be hoped, justice will be

16 Cleanth Brooks and J. E. Hardy, *Poems of Mr. John Milton* (1645) (1951), 242.

done to such poets as Blunden and Edward Thomas. The Spenserians, like these two, combine with their traditionalism a robust independence and strength: they are, after all their imitativeness, uniquely and happily themselves. Their very derivativeness, as I suggested earlier, seems to set them free to accomplish something new. They are undisciplined writers, but, because of this, expansive ones: their personalities and spirits alike expand in their poetry, for the writing of poetry is for them a supremely enjoyable activity, releasing and invigorating. In addition, they have real gifts, of feeling and imagination. They sought to be at once the amateurs and professionals of poetry, amateurs in their rejection of discipline, their insistent self-pleasing; professionals in their emphasis on the distinction of the poet's office. Among seventeenth-century poets, they more than anyone (and largely because of the freedom they take to themselves) have recognisable and genuine affinities with the Romantics, in mood and in manner. Obviously there are important differences too, yet it is not hard to understand the Romantics' liking for them. 'We were the *first* Romantics' would be an exaggerated claim for them, but one not wholly ridiculous.

These statements I hope to substantiate in the course of this study. Meanwhile, since these poets are still so little known, it may be helpful to the reader if I give here the principal facts concerning their work and careers. This will involve some discussion of the question of status, of their relationship with patrons and public, a matter which was always of great moment to the Spenserians.

Drayton, the oldest of them (1563-1631), began publishing early in the fifteen-nineties. He was a professional in the strict sense: poetry, that is, was his vocation, and he sought to earn his living by it. He wrote to publish, not to keep his verses 'in cabinets' and pass them round only 'by transcription', as he complained in 1612 was the new fashion. As a professional, he sought to achieve mastery in most of the poetic 'kinds': sonnet, pastoral, erotic epyllion, tragical legend, heroical epistle, historical poem, ode, satire, and epic (if *Poly-Olbion* may be so regarded). The study of his work is complicated by re-publications and revisions which are often so drastic as to amount to re-writing. His pastorals, *Idea The Shepheards Garland* (1593), were later altered and enlarged to become the *Eglogs* of 1606. His sonnet-sequence, *Ideas Mirrour* (1594), later *Idea*, underwent various changes and augmentations through successive editions, up to and including that of 1619. *Endimion and Phœbe* (1595), his contribution to the genre of mythological love-narrative popularised by Marlowe and Shakespeare, reappeared, having undergone a metamorphosis startling as any in Ovid, as *The Man in the Moone* (1606). *Mortimeriados*, his heroic historical poem on the reign of Edward II (1596), was re-cast and largely rewritten as *The Barons Warres* (1603). British history was always for him *the* subject; it led also to his *Legends*, of *Matilda, Peirs Gaveston*, and *Robert of Normandy*, for all of which substantially different versions exist, dating variously from 1593 to 1619, and to one other, the *Legend of Great Cromwell* (1607), which underwent relatively little change in successive editions. This historical interest bore late fruit in *The Battaile of Agincourt* and *The Miseries of Queene Margarite* (both 1627), but undoubtedly its choicest product was *Englands Heroicall Epistles*, first published in 1597, but re-published, augmented, and, inevitably, revised subsequently, though rather less drastically than usual.

Most of the poems so far mentioned belong originally to the reign of Elizabeth. Drayton's *magnum opus*, the chorographical *Poly-Olbion*, was also begun then (before 1600), but was not published until 1612 (eighteen songs) and 1622 (thirty songs). It was during James's reign that Drayton produced his most embittered poems, the satires *The Owle* (1604) and *The Moone-Calfe* (1627), and his most serene, the lovely *Shepheards Sirena* and *Quest of Cynthia* (both 1627), and *The Muses Elizium* (1630). *Nimphidia* too belongs to this period, as do his various odes and elegies, and the Biblical narratives, *Moses his Birth and Miracles* (a revision of an earlier poem), *David and Goliath*, and *Noahs Floud*. Parts of some of these poems probably antedate their publication by a number of years; the last part of *The Shepheards Sirena*, for example, was probably written in 1614.[17]

Drayton's endeavours to live by his pen (we never hear of his seeking office or preferment of any kind) also led him for a time into dramatic collaboration, in the service of Henslowe. Of the two dozen plays upon which he collaborated only one, *Sir John Oldcastle*, survives. He appears to have depended a good deal on his patrons and friends, and to have preferred it when they were one and the same, as indeed they often were. He made much use of the Dedication, but without ever becom-

---

[17] See Kathleen Tillotson, Hebel, V, 207-8.

ing servile; he saw it as more than a formality, as something which honoured the recipient as much as the donor:

Some say this use beganne by the *Heroes* and brave spirits of the old world, which were desirous to bee thought to patronize learning; and men in requitall honour the names of those brave Princes.[18]

It is typical of him therefore that *The Battaile of Agincourt* should be dedicated

To you those Noblest of Gentlemen, of these Renowned Kingdomes of Great *Britaine:* who in these declining times, have yet in your brave bosomes the sparkes of that sprightly fire, of your couragious Ancestors.[19]

One such noble gentleman was Sir Walter Aston, a frequent recipient of Drayton's dedications, from 1602 to the collected edition of 1619. Others included Henry Cavendish, step-son of the Earl of Shrewsbury, and Lucy Harington, Countess of Bedford, to whom some of Drayton's earliest poems were dedicated. But Cavendish, whom he describes as a Maecenas, appears to have disappointed him, and the Countess offended him, and their names accordingly quickly disappear from his pages. Drayton could be as spirited and proud as Dr. Johnson in these matters. His one serious blunder was in rushing to celebrate James I's accession in a poem, *To the Majestie of King James*, without first lamenting Elizabeth. It was an attempt to forestall all comers in the bid for royal patronage, but earned Drayton only a royal snub, which soured James's reign for him from the start.

Drayton's most constant patrons were, of course, the Goodere family – first, Sir Henry, in whose home at Polesworth Hall in Warwickshire he had served as a page, then Sir Henry's descendants, his daughter Frances and her cousin and husband Sir Henry Goodere (friend of Donne), and above all Anne, his younger daughter, and her husband Sir Henry Rainsford. Drayton's life-long devotion to Anne Goodere, a truly Platonic affection – she was the *Idea* of his sonnets – yet warm and human too, is impressive and endearing. ('Where I love, I love for years,' he wrote to Drummond of Hawthornden.) Throughout his adult life he was accustomed to spend the summer months at

[18] Dedication to 'Maister *James Huish*', Epistles of Elinor Cobham and Duke Humphrey, *E.H.E.* (1599). Reprinted Bernard H. Newdigate, *Michael Drayton and his Circle* (1941), 85.
[19] Hebel, III, 2.

her house in the village of Clifford Chambers. He continued too to visit
the family house at Polesworth, occupied by Frances and the younger
Sir Henry. Thus, though he was often in London, Drayton, like Shakespeare, never lost touch with his native Warwickshire; part of him, at
least, remained 'rooted in one dear perpetual place'.

Earlier, I compared Drayton with Yeats for the assiduity of his
revisions and re-writings. It is tempting to extend the comparison and
to see in Anne Goodere an Elizabethan parallel to Maud Gonne.
Certainly, though the passion she inspired was clearly much less
feverish, Anne Goodere was the activating force – the patron-saint as
well as the patron – of Drayton's poetry, as Maud Gonne was of
Yeats's. When we think, however, of Drayton's visits to her home and
calm relationship with herself and her husband, she becomes, rather,
his Lady Gregory. Such resemblances are the result equally of temperament and circumstance. In both Drayton's case and Yeats's, a romantic,
ardent nature led the poet to a single-minded, life-long devotion to
poetry as well as to a woman; and, each poet being penniless, each was
led into a dependence on patronage and friendship to supplement the
uncertain rewards of print.

Drayton had many friends and acquaintances among contemporary
poets, including Shakespeare, Jonson, and Chapman. A commendatory
poem by Christopher Brooke before his *Legend of Great Cromwell* (1607)
shows that his friendship with Brooke dates at least from this time.
Brooke was an Inns of Court man, and it may have been he who first
introduced Drayton to William Browne, who, when he began to
publish, was a student at the Inner Temple. It may equally well have
been the jurist, John Selden, who supplied notes to the first part of
Poly-Olbion (1612), and the following year ventured into verse to
praise Browne's *Britannia's Pastorals;* a note on Browne's very first page
mentions 'my very learned friend Mr. Selden'. The nature of the
literary group centred on the Inns of Court, which flourished round
about the years 1612-1615 and had Drayton, Browne, Brooke, Wither,
and John Davies of Hereford as its chief members, will be discussed in
Chapter IV (on Pastoral). A word may be said here about the friendship between Browne and Brooke, which developed for a time into
almost a literary alliance. Brooke, the close friend of Donne and witness
of his marriage, addressed by him at the beginning of 'The Storme' as
'Thou which art I', was considerably Browne's senior. He and Browne
appeared together in print with their *Two Elegies* on the death of

Prince Henry (1613). Then in *The Shepheards Pipe* (1614), Browne addressed an eclogue to Brooke, and Brooke one to him. Verses by the two poets also appear in close proximity in the 1614 edition of *Englands Helicon*. In his eclogue, Browne urges Brooke to produce something in the heroic vein of which he is capable. Brooke's answer to the appeal, it would appear, is *The Ghost of Richard III*, which also appeared in 1614, accompanied by commendatory verses from Browne. Browne seems to have thought highly of Brooke's talents, more highly, perhaps, than any other reader before or since. He writes generally in a grave, moralising way that links him with such writers as Chapman and Greville. *The Ghost*, as its title suggests, belongs to the old-fashioned genre of the tragical legend. Brooke is a competent versifier, but no poet. One wonders what Donne thought of his friend's literary efforts. I shall not consider Brooke further in this study, but his place in the picture, even if low down in the corner, should be remembered.

Davies of Hereford was another contributor to *The Shepheards Pipe* who belonged to the older generation. His sombre allegory, *Humours Heav'n on Earth*, might have given him a place in this study, but on the whole neither his allegiance to Spenser nor his quality seemed to warrant it. It is interesting to notice the encouragement given to the young Browne and Wither by these three elder writers. No doubt they saw in them the hope for poetry among the younger generation. Drayton's friendship for Browne developed into a permanent and deep affection: in the Elegy addressed to Henry Reynolds (1627) he is named as 'my Browne', one of

> My deare companions whom I freely chose
> My bosome friends.

The first book of Browne's *Britannia's Pastorals* appeared in 1613. It was reprinted, along with the second book, in 1616. There was a further edition in 1625. A fragmentary third exists in manuscript in Salisbury Cathedral. Browne's other large-scale work, not so far mentioned, is the *Inner Temple Masque*, which was written for performance in January, 1615, but not printed until 1772. In addition, he wrote many short poems – elegies, epistles, odes, sonnets – which are collected in Lansdowne Manuscript 777, in the British Museum.

The fact that Browne left almost as much verse in manuscript as he did in print suggests that he was less of a professional in poetry than

Drayton. He was also more successful in obtaining powerful patronage. We have only Anthony à Wood's statement as testimony to the fact that Browne ever lived in the Herbert household at Wilton. The many poems he wrote commemorating members of the Herbert family would seem to verify it however. Although the 1616 edition of the *Pastorals* was dedicated to William Herbert, Earl of Pembroke, it seems in fact to have been Pembroke's brother, Philip, Earl of Montgomery, who did most for Browne. Montgomery was guardian and later father-in-law of Robert Dormer, later Earl of Carnarvon, to whome Browne was tutor at Eton and then at Oxford (1623-4). In 1640 we find Browne still praying for 'my honoured lord the Lord Chamberlain' (Philip Herbert, now Earl of Pembroke), and 'my good lord and master the Earl of Carnarvon'.[20]

Wither's history is more complicated. His works fill twenty volumes in the Spenser Society reprint (1871-82), but they include practically everything up to the *Fragmenta Prophetica* of 1667. I limit myself to the early works, up to and including *Haleluiah* (1641). These are sufficiently numerous: they include *Faire-Virtue, the Mistress of Phil'Arete*, written according to Wither when he was very young, but not printed until 1622, probably having undergone some revision; *Abuses Stript and Whipt*, a collection of satires, apparently first published in 1613, when it brought imprisonment upon the author (there *may* have been an earlier edition in 1611); *The Shepheards Hunting* (1615), a collection of eclogues celebrating both his satires and his imprisonment; *Fidelia* (1615), a long verse-epistle 'to her unconstant friend'; and *Wither's Motto* (1621), a long, moralising, partly satirical verse-essay. It will be seen from this list that the satyr and shepherd who appear together on the title-page of his collected *Juvenilia* (1622) were appropriate insignia. But Wither also has a reputation as a hymn-writer and metrical translator of the psalms, his chief works in this category being the *Hymnes and Songs of the Church* (1623), the *Psalms of David* (1632), and *Haleluiah*. Other works of his which I shall take into consideration are *Britain's Remembrancer* (1628), a description of the plague of 1625 containing prophecies concerning his country's future, of the accuracy of which Wither was always proud, and the *Collection of Emblemes* (1635).

Wither had a stormy career as a writer, and a strange one. The strangeness lies in the fact that, although his writings were mostly

---

[20] Letter to Sir Benjamin Rudyard, printed by A. H. Bullen, Introduction to Muses Library edn., I, xxv.

aimed at a popular audience – he speaks of 'vulgar capacities', 'the common people's capacities' – they sought, and often found, royal or noble patronage and protection. The rôle of popular teacher seems to have been one that he assumed increasingly as his enemies of a higher social class, irritated by his vaunted plain speech, increased also, rather than one sought deliberately from the start. Wither was, after all, an educated man of some scholarship, and his earliest works were addressed to readers of similar interests and culture. On the other hand, they quickly won a wider audience: *Abuses Stript and Whipt* ran into at least five editions in 1613, and another five during the next ten years. In *The Shepheards Hunting* Wither hints at popular sympathy for him in his imprisonment.

He could win sympathy in other quarters too. Princess Elizabeth, later Queen of Bohemia, was one of his earliest protectors; Wither remembers this in dedicating his *Psalms of David* to her in 1632. Wither's dedications are almost always addressed to the highest in the realm – to King James and his Queen, to Prince and, after his accession, King Charles, and to Queen Henrietta, and of course to such influential persons as the Herberts. (With a consistency more real than apparent, *Haleluiah* (1641) was dedicated to 'the Thrice Honourable The High Courts of Parliament, now assembled in the triple empire of the British Isles'.) In spite of this, he was twice imprisoned in this early period of his life: in 1614 for *Abuses Stript and Whipt*, and in 1621 for *Wither's Motto*. The former imprisonment was apparently procured by the machinations of his enemy, the Earl of Northampton, but can hardly have been, as John Peter suggests, for his 'uncomplimentary references to kings',[21] since Wither's royalist sympathies were at this date not in doubt. Neither imprisonment was for long, and from remarks made in a dedicatory poem to Philip Herbert before the *Emblemes* it appears that William Herbert, Earl of Pembroke, was instrumental on the second occasion in procuring his release and reconciling him to the king. So complete was the reconciliation that James 'bestow'd A Gift upon mee, which his *Bountie* show'd'.[22] This gift was a patent granting Wither sole rights – a monopoly for fifty-one years – in his *Hymnes and Songs of the Church*, then in preparation. (It was rare in those days for an author to maintain any right over his own work.) A further patent ordered that no copy of the Psalms in metre should be printed without

[21] John Peter, *Complaint and Satire in Early English Literature* (1956), 156.
[22] *A Collection of Emblemes* (1635), Fourth Book, sig. (x).

Wither's work too. Instead of the financial profit he had hoped for, all that this brought Wither was a prolonged quarrel with the Stationers' Company, in whose privilege the metrical psalter lay. The quarrel continued until 1635, when, according to the most recent investigator, Mr. Allan Pritchard, Wither conceded victory to the Stationers.[23] Meanwhile, Wither had been driven to 'imprint every sheet' of his *Britain's Remembrancer* 'with his own hand', because he could not get licence or help to do it.

This affair seems to mark the start of the decline of Wither's fortunes, his reputation, his talent; almost, in some degree, of his reason. The Dedications in his *Emblemes*, to the high and mighty of the land, have in them a note of desperation. The first is addressed to Charles and his queen, and signed 'Your MAIESTIES most Loyall Subject'. In the Civil War, Wither fought on the parliamentary side, but was not, it seems, an anti-monarchist. His addresses to Charles were from the start accompanied by outspoken criticism of him; he will ask him to be his Maecenas, as in *Britain's Remembrancer*, even while reproving his conduct. Small wonder that he ends that poem,

> I know, God will release
> My Body, or my Soule, againe in peace.
> To him alone, for *Patronage*, I run:
> *Lord, let thy* pleasure, *and thy* will *be done.*

The last twenty years or so of Wither's life are a record of poverty, petitions, 'grievances and longsufferings', and further imprisonments, accompanied by an endless flowing lava of verse. His position as an author in his early years, contending for court patronage yet seeking to instruct the people, is an interesting one. He was never, properly speaking, a hack-writer, since his poems were always the product of his own tastes and ideals. He seems to bestraddle many sections of Jacobean literary society, as for instance it has been described by Phoebe Sheavyn in her *Literary Profession in the Elizabethan Age*.

There remain the brothers, Giles and Phineas Fletcher. They both became clergymen, a fact which in itself sets them apart from the poets just considered. Both went to Cambridge, Phineas, the elder of the two, to King's College, Giles to Trinity, and both remained there for a

[23] Allan Pritchard, 'George Wither's Quarrel with the Stationers', *Studies in Bibliography*, XVI (1963), 30.

number of years, wearing out their lives and spirits in hopes of an academic preferment which finally eluded them, as it had eluded their father, Giles Fletcher the elder. Giles came nearer to success than Phineas: he became a preacher at St. Mary's, preached before King James in May, 1615, and in 1618 was appointed Reader in Greek at Trinity. Yet in 1619 he left Cambridge to become parish priest of the village of Alderton in Suffolk, where he died four years later. Similarly, Phineas finally resigned himself to the priesthood: after being chaplain in the household of Sir Henry Willoughby at Risley in Derbyshire from 1615 to 1621, he became Rector of Hilgay in Norfolk, remaining there for the rest of his life, and becoming, his prose devotional works seem to suggest, an exemplary pastor of his flock.

Giles Fletcher's poem *Christs Victorie, and Triumph* (he is virtually the poet of a single poem), was published in 1610. Fletcher was by then twenty-five. The dedication to Thomas Neville, Master of Trinity, speaks of a benefit conferred that is both 'fruitfull, and contenting for the time that is present' and 'hopefull, and promising for the time that is to come', which rather neatly makes of the poem both a thanks-offering and a solicitation. (It may have been Neville's death in 1615 that dashed his hopes.) Langdale, Phineas's biographer, is probably right in saying that both the Fletchers hoped to make their poetic talent the avenue of academic advancement, though it is difficult to know how much reliance they put upon it. Phineas has a Latin poem addressed to Sir Henry Wotton while the latter was ambassador at Venice, which is quite frankly a plea to be taken into his service, no doubt as one of his secretaries. His major Latin poem *Locustae* survives in three autograph manuscripts, dedicated respectively to the Bishop of Bath and Wells, to Prince Henry, and to Thomas Murray, tutor to Prince Charles. This looks like economy, but is rather a proof of desperate straits. The dedication to the Bishop speaks of his father's death and of his mother's plight, left with ten children to bring up. The bitterness and anguish of that to Murray bring vividly home to us his predicament, and that of others like him. Fletcher speaks of himself as a beggar, and of his 'Muses' as 'fellow-beggars with me'. 'Hard, even iron necessity,' he writes, 'has driven me to have recourse to thee, a man known to me by face only and by fame, and whom I have seen but once, and bound to me by no claim – and timidly to solicit a donation . . .'[24]

[24] Grosart, *The Poems of Phineas Fletcher, B.D.,I* (1869), lxviii. The original Latin is in Boas, I, 281–2.

Phineas Fletcher did not rush into print. Probably all his poems were written before he left Cambridge, though they may have been revised later, but none of them (apart from tributary verses to Elizabeth and James) had then been printed. This sets him, despite his iron necessity, with the gentlemen-amateurs among poets, rather than with the professionals, like Drayton and Wither. Publication came later: *Locustae, vel Pietas Jesuitica* in 1627 together with its English paraphrase, *The Locusts, or Apollyonists; Sicelides,* his fisher-play, in 1631; *The Purple Island, or the Isle of Man: Together with Piscatorie Eclogs and Other Poeticall Miscellanies,* in 1633; the *Sylva Poetica,* also in 1633. Fletcher put his name to the *Locustae* volume, his initials to *The Purple Island* and the *Sylva,* all printed at Cambridge. *Sicelides* is unacknowledged, perhaps pirated. It is a tedious drama, owing something, it would seem, to Italian pastoral plays such as *Filli di Scirum,* and was prepared for performance before King James on his visit to Cambridge in 1615, though he left without seeing it. Fletcher did well not to own it.

The *Piscatorie Eclogs* are very personal, often autobiographical, in reference, as are many of the miscellaneous poems. Such writing, however conventional in form, is as much a private matter as were the lyrics of Donne. This is also true of the verses and translations, many of them very fine, which appeared in Fletcher's prose treatise, *A Fathers Testament,* written for the benefit of his sons and not published until 1670, twenty years after his death.

The printing of *The Purple Island* was an unusual affair. It was undertaken with the aid of Benlowes, who could be regarded as Fletcher's patron as well as his friend, and was beautifully and expensively done. Some copies, evidently for presentation, contain engravings 'of a very personal nature'.[25] It is interesting to find here even print being used in the service of friendship.

In 1628 a poem called *Brittain's Ida,* 'written by that Renowned Poet, EDMOND SPENCER', was published. To anyone familiar with Fletcher's verse, his authorship of it is immediately apparent, but proof positive came in 1923, when Miss Ethel Seaton discovered in Sion College library a manuscript containing along with other known works of his a poem called *Venus and Anchises* which is virtually the same poem as *Brittain's Ida.* 'I am certainly assured by the ablest, and most knowing men,' Walkley the publisher had written, 'that it must

25 Harold Jenkins, *Edward Benlowes* (1952), 71.

be a Worke of *Spencers*.' Quarles in his commendatory poem before *The Purple Island* was to hail Fletcher as 'The *Spencer* of this age'. Abraham Holland too had found in Drayton 'our still reviving Spencer', while Browne had been greeted before the First Book of *Britannia's Pastorals* as 'our second Colin Clout.' In the face of such pronouncements, it may be salutary to recall John Lawlor's statement,

If we had lost the text of Chaucer, Spenser and Milton what we should reconstruct from the work of their disciples would be sadly less than the master-work.[26]

On the other hand, it would also be, not simply 'less', but 'other'. 'For it is the characteristic of discipleship in every age,' Professor Lawlor continues, 'to assimilate to itself certain single and simple aspects of a master-work which has triumphed in holding many things in balance.' The nature of that 'triumph' is the subject of my next chapter. In later chapters we shall look at those 'single and simple aspects', the single threads these poets extracted from the complex web which is the work of Spenser. But we shall look more closely at the designs that, with his encouragement and example, they wove for themselves.

[26] John Lawlor, *Piers Plowman, An Essay in Criticism* (1962), 319.

The Poetry of Spenser

'Of all the poets,' said Hazlitt of Spenser, 'he is the most poetical.' We today may not wholly approve of Hazlitt's notion of the 'poetical'; nevertheless, we know what he means, and can in part agree with him. Poems like the *Epithalamion* and *Prothalamion* seem to offer us the quintessential pleasures of poetry, considered as something at the farthest possible remove from prose – from the prose of everyday speech and everyday living: a music that, like the Lady's song in *Comus*, rises 'like a steam of rich distilled perfume'; striking images; rich, evocative, sensuous language; an elaborate verbal structure; and vividly communicated emotion. Parts at least of *The Faerie Queene* and *The Shepheardes Calender* offer similar delights. On such occasions, Spenser is, we feel, in an absolute sense a Poet.

Spenser's 'poeticalness', however, extends far beyond what either Hazlitt or we, when we give a casual assent to the description, have in mind. 'E.K.' tells us before the 'October' eclogue of *The Shepheardes Calender* that in its central character Cuddie 'is set out the perfecte paterne of a Poete.' But Spenser too exemplifies that pattern, and not merely accidentally or by reason of his natural gifts, but by deliberate intent. It is reflected in both his endeavour and his achievement. Finding himself by all the signs born to be the prince of poets in his time, Spenser deliberately groomed and fashioned himself for the rôle. Thus he fulfils not merely one, Romantic and post-Romantic, idea of what constitutes the 'poetical': he fulfils *any* idea, though above all that of his own time. The word 'poet' is stamped all the way through Spenser's work, as the name of a sea-side town is through a stick of rock. Part of his uniqueness lies in his very representativeness. He was perhaps the poets' poet because he was so pre-eminently the poet.

This impression is confirmed first of all by his professionalism: not primarily in the sense that his verse was written, most of it, for publication and in hopes of profit of one kind or another, though that is true too, but rather in the sense that it is carefully executed and covers all the major 'kinds' – pastoral, epic, lyric, sonnet, satire. It manifests a range and variety of skills, exercised in traditional and conventional modes. For a writer possessed of such an ambition or such a destiny as I have suggested, it was essential to prove himself master of all trades, jack of none. Spenser's achievement is accordingly comprehensive, almost encyclopædic, in its scope: if his contemporaries were impressed by it, it must have been, in part at least, simply because it was *there*.

There is more to a poet, however, than his skills: there is the question of the use to which he puts them. Spenser accepts, fervently and with conviction, the traditional and orthodox Renaissance doctrine that the poet's function is educative and directed to the common good; it is the faith which as a poet he tries to live by.

> O what an honor is it, to restraine
> The lust of lawlesse youth with good advice:
> Or pricke them forth with pleasaunce of thy vaine,
> Whereto thou list their trayned willes entice,

cries Piers to Cuddie in the 'October' eclogue. To dismiss this as an uninspired didactic ideal, advocating what amounts to a prostitution of pure poetry, is to miss the central inspiration of Spenser's verse. For Spenser, it is important to remember, belongs wholeheartedly to the humanist tradition: he sees poetry as a form of learning, and learning as the great civilising force. In Ireland, he would like to see the sons of lords and gentlemen compulsorily educated:

For learninge hath that wonderfull power of yt self that yt can soften and temper the most stearne and salvage nature.[1]

In England, apparently, he sees this educative function as devolving upon poets. In *The Teares of the Muses* he describes the 'girlond of Nobilitie' shaped by poets and those to whom they address themselves. The poets by their wisdom inspire

> learned Impes that wont to shoote up still
> And grow to hight of kingdomes government,

---

[1] *A View of the Present State of Ireland*, ed. W. L. Renwick (1934), 205.

encouraging in them virtuous deeds, which the poets then go on to celebrate. Unfortunately, at the time he wrote the poem, Spenser saw the garland as replaced by the vicious circle: no interest in the poet's 'celestiall skill', no good deeds, and consequently Clio's complaint, 'I nothing noble have to sing.' Yet *The Faerie Queene* refutes such despondency. The explanation to Ralegh of his intention to 'fashion a gentleman or noble person in vertuous and gentle discipline'; the pious hopes expressed in the dedicatory sonnets that 'redoubted lords' such as the Earl of Cumberland, in whom the flower of chivalry is now 'bloosming faire', may be inspired by the poem to the pursuit of honour and magnanimity; the all-comprehending dedication of the poem to Elizabeth herself—all testify to Spenser's continuing faith in the alliance between poetry and 'civilitie'. The personal perfection to which the poet points the way is seen as realising itself in terms of the public good.

Professor G. K. Hunter in his *John Lyly, the Humanist as Courtier* has portrayed for us the sixteenth-century humanist dream of influencing national politics. Spenser's is a poet's version of that dream. The ideal that inspires it links *The Faerie Queene* with such works as Elyot's *Book of the Governor* and More's *Utopia*. The 'noble humanist aim' summed up by Edmund Harvel,

To make all the land know *quam sit humaniter vivendum*, help to take out all barbarous customs, and bring the realm to an antique form of good living . . .[2]

was Spenser's also. It was not self-seeking alone that led him to associate poetry so closely with what we now call the Establishment. If he sought room at the top, he sought virtue there too. A hierarchical view of the universe made it natural that the virtues of civilisation should be seen as starting at the top, and it was there accordingly – in 'Princes pallace' – that the poet should exercise his skills. It was, moreover, traditionally the poet's right as well as his duty to do so, as Jonson recalls when he looks back enviously to the time when poets 'were wont to be the care of kings and happiest monarchs.'[3]

That poets were the first civilisers of mankind was for the Renaissance a commonplace of literary history, familiarised by Horace, and

[2] Quoted by G. K. Hunter, *op. cit.*, 28, from a letter from Harvel to Thomas Starkey, 18th June, 1531.
[3] *Volpone*, Dedication.

frequently repeated. Spenser in accepting this rôle for himself was proving himself one in an apostolic succession of poets going back to Orpheus and other 'first poets', Linus, Amphion, Musaeus, but especially Orpheus. It is significant that in the passage from 'October' already referred to, the power to restrain the lusts of lawless youth is linked with an Orphean power to bereave 'their soule of sence'. In one of the commendatory poems before *The Faerie Queene*, a certain 'R.S.' actually calls Spenser 'this Bryttane *Orpheus*', showing moreover by allusions to Spenser's 'hye drifts' and 'deepe conceites' that he recognises that he deserves the name for his matter, not merely for his ravishing melody. Spenser himself clearly intended the poem to be a modern equivalent of Orpheus's song, equally ravishing, equally influential. If Orpheus is the prime example – the 'perfecte paterne' – of a poet, then Spenser will be an *Orpheus Redivivus*.

Yet Orpheus was known to be more even than simply a teacher of morals and manners, and a captivating singer: tradition had it that he had been divinely inspired and had hymned the secrets of Creation. Spenser too hints that the knowledge revealed in *The Faerie Queene* is in origin secret, mysterious, fundamental, and not acquired by normal human means. His fullest statement on this matter comes in the Prologue to Book VI, in his plea to the Muses:

> Revele to me the sacred noursery
> Of vertue, which with you doth there remaine,
> Where it in silver bowre does hidden ly
> From view of men, and wicked worlds disda'ne.

Of Spenser's attitude to the Muses, Professor W. L. Renwick writes:

. . . the new poets believed. To the Pléiade and to Spenser the Muses represent something more real and more powerful than the decorative image they soon became in the neo-classic poetry of both countries, for, . . . they represent the power of God.[4]

C. S. Lewis agrees with him:

The invocation of the Muse hardly seems to be a convention in Spenser. We feel that his poetry has really tapped sources not easily accessible to discursive thought.[5]

[4] Renwick, *Edmund Spenser* (1957 edn.), 187.
[5] C. S. Lewis, *The Allegory of Love* (1953 edn.), 358.

I think that these two critics are right. Spenser's sense of the 'secret comfort' and 'heavenly pleasures' sent 'welling' into his mind by the mysterious access of poetic inspiration is too overwhelming for his statements concerning the Muses to be 'expressions merely tropical'. The Muses were for him not so much a fable as a necessary imaginative hypothesis. Through them he could express his feeling that the matters revealed in his poetry really did come to him from 'out there'. Thus in the invocation to Book I of *The Faerie Queene* he appears before us as a kind of antiquarian, transcribing material (truly primary material) provided by the Muse:

> Lay forth out of thine everlasting scryne
> The antique rolles, which there lye hidden still,
> Of Faerie knights and fairest *Tanaquill* . . .

Here he closely anticipates Blake, who says of his own 'Sublime Allegory',

I may praise it, since I dare not pretend to be any other than the Secretary; the Authors are in Eternity.[6]

And in Blake we recognise the Muse-poet, the Bard who present, past, and future sees. The description may be extended to Spenser also. Turn the Idea of the Poet which way we will, we still find Spenser answering to it.

But if Spenser is *vates*, he is also *poeta*, a maker, in Puttenham's sense ('because he makes verses'), but above all in Sidney's. Spenser's conformity to the idea of the poet presented in Sidney's *Apology* is so complete that it might be modelled upon it. *The Faerie Queene*, as Mr. A. C. Hamilton has shown, provides those images of a golden world which Sidney suggests are characteristic of the poet, images which, imitating the *noumenon* rather than the *phenomenon*, make the *poeta* one with the *vates*.[7] It provides too the outstanding Elizabethan example of 'that feigning notable images of virtues, vices, or what else, with that delightful teaching' which in his 'more ordinary opening' of the subject Sidney makes 'right distinguishing marks' to know a poet by. It provides the story which captures old and young alike: 'With a tale he

---

[6] *The Complete Writings of William Blake*, ed. Geoffrey Keynes (1957), 825.
[7] A. C. Hamilton, *The Structure of Allegory in The Faerie Queene* (1961), 15–29.

cometh to you, with a tale that holdeth children from play and old men from the chimney corner.' Spenser, as those who compare him with Donne too often forget, is a poet in this fundamental sense; he is a maker of *fictions*. He 'makes' people and places and stories, and apparently effortlessly and endlessly. In this respect a juster comparison would be with Dickens or Fielding rather than with Donne. Spenser has creative 'abundance' (the word is his own). In this, his endless inventiveness, we see most clearly the 'divine gift and heavenly instinct not to bee gotten by laboure and learning, but adorned with both' of which E. K. speaks before 'October'. Of *The Faerie Queene* we could say, as Dryden says of Chaucer, 'Here is God's plenty', and for Spenser such a comment would perhaps form the supreme recognition of his power as a poet. Scaliger, Sidney, Puttenham and others had pointed out in a general way the parallel between the poet's act of creation and God's. Tasso, however, in his *Discourses on the Heroic Poem* (1594) made the comparison explicitly dependent on the abundance and variety-in-unity of the worlds which both God and the heroic poet create.[8] Spenser fulfils the perfect pattern of a poet above all by being a creator of this kind.

Much in this preliminary account of Spenser may seem sufficiently obvious, though it is not, perhaps, always sufficiently remembered. As a poet, Spenser is conscious, literary, and artistic; respectful of convention and deeply devoted to tradition. But he is also creatively fecund, instinctive: poetry *does* come to him as naturally as leaves to a tree, though he is not prepared to let it grow like a primaeval forest, untended. It is not only in *The Faerie Queene* and its seemingly effortless, endless flow that this fecundity appears. The Letters to Harvey (1580), with their excited concern over work completed, in progress, or planned – his *Dreames*, his *Nine Comedies*, and 'parcels' of *The Faerie Queene* – are themselves testimony to the teeming brain, the mind, like Keats's, 'stuff'd like a cricket ball'. And all Spenser's work, whatever the degree of conscious artistry involved in it, has a fullness suggestive of unlimited resources, of powers generously used yet still unexhausted.

[8] A. H. Gilbert, *Literary Criticism from Plato to Dryden* (New York, 1940), 500.

Art, in Spenser's verse, does not inhibit Nature; rather, it directs and controls it.

The Shepheardes Calender (1579), Spenser's first published poem apart from the early verse-translations for the Dutchman Van Der Noodt, already illustrates much of this. It is a work, most would agree, of almost unlimited technical richness. It has to my mind, though I know that all would not agree on this, an equal imaginative richness. Its importance in Spenser's work can hardly be over-stressed; it is, as Mr. A. C. Hamilton, borrowing one of Spenser's own phrases, calls it, 'the wel-head of the history'. For it first establishes Spenser as the Poet, and gives him the persona – that of Colin Clout – that is to last him throughout his literary career. Spenser established his poetic orthodoxy by beginning with a pastoral, but in doing so he also found his métier. For the central idea in pastoral is poetry itself. Poetic self-consciousness is its integrating principle: to write it is to affirm oneself professionally a poet. This Spenser did, with a display of technical virtuosity and literary imitativeness that dazzled his contemporaries. But he did more: he made Colin Clout, quite legitimately, lover as well as poet, and he made him English, even in his name, and deeply melancholy. And he set him in a rounded, vivid, fully existent world, a world distinct from yet related to the actual world and as English as Colin's name. In other words, he gave reality to Colin and to his world. The reality persisted: the image of Colin, poet, shepherd, lover, melancholy idealist, inhabitant yet creator of imagined worlds, stays with Spenser, and with his reader, throughout the whole of his work. Despite his announcement in the Prologue to *The Faerie Queene* of his change of instrument (from 'oaten reeds' to 'trumpets sterne'), he never really loses his 'Shepheards weeds'. We can read Virgil's *Aeneid* without remembering the Tityrus of the Eclogues, but there is no discarding of the image of Colin. He persists in the humility of the Prologues (in that before Book III the poet's is still a 'rusticke Muse'), in the surviving pastoral landscapes and episodes in parts of the poem, and, more generally, in the odd, strangely distanced world of the poem, the product of a particular union of language and sentiment that we recognise as Colin's own. In Book VI, of course, Spenser brings Colin directly back into the poem, in the beautiful episode on Mount Acidale. No mention here of trumpets: Colin pipes apace, and only breaks his pipes when his vision is rudely shattered by Sir Calidore, intruder from the outside world.

B

The image of the pastoral poet, then, is central to Spenser's poetry, and is virtually one with the image of the Poet. Is sums up in itself much of both the character and tone of the work. It establishes, for instance, its formalism. There is no Ted Spenser in Spenser's verse, no voice immediately expressive of 'the bundle of accident and incoherence that sits down to breakfast'.[9] Instead there is guise and disguise, the ritual of the Poet. But to suppose because it is not expressive in this way that it is not expressive at all would be utterly mistaken. The world *The Shepheardes Calender* creates exists to be contemplated rather than entered; it presents to us a pure art-image, graceful and remote. Yet the poem is at the same time saturated with feeling, feeling about love, about England, about poetry, and above all about mutability. Spenser's use of the calendar structure to show us the poet – man himself – ageing with the year makes of the poem a true verbal icon, and a very moving one. And of course these feelings are all the feelings of Spenser himself: he is not less, but rather, more himself for having been 'reborn as an idea, something intended, complete'.[10]

For Mr. A. C. Hamilton, the precise allegorical allusions in much of *The Shepheardes Calender* reduce the autonomy of the world it creates, at any rate in comparison with that of *The Faerie Queene*. 'While the reader may seek some reality behind Morrell,' he writes, 'he must allow that Acrasia exists only in a poetic world.'[11] This is true, of course; the discussions, in the July and September eclogues especially, complete their meanings by reference to situations outside the world of the poem. But a poetic world does not, by meaning something, cease therefore to *be*, and the world of *The Shepheardes Calender* seems to me to be vital and complete. It is a world compounded of many elements, but owes its substantiality and distinctness above all to its language, which is the material, the very fabric, out of which it has been built. The 'old rustic language' about which Sidney was uneasy serves many functions. Its oldness helps to suggest that both this pastoral world and the poetry Spenser is writing have long roots in the past; its rusticity gives it an authentic 'homeliness', where 'homely' implies 'native' as well as 'unpretentious'. For Spenser has here crossed the Sicily of Theocritus and Virgil's Mantua-Arcadia with the England of Chaucer and Langland, to create an England transmogrified, familiar as English weather and hawthorn buds and bramble bush and daffadowndillies,

---

[9] W. B. Yeats, *Essays and Introductions* (1961), 509.   [10] *ibid.*
[11] Hamilton, *op. cit.*, 49.

And Cowslips, and Kingcups, and loved Lillies,

yet shot through with vision, haunted, like Mount Acidale later, by the Graces. And this is largely a creation of the language – of those 'rough and harsh termes' which, gnarled as a hawthorn and often impenetrable as a bramble, suggest, however vaguely and inaccurately, the language of the Anglo-Saxon; but also of the 'brightnesse of brave and glorious words', to which is often due a strangeness of vision and scene, as in these lines from the April eclogue:

> I see *Calliope* speede her to the place,
>   where my Goddesse shines:
> And after her the other Muses trace,
>   with their Violines.

Here 'speede', 'trace', and 'Violines' are the transfiguring words, creating a world in which the Muses really tread the greensward, and give open-air concert performances. In such writing Spenser is asserting his literary allegiances, refusing to equate the 'native' with the 'barbarous', and yet making a contribution to the English literary Renaissance. Yet he is also creating an imaginative world to be enjoyed for its own sake, as other such worlds are enjoyed – those of Lewis Carroll, for example, or of the writers of fairy-tale.

In 1595 Spenser published *Colin Clouts Come Home Againe*, a poem in which he commemorates his return to Ireland, after his visit to England in 1589-90 in the company of Ralegh, and records his impressions of the English court. This relaxed, discursive narrative is proof of his flexibility in the handling of pastoral: here at least we might exclaim 'Natural, easy Spenser!' The pastoral dress is worn lightly, easily; 'real life' is closer to the surface, and the pastoral world is continuous with the ordinary world, not, like that of *The Shepheardes Calender*, separated from it. It is, in fact, Ireland, an Ireland beautifully evoked in Hobbinol's lament, 'The running waters wept for thy returne', as well as in the allusion to 'the greene alders by the *Mullaes* shore'. Colin has changed from the solitary, introspective figure of the *Calender* into a more relaxed, sociable person, more confident and more loquacious, the returned traveller entertaining his fellow-shepherds who 'all gan throng about him neare', with the tale of his experiences. The shepherds, including Colin himself, seem simpler than their counterparts in the earlier poem. Their ignorance of and open-mouthed wonder at the sea and the sailing-ships is a nice touch of make-believe, and has the effect of making them seem, though less 'out of this world' than the shepherds of the *Calender*, more remote from civilisation. At the same time, they are seen to uphold the values of civilisation better than many of the representatives of sophisticated court-society. And this is essentially a poem about values, weighing the private, provincial life against that of the court, the virtues of court-life against its corruptions. (Incidentally, its use of the court-country contrast gives it an affinity with Renaissance pastoral narrative and drama – for example *As You Like It* – lacking in *The Shepheardes Calender*.) For all its carefree pastoral make-believe, *Colin Clouts Come Home Againe* is a serious poem, sharing the same moral temper and climate as *The Faerie Queene*, and dealing directly, straight from life, with much of the material – the 'vaine votaries of laesie love', for example – which the greater poem comments on and portrays in figurative fashion. The shrewd, disenchanted picture of courtly vice links the poem also with Spenser's one wholly satirical work, *Mother Hubberds Tale;* the rapturous testimony to the power of love with which it concludes, on the other hand, recalls the mood of the *Fowre Hymnes*. The poem could in fact be taken as Spenser's *credo*, a re-affirmation of his beliefs, both moral and literary (and hence a 'coming home'). In its 'deliberate self-delighting happiness', the pastoral make-believe here exemplifies that overflowing generosity of the creative spirit which Yeats sees as the secret of 'style': 'it is, as it were, the foam upon the cup, the long pheasant's feather on the horse's head, the spread peacock over the pasty.'[12] In this sense – in being partly play – it has its own touch of *sprezzatura*. It is play seriously meant, however, for Spenser is here using the shepherd-image, as in Book VI of *The Faerie Queene*, to symbolise true innocence and courtesy.

With the publication of the first three books of *The Faerie Queene* in 1590, however, it at once became clear that, however significant, revealing, and delightful Spenser's minor poems might be, this was to be his life's work, the colossus upon which were concentrated all his

12 Yeats, *op. cit.*, 254.

creative energies and ambitions, the embodiment of all that was of most moment to him in experience and in philosophy. Had it been completed, it would have been overpowering in its hugeness, like a baroque cathedral, and our first impressions would perhaps have been of Spenser as an architect of the vast. (He shows his architectonic skill in little in the *Epithalamion*.) As it is, we see it as something developing and continuous, not as something static; as poetry rather than as poem. The refrain of the *Prothalamion*, 'Sweete *Thammes* runne softly, till I end my Song', seems even more appropriate here, for the poem does run on like a river, in a state of continuous creation. The comparison could be with the river of life, for there is something like the flow of life itself in the movement of the poem, not simply in its composition, the steady procession of stanza following stanza, verse following verse, as week follows week, one day another day, but also in the insistence on movement within the narrative itself, where, from the moment the gentle knight first comes before us, 'pricking on the plaine', we are seldom without a sense of horses' heads or human feet turned in a forward direction. Thus, as Professor Geoffrey Tillotson says of *Vanity Fair*, we feel at the beginning the 'rest of the vast [poem] stretching out before us like the rest of our own life', and see in it a reflection of 'the streaming-ness of existence'.[13] This, once more, enhances our sense of Spenser as poet-creator. At the same time, it increases the difficulty of describing the poem, for if on the one hand it is a formal literary imitation of certain specific models, it seems on the other to be shaped by an instinctive, elemental force. But Spenser presents us with many such paradoxes.

The Faerie Queene is Spenser's heroic poem, and as such its chief models are the *Orlando Furioso* and *Gerusalemme Liberata*. It belongs, that is, to the genre of romantic epic. Apart from actual borrowings, the variety and complexity in plot and setting, the interweaving of stories, the multiplication of heroes, and the brilliant colouring of some of the episodes all make the affinity plain. Rosamond Tuve, however, has recently argued that the romance of *The Faerie Queene* owes far more both in substance and spirit to the actual mediaeval romances than it does to these sixteenth-century chivalric imitations.[14] To a large extent, the two interests work together to a single end – Spenser's was always a method of inclusion, not exclusion – but it is good to have the

[13] G. Tillotson, *Thackeray the Novelist* (1954), 165, 32.
[14] Rosamond Tuve, *Allegorical Imagery* (Princeton, 1966) chapter 5, 'Romances'.

relevance to *The Faerie Queene* of Malory and similar works recognised at last. If Spenser had the sound of *these* ancient authors ringing in his ears, that would account for the much greater sense we have in his poem than in either Ariosto's or Tasso's of actually being back in a mediaeval world. *Orlando Furioso* is a mediaeval charade, whereas *The Faerie Queene* is, in part, a mediaeval re-creation. And, as Miss Tuve argues, this is largely due to the simple realistic detail of much of his narrative, the element of plain, almost routine ordinariness in his account of the comings and goings of his heroes, which suggests that he had learned (from such writers as Malory),

to imagine things as if they were taking place in a real and ordinary medieval world where chivalry, and the way of living that went with it, was a common and living institution.[15]

Spenser's powers of imaginative assimilation – not simply of conscious imitation – were indeed immense, and contributed much to the substance of his poem, to the material out of which its special world was built. Spenser was, it seems, the kind of poet whose imagination is nourished by the imaginings of others (though not, of course, by them alone). This does not necessarily make him merely 'literary' and inferior; literary experience *is* experience, and may stimulate the imagination as powerfully as other experiences. For Spenser it did so: in his capacity to enter and possess the worlds of others, he was indeed the 'chameleon poet'. Our experience of his poem therefore becomes in its turn a journey back into the past, into the worlds, imaginary and real, of other men (worlds now, however, united to form yet another, unique and distinct from them all). One really needs a transverse section to appreciate the constitution of the poem in this respect. For just as the brilliant, enchanted world of the Italians falls back onto and merges with the graver, more solidly based world of Malory, so that in its turn gives way to a yet more antique time, to a golden age in which such personages as Bacchus and Hercules appear as 'servants unto right'. And across them all falls the shadow of the *Aeneid*, and hauntings from the worlds of classical and Celtic mythology. Spenser's imagination, I have said, worked in this way, devouring disparate (literary) experiences; but it worked to a purpose, and not haphazardly. For *The Faerie Queene* has its setting, in so far as this can be measured

[15] *ibid.*, 380.

chronologically at all, not in the age of Chaucer (or Malory), but in the beginning of Time. It takes us back to 'the sacred noursery Of vertue', where the seeds of all subsequent virtuous actions can be found. Spenser is in this sense a 'Poet historical', as he indicates in his letter to Ralegh, and one of distinctly Platonic mould. His 'history' goes as far back as it can, to give us 'brave ensamples of long passed daies', 'old Heroes' like Arthur and Artegall, in whom may be found archetypal patterns of the virtues. Miss Isabel E. Rathborne may well be right in her suggestion that Spenser's Fairyland is a land of fame, resembling the classical Elysium, in which 'the fairies are the race of gods and heroes who in their earthly lives anticipated the fame of Arthur and the future worthies who were destined to revive it.'[16]

Spenser repeatedly stresses the fact that his poem is an 'image of the antique world',

> When as mans age was in his freshest prime,
> And the first blossome of faire vertue bare.
>
> (F.Q., V, Prol.)

The introduction of Arthur makes it at one level specifically England, and in his dedicatory sonnets Spenser often reminds the recipients that they may find in it portraits of their forefathers. This reminder has to be taken seriously, if not literally, for it emphasises Spenser's Virgilian intentions. Properly understood, the poem is a national epic similar in certain fundamental respects to the Aeneid: its story is, like that of the Aeneid, a story 'doctrinal to a nation', set 'in the dark backward and abysm of time'; Elizabeth is shadowed in Gloriana as Augustus is in Aeneas; Prince Arthur and the other leading knights provide 'ensamples' of virtuous conduct for the patriotic Englishman, as Aeneas and his companions had provided them for the patriotic Roman, and Spenser clearly wants his readers to experience a sense of continuity, of virtue flowing directly from past to present, or past and present 'bracketed in a single whole', as C. M. Bowra says of the Aeneid.[17] E. M. W. Tillyard is right, I think, to find in The Faerie Queene 'a recurrent political fervour bordering on the religious'.[18]

---

[16] Isabel E. Rathborne, The Meaning of Spenser's Fairyland (New York, 1937), 'Foreword' vii.
[17] C. M. Bowra, From Virgil to Milton (1945), 15.
[18] E. M. W. Tillyard, The English Epic and its Background (1954), 287.

For Spenser the *politice* and the *ethice* easily merged into each other, since love of country involved both:

> How brutish is it not to understand,
> How much to her we owe, that all us gave,
> That gave unto us all, what ever good we have.
>
> (*F.Q.*, II.x.69)

To prevent and correct such brutishness, especially in present and future 'governors' of the country, is, as we have seen, one of the poem's main purposes. Thus the patriotic and the ethical naturally combine in a single focus. How perfectly Spenser's historical imagination is working in harmony with his conscious intention is seen in the fact that Bacchus and Hercules, those two 'old Heroes' who are ultimately the model and archetype of Spenser's knights (he mentions them specifically in V, I, 1–2), both embody ideals of public service such as Spenser is trying to inculcate, Hercules in particular being recommended by Cicero as the example of one who was willing to 'undergo the greatest toil and trouble for the sake of aiding and saving the world'.[19]

The Faerie Queene does therefore provide for its readers 'a lofty image of such worthies as most inflameth the mind with desire to be worthy', as Sidney says it is the business of the heroic poem to do. Although they have, as we have seen, ancestors more remote, the immediate model for these worthies, both in their character and their story, is provided by King Arthur and his knights, from whom, as Caxton had said, 'noble men may see and lerne the noble actes of chyvalrye, the jentyl and vertuous dedes that somme knyghtes used in tho dayes.'[20] Their deeds of heroism and chivalry – the Red Cross Knight's fight with the dragon, Britomart's rescue of Amoret, the numerous battles against odds – are intended to arouse admiration in a quite straightforward way. Our reaction to these characters, however, can never be quite straightforward, for the simple reason that they are, and are known to us to be, allegorical. It is now no longer necessary, thank goodness, to defend Spenser for using allegory. As recently as 1947 Professor W. L. Renwick could write, ironically, 'It has long been clearly understood that allegory is a crude mediaeval device which Spenser should never have adopted.'[21] Twenty years later, those who

---

[19] Cicero, *De Officiis*, Book III, chapter 25 (Loeb edn, 1956), 291.
[20] *The Works of Sir Thomas Malory*, ed. Eugène Vinaver (1954), Caxton's Preface, xvii.
[21] Renwick, '*Spenser's Faerie Queene*', *Warton Lecture on English Poetry* (1947), 9.

confuse Spenser's allegory with what we have learned from Professor Northrop Frye to call naive allegory seem themselves naive. For of course Spenser's allegorical purpose is the great transfiguring force at work in the poem, breathing upon the Arthurian and other material and moulding it to a new life. It is in the allegory that the mystery and the power of Spenser's genius, the strange workings of his imagination, are apprehended most keenly.

One erroneous impression, still occasionally met with today, is that Spenser uses allegory in *The Faerie Queene* simply to inculcate rules of conduct, in a pageant of dressed-up admonitions and prohibitions. Whatever his conscious intention (as expressed in the letter to Ralegh), this is not the way in which his poem works. If it teaches what men ought to do, it also shows what they do, and are; it is, to borrow Rosamond Tuve's description of *Five Poems by Milton*, 'a profound figurative vision of the realities of man's life'.[22] It offers, certainly, a guide to conduct by recommending those virtues desirable to us both as individuals and as social beings and suggesting how we may attain them, but in doing so it also portrays the context, moral and psychological, in which they will have to be won. And it is here, in his presentation of the 'difficulty of the way', that Spenser's insight into the human condition is most apparent.

But it is the *method* of Spenser's allegory that still most requires explanation – naturally enough, considering its complexity. What we have to be on our guard against is 'any irritable reaching' (or, for that matter, any good-humoured reaching) after interpretations and meanings. Obviously Spenser's subtle mind has at some stage consciously worked on and shaped his material, loading many rifts with ore of meaning, much of it now being uncovered by modern scholarship. But to see the poem wholly in terms of a traffic between a conscious planning mind on the one hand and a conscious interpreting mind on the other is surely a mistake. 'The ethical effect comes not from hidden meanings detected by a watchful mind, but by an instantaneous effect upon feeling and imagination.'[23] K. O. Myrick writes thus of 'representative fiction', contrasting it with the allegorical variety, especially Spenser's. Yet the statement (except that we need not jettison the 'hidden meanings') seems to me equally true of Spenser's allegorical fiction. Spenser's allegory offers us first of all an *experience*,

---

[22] Tuve, *Images and Themes in Five Poems by Milton* (1957), 7.
[23] K. O. Myrick, *Sir Philip Sidney as a Literary Craftsman* (Cambridge, Mass., 1935), 199.

B*

and its significance emerges from that experience, whether we are watching Pyrochles leaping into the Idle Lake crying 'I burne, I burne, I burne', or are looking at Amoret, tied to the pillar in Busyrane's flame-surrounded palace, her heart transfixed with a knife, or moving with Sir Guyon through the cave of Mammon. Reflection on such images may deepen and enlarge our understanding of them, as happens in the reading of any kind of literature, but it is the first, imaginative impact that gives them their power and validity.

Myrick's argument that with representative or imitative art 'there is no meaning but the literal, and the lesson cannot be separated from the imaginative effect of the fiction', whereas in allegory the fiction is distinct from the lesson so that it need have no congruity with it, seems likewise to be inapplicable to *The Faerie Queene*.[24] My own view, in common with that of many present-day critics of Spenser, is precisely that in his allegory 'the lesson cannot be separated from the imaginative effect of the fiction', using 'fiction' now to signify the total structure of the poem, not just the separate images. Our willingness to admit this, perhaps, depends on the kind of credence we give his story. Its non-naturalistic character, for instance, may itself seem to invite us not to take it seriously *as* a story, to assume, that is, that an action so obviously making no claim to plausibility *must* be without value in itself. But this is to make imaginative experience conditional upon verisimilitude. Spenser offers us an imaginative experience in *The Faerie Queene*, but he offers it on his own terms, which are those of the fairy tale and the romance, not of the realistic novel or drama. He creates a special and distinct world and demands our surrender to it, and understanding of his meanings comes, in the first place, through that surrender. For surrender to his world involves recognition of its 'daemonic' character – intuitive, not necessarily conscious, recognition.[25] His Faery land is not merely a Country of the Mind; it *is* the mind. Many people have felt its kinship with dream – Lamb, for instance, found in the episode of the Cave of Mammon 'a copy of the mind's conceptions in sleep', 'the shifting mutations of the most rambling dream', mutations, moreover, which the judgement 'all the time awake' still ratified.[26] Recently Professor Graham Hough has asserted that

[24] *ibid.*
[25] I borrow the word 'daemonic' from Angus Fletcher, *Allegory, The Theory of a Symbolic Mode* (Cornell University Press, 1964).
[26] See his essay, 'The Sanity of True Genius', in *Last Essays of Elia*.

there is a far greater quantity of psychic material behind Spenser's romance-figures than a simple translation of them into the obvious moral terms would suggest, . . .[27]

and has used Freud's *Interpretation of Dreams* to demonstrate this. To accept this argument (as I do) is to go some way towards understanding the grip which Spenser's images, whether of background, character, or action, so often have on us. It helps to explain why, for example, C. S. Lewis could feel that in this poem what we have is not so much a poet writing about the fundamental forms of life 'as those forms themselves spontaneously displaying their activities to us through the imagination of a poet'.[28] A poem of Theodore Roethke's seems relevant here:

> When I saw that clumsy crow
> Flap from a wasted tree,
> A shape in the mind rose up:
> Over the gulfs of dream
> Flew a tremendous bird
> Further and further away
> Into a moonless black,
> Deep in the brain, far back.[29]

Spenser's images too have their origin 'deep in the brain, far back', and the shapes that rise up in *our* minds at the sight of his clumsy crows – Despair, Mammon, Maleger, Malbecco – appear in some indefinable way to be 'almost a Remembrance'; they are at once strange and familiar. As Janet Spens says, Spenser's presentation of the temptations (it is the temptations rather than the virtues – that is, experiences, rather than ideals – that call forth this power in him) 'is subtle, manifold, opening out vistas in the mysterious forest of human personality.'[30]

While however the psychical and archetypal content of Spenser's images is important, their success in embodying his allegorical meaning is not due to this alone. Their precision is as important as their evocativeness. They are at their best 'the exact verbal equivalents of states of mind and feeling'. Professor Hough in his well-known chapter on 'the allegorical circle' reserves the term 'incarnational' for the Shakespearian

[27] Graham Hough, *A Preface to The Faerie Queene* (1962), 133.
[28] Lewis, *op. cit.*, 358.
[29] Theodore Roethke, 'Night Crow', *Words for the Wind* (1958), 58.
[30] Janet Spens, *Spenser's Faerie Queene* (1934), 121.

form of writing in which 'theme and image seem equally balanced', but in that he is able to give shape and life to the abstract and intangible, it fits Spenser too. Sometimes the effect desired (and achieved) is a relatively superficial one, a vivid momentary 'incarnation' by means of emblem or attribute, significant feature or gesture. At such times Spenser exercises the traditional skill of the allegorist, and our pleasure is perhaps mainly in his skill, in the happy rightness of his choice of symbol. In his Masque of Cupid, for instance, the 'lovely boy', Fancy, appears in a garment that is neither 'of silke nor say',

> But painted plumes, in goodly order dight,
> Like as the sunburnt *Indians* do aray
> Their tawney bodies, in their proudest plight,

and he carries a 'windy fan', moving here and there 'in the idle aire'. This is a felicitous picture; its rightness is confirmed by our own epithet for a similar mental state, 'feather-brained'. Earlier in the poem Spenser had introduced Phaedria, the personification of 'immodest Merth', and by means of her 'little Gondelay', the 'shallow ship' in which she skims the Idle Lake, had managed to suggest a lightness not unlike that of Fancy. (Both, after all, are associated with the idea of love-in-idleness.) But the portrayal of Phaedria is altogether more complex, more psychologically revealing, and of course more extensive; it is full of telling detail. Here we both recognise Phaedria because we know the state she represents, and learn more about that state through her delineation. And this combination of recognition and revelation characterises all Spenser's major allegorical images. It is felt very strongly in, for instance, the encounter with Despair, where everything – the dreary wasteland round Despair's cave, his honeyed eloquence, his knowledge of his victim's life and inmost thoughts – serves to enforce it.

Dryden, in his plea for 'the fairy way of writing', states that it is permissible for a poet to describe things which do not really exist, if they are founded on popular belief. 'For 'tis still an imitation, though of other men's fancies.'[31] That *The Faerie Queene* is such an imitation is now generally acknowledged. C. S. Lewis declared 'What lies next beneath the surface of Spenser's poem is the world of popular imagina-

---

[31] Dryden, 'The Author's Apology for Heroic Poetry', *Critical Essays*, ed. George Watson (1962) I, 204.

tion.'[32] Professor Northrop Frye and his disciples have uncovered (with varying degrees of conviction) some of the poem's underlying myths. Spenser's creativeness, it seems, even at its most spontaneous and intuitive, draws upon the imaginative creations of other men in whatever form they exist, whether as oral tradition or in the written word. This is not to suggest, as Mr. Alvarez has suggested, that his inspiration is merely literary. Rather, it is to recognise that a fundamental part of his inspiration comes from the mind of man, from his mental fashionings as well as from his mental experiences. Thus he draws from the mental life both his themes and his manner of treatment of them. In a fundamental sense, his poetry originates in poetry.

The elements of fairy-tale and romance, therefore, in both incident and structure, are not to be brushed aside as mere excrescences or escapist irrelevancies, unimportant to the poem's serious intents. Rather, they are indispensable aids to the achievement of its own special and unique high seriousness. Whether it was Ariosto, or Malory, or the Accession Day tilts, or all three working together that led Spenser to choose the chivalric romance for the form of his poem, he could not have done better, for this is one of the basic story-types for expressing the moral struggle, as its survival in popular form in the 'western' of today still shows. It also allowed him scope to vary the levels of reality in his narrative: the plain, like the prairie, is 'spacious and wide', and anything can happen there. Everything in *The Faerie Queene* is not a phantasmagoria. Much of the action takes place at the level of ordinary, every-day experience; it is presented to us as the fully realised social and inner life of substantial personalities. The world we know does not *disappear* when we read *The Faerie Queene*: it simply expands to include or unite with other less usual forms. If Spenser's method is not, ultimately, that of the 'realist', this is not because the methods of realism were beyond his grasp. One of the things his poem is richest in is shrewd yet sympathetic observation of human conduct, expressed both in portraiture and in comment. We are very early introduced to this aspect of Spenser's art, when in Book I after the totally allegorical incident of the fight with Error, we move on to the description of Archimago's 'brain-washing' of the Red Cross Knight, which is to separate him from Una. This is, for the most part, presented naturalistically. The knight's dreams, whether brought by demons or not, are of a kind known to human experience; and when later a

[32] Lewis, *op. cit.*, 312.

deception is practised on him similar to that practised on Claudio in *Much Ado About Nothing*, his reactions are equally lifelike and natural. The Red Cross Knight is here a lover, as well as holiness, and it is in the depiction of his lovers that Spenser most often resorts to naturalism. He is a great realist, as well as idealist, in his treatment of love.

The presence of these elements of realism in the poem does not, in my opinion, necessitate our seeing it as a 'discontinuous allegory' similar to Ariosto's, as Professor Hough does. Although the allegorical content of the action constantly varies, swelling out or dwindling like a flame in the breeze, there is a unifying factor that gives continuity to the 'dark conceit', in the consistency of the world Spenser has created. All the action, whatever its character, takes place in this world and is absorbed into it without fuss. We do not switch worlds, as in some fairy-tales – John Masefield's *Box of Delights*, for example, where the hero slips backward and forward between a real world of policemen and bishops and a fantastic, magical world of the imagination. Spenser's world accommodates the real and the fantastic in a single, continuous whole from which meaning naturally arises. How inseparable they are may be illustrated by the fine though bitter ending of Book V, where, after Sir Artegall has successfully completed his mission, Envy and Detraction wait for him on the shore and set the Blatant Beast to bellow after him. Envy and Detraction are as allegorical as the earlier-appearing Ate, yet they are acceptable too as a couple of old cockle-women or fish-wives, and the whole incident is a moving representation of the loneliness and isolation of the man of life upright, and of the *injustice* of man to man, in which we move rapidly from the 'real' to the symbolic and back again.

The good sense and fine fabling of Spenser's poem are inseparable. It is the fullness of life that Spenser has given to his personages, however conceived, that distinguishes *The Faerie Queene* from more ordinary allegories such as Lydgate's *Reason and Sensuality* or Stephen Hawes's *The Passetyme of Pleasure*. These have pictorial vividness and even a certain narrative interest, but in our reading of them we are always conscious of the figurative meaning as predominant and that the story subserves this. But in Spenser the story has really 'come alive', and truly expresses and embodies the poet's vision, to comprehend which we are asked, not so much to *translate*, as to *see* and *experience*. Perhaps this is the sort of response C. S. Lewis had in mind when he observed of the poem,

The things we read about in it are not like life, but the experience of reading it is like living.[33]

They are not 'like life': the world which Spenser has created, though it gives life, also restricts and confines it, and his characters, however humanised, are unimaginable in the actual world. (No-one would ever say he knew Sir Artegall, as the seaman knew Captain Gulliver.) Aesthetic distancing keeps them smaller than life, like reflections in a crystal, perfect, but reduced in size. The impression that the entire poem is such a crystal is strong; it resembles the 'glassie globe' of Merlin, which

round and hollow shaped was
Like to the world it selfe, and seem'd a world of glas.[34]
(*F.Q.*, III.ii.19)

The world of *The Faerie Queene* is a world of images, like the world on Keats's Grecian Urn; it is Spenser's distinction that, while preserving the remoteness of those images, he yet makes them warm and vital.

This account of Spenser's work has necessarily omitted much. I have tried to concentrate on those features of it which express the essence and uniqueness of the poet, and which at the same time offer the most significant comparisons and contrasts with the work of his followers. Spenser is a poet for whom the mental life is paramount. Yet he is no idle dreamer or escapist: *The Faerie Queene* is based on social observation, not simply on introspection. To make the external internal, the internal external, which Coleridge describes as 'the mystery of genius in the Fine Arts', appears to have been the poem's artistic aim. Spenser's mind seems to work somewhat like that 'immense sensibility' described by Henry James as 'a kind of huge spider-web of the finest silken threads suspended in the chamber of consciousness, and catching every air-borne particle in its tissue',[35] –

---

[33] *ibid.*, 358.
[34] Since this chapter was written, Miss Kathleen Williams's excellent study, *Spenser's Faerie Queene, The World of Glass* has appeared (London, 1966).
[35] James, *The Art of Fiction* (New York, 1948), 10.

although we should add that Spenser's spider, like Donne's, 'transubstantiates all'. Spenser is also sane and shrewd, even prosaic: James Sutherland's comment,

It may seem an odd thing to say of 'the poet's poet'; but the virtues of Spenser – the unfailing lucidity, the steady progress, the mind continually looking forward and organizing the argument – are the characteristic virtues of good prose . . .[36]

deserves enthusiastic endorsement. Recollection of a few outstanding passages tends to fix Spenser in the memory as more exclusively a poet of luscious, dreamy description than he actually is. He does not always wear purple and gold: he dresses for the occasion when there *is* an occasion (his own wedding, for example: 'Song made in lieu of many ornaments, With which my love should duly have bene dect'), but his normal style is quite plain and work-a-day. It is the combination of archaisms with plainness that, in *The Faerie Queene* especially, helps to give at once strangeness and substantiality to the world that is created: to distance it, and yet by the provision of a style of narration that is down-to-earth if not downright earthy, to confer upon it something of the solidity of earth.

Spenser lavished some of his best and richest poetry upon his description of Acrasia's bower, and in doing so managed to distort our image of him. Largely because of this description, he has become for many readers pre-eminently 'a poet of the delighted senses'. This he certainly is, but he is much else besides. He drew 'arbitrary images of virtue', Yeats tells us, while thinking all the while 'of nothing but lovers whose bodies are quivering with the memory or hope of long embraces'.[37] This is nonsense. Even as an account of Spenser's treatment of love, it is inadequate, omitting as it does any acknowledgment of his insight into his lovers' hearts, into the secrets that they carry so painfully around with them. Spenser's attitude to sexual love is joyous and affirmative; this we see, not so much from the portrayal of love-in-idleness in Acrasia's bower, as from the episode in Venus's Temple, where Venus laughs upon Scudamour as he seizes Amoret, or from his frank confession in his description of the Garden of Adonis that he knows from personal experience the pleasures of the Garden. But there are other things he feels passionately and

---

[36] J. R. Sutherland, *On English Prose* (University of Toronto, 1957), 9.
[37] Yeats, 'Edmund Spenser' (1902), reprinted in *Essays and Introductions* (1961), 369.

affirmatively about too, and these include virtue, and the well-being of England. Comprehensive as it is, Spenser's work requires to be judged by the whole, not by the part. It is because, one suspects, they had been too much affected by Acrasia that those 'ablest, and most knowing men' mentioned at the end of the last chapter made the mistake of attributing *Brittain's Ida* to him.

The Spenserians: attitudes
to poetry

To begin a discussion of the Spenserian poets by examining their views on poetry seems logical and fitting, since poetry itself is the subject of much of their verse. They all love poetry, and say so repeatedly: to write poetry and to express their delight in writing it were simultaneous impulses with them. In their attitude to poetry, moreover, they exhibit a high degree of unanimity. There are deviations on one or two issues, but on the whole the area of agreement between them here is so great as to provide one of the main justifications for treating them as a group. As might be expected, the 'poetic' they accept and make the basis of their work is in the main the traditional, orthodox poetic of Spenser and Sidney. They accept Spenser's view of the poet's function in society, as also, to a large extent, his aims and methods. They share his sense of 'the great tradition', and are aware, with him, of the making of literature as a continuous process, in which one artist provides material for another; not as a series of fresh starts, like Penelope's web. They share his devotion to the Muse, his preference for narrative and for the creation of distinct poetic 'worlds', his assumption that the truest poetry is the most feigning. They thus carry over into the seventeenth century the literary values for which he stood.

These values differ considerably from the values represented by Donne and the Metaphysicals. Here we may recall Rosamond Tuve's statement,

· . . it is highly inaccurate to affirm and reaffirm, as our handbooks have done for years, that important differences in poetic separated the Spenserians from the Metaphysicals.[1]

Professor Tuve is here using 'Spenserian' in a wider sense than I am,

[1] Tuve, *Elizabethan and Metaphysical Imagery* (1947), 226.

to include Spenser himself and all those Elizabethan poets who in a general way shared his method. She also means something rather different by 'poetic'. She is thinking mainly of style and rhetorical method; her book, *Elizabethan and Metaphysical Imagery*, is largely a demonstration of how much common ground there is between Elizabethans and Metaphysicals in these matters. Nevertheless, we are not wrong to see Spenser and his followers on the one hand, and Donne and his on the other as representing in some ways opposing ideals in poetry. For however close they may be in technique and rhetorical training, in matters of taste and creed there are real and important differences between them. These differences will be discussed in the course of the chapter, so need not be detailed here. I mention them merely to make the point that in matters of taste and creed the Spenserians stand out as being, by contrast with the Metaphysicals, distinctly orthodox, traditional and conservative.

In recognising this, however, it is important to note that they are not *merely* orthodox. The emphasis in this chapter will, in fact, be on what is new and peculiar in them – that is, in their creed, their attitude to poetry. For what we find in these Spenserians is an insistence on orthodox and traditional views carried to such lengths that it becomes an extreme traditionalism, an ultra-orthodoxy, in which the normal orthodoxies and traditions are so transformed as to become virtually something new. The Spenserians develop positions held by Spenser far beyond anything envisaged by Spenser himself. It could almost be said that their Spenserian orthodoxy disintegrates even in their affirmation of it. Again, these are statements which the rest of the chapter will, I hope, substantiate. What must be added here is that, although this tendency in the Spenserians comes partly from within themselves, partly from the pressure of the times, it is also due in large measure to the example of another poet, or another poet and his translator, who, although they seldom imitated him so deliberately and at such length as they imitated Spenser, had undoubtedly a very great influence on them. I refer to the French poet, Salluste Du Bartas, author of *La Sepmaine* (1578) and *La Seconde Sepmaine* (1584–1608), and to his translator, Joshua Sylvester. Although the influence of *The Divine Weeks and Works* on the style, especially the diction and imagery, of seventeenth-century poetry has long been recognised, I think the effect it had in modifying people's feelings about poetry, about its nature and objectives, in other words its *general* effect upon taste, it still not sufficiently acknowledged. Certainly the poets I have called 'Spenserians' could equally well have been called 'Bartasians' or 'Sylvestrians', though one is thankful that they never have been.

It is also in their attitude to poetry that we find the Spenserians at times anticipating the Romantics, more strikingly, I think, than do any other Elizabethan poets. The resemblance can probably be explained by the convergence in the Spenserian poets, as in the Romantics, of three impulses or desires: an impulse, on the one hand, to the creation of fictions or myth-making; on the other, to personal statement or self-expression, which means, essentially, to lyrical expression; and, at all times, an impulse to celebrate in lyrical terms poetry and the poet.[2] In Romantics and Spenserians alike the strong lyric feeling – and it is a feeling chiefly about *poetry* – tends to turn narrative into effusion. In Spenser, such impulses and feelings are kept under control by the discipline of convention. In the Spenserians this discipline is breaking down – again partly through Du Bartas's influence and example.

An account of the Spenserians' attitude to poetry must begin, then, with their love of poetry itself. This is remarkable for its ardour and enthusiasm. The Spenserians are not just lovers of poetry: they are poetry-addicts. Poetry, both the writing and the reading of it, but especially perhaps the writing, is their ruling passion. If Spenser is the poets' poet, then they are Poetry's poets. In this respect they might be said to out-Spenser Spenser.

As my remarks concerning their affinity with the Romantics suggest, this sheer delight in poetry encourages a pronounced lyricism in these writers. Their pleasure in the act of writing infuses itself everywhere, and is a major determinant of style. We should know that they felt this pleasure even without their telling us so: it is evident in the constant sparkle and fervour of the writing, the rhetorical brilliance, and, negatively, in the general indifference to and failure to cultivate the more 'prosaic' virtues of Spenser, such as the plain, homespun manner which he employs to drive on his narrative. But in fact they do tell us of their pleasure, repeatedly. Personal statement in their poetry takes the form, most often, of statement about poetry: their love of poetry

[2] Of these impulses in the Romantics and their effect upon their work, A. C. Bradley has written in his essay, 'The Long Poem in the Age of Wordsworth', *Oxford Lectures on Poetry* (1965 edn.), 177–205. Bradley's argument concerning the extension of the 'subjective' spirit into the long poem (182–7) is particularly relevant.

impels them to sudden outbursts, at once confiding and rapturous. Passages expressive of his admiration for poetry occur, for instance, in many of Drayton's poems, including even his satires. His commendations, however, are usually general in character, praise for poetry's self, seen, for example, as

> The language, which the Spheares and Angels speake,
> In which their minde they to poore Mortalls breake
> By Gods great power, into rich soules infus'd.
>
> (*The Moone-Calfe*, 377–9)

With the others, it is most characteristically their delight in their own skill, in the poem which they are actually writing, that they like to stress. Wither's *Faire-Virtue* and *The Shepheards Hunting* are full of expressions of his pleasure and content at the work he is producing. Browne, repeatedly moved to exclamations of delight, apologises to the reader:

> So if to please my selfe I somewhat sing,
> Let it not be to you lesse pleasuring.
>
> (*B.P.*, II, sig. N1^r)

Writing is his hobby, he explains: he prefers 'the pleasing cadence of a line Strucke by the consort of the sacred *Nine*' to the noise of hounds, and takes 'more pleasure To heare a Verse keepe time and equall measure' than he does in courtly dancing:

> In this can I as oft as I will chuse
> Hug sweet content by my retyred *Muse*,
> And in a study finde as much to please
> As others in the greatest *Pallaces*.   (*ibid.*)

Similarly, Giles and Phineas Fletcher watch themselves at work, striking conventional attitudes of humility, behind which their pleasure in their achievement is still quite apparent.

Phineas Fletcher wrote of himself in a letter to Thomas Murray as 'from my very childhood serving Poetry with all fidelity'. All the Spenserians could say the same; most of them did. Drayton's statement comes in his elegy, 'To My Most Dearely-loved Friend Henery Reynolds Esquire':

> For from my cradle (you must know that) I,
> Was still inclin'd to noble Poesie,

and is followed by the story of how, 'Much like a Pigmy, scarse ten yeares of age', he clasped his tutor round the thigh, and begged him, 'Make me a Poet, doe it; if you can.' His tutor's answer was to read Mantuan and Virgil's Eclogues to him. 'Me thought I straight had mounted *Pegasus*,' Drayton adds. All the Spenserians accepted imitation as the proper road to Parnassus for them, not simply because this was orthodox doctrine, but because they loved other poets so much, they wanted to imitate them. Wither, it is true, repudiated imitation as a doctrine and directive:

> *Pedants* shall not tye my straines
> To our Antique *Poets* vaines;
> As if we, in latter dayes,
> Knew to love, but not to praise.
> Being borne as free as these,
> I will sing, as I shall please;
> Who, as well new paths may run,
> As the best before have done,   (*F.V.*, sig. C3ʳ)

an attitude of sturdy independence which he maintains even more aggressively later, in *Britain's Remembrancer* and elsewhere. But although Wither's verse is remarkably unclotted and free from classical allusion, it is still a treasury of poetic clichés, used with so blithe an ignorance of what they are that they almost thereby achieve the freshness Wither claims for them. Moreover, Wither does imitate – if not 'antique' poets, certainly modern ones, especially (in *Faire-Virtue*) Sidney. And he loves to praise his fellow-poets: in *Faire-Virtue* Drayton, Browne, Spenser and Sidney; in *Abuses Stript and Whipt* Daniel, Drayton, Jonson, Chapman, and Sylvester. Most of the others have similar lists somewhere in their work. By introducing a Festival of Poets into *Britannia's Pastorals*, Browne is able to make an international as well as a national survey. (It is to him we owe 'well-languag'd Daniel'.) Phineas Fletcher's roll-call, at the beginning of *The Purple Island*, to prove how little 'our father-ages Have left succeeding times to play upon' is thoroughly cosmopolitan: it includes Virgil, Ovid, Sannazaro, and Du Bartas. He also praises his brother Giles, just as Browne and

Wither praise each other. All this celebration of other poets, which culminates in Drayton's truly noble 'essay in criticism', the Elegy to Henry Reynolds cited above, is for these poets another means by which their intense love of poetry finds an outlet.

Mr. Owen Barfield, writing on literary imitation, particularly as practised by minor poets, has a statement so appropriate here that it almost seems made for these poets. He writes:

The minor poet is appreciator rather than creator. He imitates, because he must have his idiom established, acknowledged, labelled in his own consciousness as 'poetic' before he can feel that he is writing poetry. He is always trying to give himself the sensations which he has received from reading the works of greater poets. And since his energies go more into contemplating than creating, it is even possible that he extracts more aesthetic *pleasure* from his own work than the great poet does.[3]

Although Drayton's achievement is too varied and substantial to fit this description entirely, its accuracy in relation to the other Spenserians is beyond question.

Further consideration suggests, however, that Mr. Barfield's statement is a description of many degrees of minor poet. It is, for example the way of writing of most young poets, as a glance at almost anyone's *juvenilia* will show, and in that sense even a major poet is a minor one when he begins. Browne, Wither, and the Fletchers were all young poets, at least when they wrote the works for which they are remembered. They themselves are fond of stressing their precosity. In *The Purple Island* Phineas Fletcher draws elaborate attention to his youth and prays for gentle forbearance for 'these infantine beginnings'. Browne may have been twenty-two when he published the first part of *Britannia's Pastorals*; according to his own testimony he was only nineteen when he wrote it:

> Here could I spend that spring of *Poesie*,
> Which not *twice ten Sunnes* have bestow'd on me;
> And tell the world, the *Muses* love appeares
> In nonag'd youth, as in the length of yeeres.

> > (B.P., I, sig. M4^{r})

Wither was twenty-three when his first poem *Prince Henries Obsequies*

[3] Barfield, *Poetic Diction* (1952 edn.), 159.

was published, in 1612, and may have been even younger when he
wrote, or began, *Faire-Virtue*, which he says was composed 'in my
childhood'. In publishing his *Juvenilia* for the first time, in 1622, he
acknowledges the 'childishness' of the poems and their lack of learning,
but his pride in his achievement is clear:

> For, when he this composed it was more,
> Then he had read in twice-twelve Moneths before.
> And, by his latter Studies, some discerne,
> That, first he writ, and then beganne to learne.
>
> ('To the Reader', no sig.)

This pride is perfectly justified. Wither's and Phineas Fletcher's poems
may have been revised for publication (Fletcher, after all, was fifty-one
when *The Purple Island* was printed), but even allowing for this, the
achievement of all four writers, considering their youth, is remarkable.
Browne especially must have seemed to contemporary readers to
promise great things. Keats at the same age had published only the
Poems of 1817 and *Endymion*, with either of which *Britannia's Pastorals*,
Book I, will stand comparison.

   In all the Spenserians except Drayton, then, we meet the ready
sensibility and undeveloped critical intelligence of the young poet. It
is this, partly, that accounts for their curious anticipation, at times, of
the Romantics. They respond eagerly to experience, particularly
literary experience, and express that response in their verse with an
ardour and impetuosity and (on occasion) brashness suggestive of the
young Keats or Shelley. They are full of high hopes and enthusiasm
about the masterpieces they are *going* to write.

> ... and though in accents rare
> I misse the glory of a charming ayre,
> My *Muse* may one day make the Courtly Swaines
> Enamour'd on the *Musicke* of the Plaines,
> And as upon a hill shee bravely sings,
> Teach humble Dales to weepe in Christall Springs.
>
> (*B.P.*, I, sig. P2ᵛ)

Thus Browne concludes his poem as published in 1613. Similarly in
'Sleep and Poetry' Keats looks ahead:

> O for ten years, that I may overwhelm
> Myself in poesy! so I may do the deed
> That my own soul has to itself decreed.

The consciousness of bursting powers, of poetic fertility, which Keats felt at the time of *Endymion* and expressed in the sonnet 'When I have fears':

> When I have fears that I may cease to be,
> Before my pen has glean'd my teeming brain . . .,

is a feeling shared by these Spenserian poets. With the sense of plenitude expressed in these lines of Keats we might compare Phineas Fletcher's description of the visitations of his Muse:

> Oft therefore have I chid my tender Muse;
> Oft my chill breast beats off her fluttering wing:
> Yet when new spring her gentle rayes infuse,
> All storms are laid, I 'gin to chirp and sing:
>   At length soft fires disperst in every vein,
>   Yeeld open passage to the thronging train,
> And swelling numbers tide rolls like the surging main,
>   (*P.I.*, I, 22)

or Browne's declaration at the beginning of *Britannia's Pastorals*, Book II:

> . . . a hundred Theames come on,
> And hale my Barke a-new for *Helicon*,   (sig. B1ᵛ)

or again Wither's

> Boy, ha' done; for now my braine
> Is inspir'd afresh againe,
> And new Raptures pressing are,
> To be sung in praise of her.   (*F.V.*, sig. E8ᵛ)

Fluidity of fancy and facility in versifying combine with the love of poetry to make the activity of writing a sensuous, not merely a mental, pleasure for them, as is clear from the images they use to describe that pleasure. The lines quoted above, for instance, in which Phineas Fletcher describes his possession by the Muse, are anticipatory less of the Romantics than of certain parts of *Lady Chatterley's Lover*. Similarly Wither's references in *Faire-Virtue* to the 'ravishings', the 'pleasures not to be exprest', the 'sweets', of poetry have something of the ambiguity of Crashaw's Hymn to St. Theresa. Browne too has an address to the Muses which makes the sensuous nature of his pleasure unmistakable:

> *Piërian* Singers! O yee blessed *Muses*!
> Who as a Iem too deare the world refuses!
> Whose truest lovers never clip with age,
> O be propitious in my *Pilgrimage*! ...
>
> Cause every coupling cadence flow in blisses,
> And fill the world with envy of such kisses.
> Make all the rarest Beauties of our *Clyme*,
> That deigne a sweet looke on my younger ryme,
> To linger on each lines inticing graces,
> As on their *Lovers* lips and chaste imbraces!
>
> (*B.P.* II, sig. B1ᵛ)

Keats's association of poetry with 'luxuries' in 'Sleep and Poetry' and other early verse, and his ecstatic celebration of its 'overwhelming sweets', provide a parallel with this.[4] Or can we forget his 'I look upon fine phrases like a lover'?

That these young poets found in the writing of poetry an outlet for their sexual feelings seems highly probable. Wither acknowledges as much; addressing any possible carping critics, he tells them,

> While their *Desires* (perhaps) they looselier spent;
> I gave my heats of Youth, this better vent.
> And, oft by writing thus, the bloud have tam'd;
> Which some, with reading wanton *Layes* enflam'd.
>
> (*F.V.*, sig. N8ʳ)

---

[4] Keats's expression of his feelings about poetry in 'Sleep and Poetry' and the three Epistles of the 1817 volume may owe something in manner to the Spenserians' example. The quotation from Browne before the Epistle 'To George Felton Mathew' suggests this. With the last quotation from Browne, cf. also Keats, 'Isabella':
> So said, his erewhile timid lips grew bold,
> And poesied with hers in dewy rhyme.

This is not in itself, however, an adequate explanation of the characteristics under discussion. The expressions used have a literary as well as
a psychological significance. They are attempts to define, to capture on
paper, the nature of the poetic act. For the Spenserians, like the Romantics, are aware of the special activity that writing a poem and *being* a
poet involves, and in their own fitful, rudimentary, half-accidental
way they try to find words to express that perception.

Had they actually been Romantics, they would probably have
written of 'imagination', 'sensibility', and so on, or gone wandering
at the beck of 'Two starry eyes, hung in the gloom of thought'. As it
is, they make do with that (for them) not yet defunct piece of divinity,
the Muse. Through her they are able to express their various feelings
concerning their own poetic powers, and their relationship to those
powers.

At times she is simply a figure of speech for the poem itself, the act
of composition. She is then a means by which the poet can comment
on his own proceedings, and express his satisfaction at them. This is
Browne's usage:

> But stay sweet *Muse*! forbeare this harsher straine,
> Keepe with the Shepheards; leave the *Satyres* veyne . . .
> $\qquad$ (*B.P.*, II, sig. D4^v)

> But let us leave (faire Muse) the bankes of *Po:*   (sig. E1^r)

> On now, my loved *Muse*, and let us bring
> *Thetis* to heare the *Cornish Michael* sing.   (sig. N1^v)

Browne's epithets for her are always expressive of his delight in
writing – 'fair', 'sweet', 'gentle', 'loved'. Drayton too uses the Muse to
comment on his activities and progress, especially in *Poly-Olbion*.
His epithets – 'th' industrious Muse', 'the laborious Muse'. 'the active
Muse', 'the ever labouring Muse' – though very different from Browne's
equally bespeak his pride in the work. Both poets (Browne possibly
imitating Drayton) send their Muses travelling, often on foot. Phineas
Fletcher's Muse is the more familiar, winged kind. She is 'ungrown'
and 'downy' (thus emphasising his youth); she creeps, flags, or tries to
soar. Fletcher's manner of speaking of her makes her like Browne's a

metaphor for his delight in composition: she is, for instance, his 'sweet numerous Muse'. But Fletcher's Muse, like Wither's, is more than simply his craft objectified and personified; she is also an external power that possesses him, lodging herself in his breast and inspiring him to sing.

Wither, writing of the solace he derived from poetic composition during his imprisonment, at times uses the Muse to signify, virtually, the poem itself:

> But, though that all the world's delight forsake me,
> I have a *Muse*, and she shall Musicke make me:
> Whose ayrie Notes, in spight of closest cages,
> Shall give content to me, and after ages.   (*S.H.*, sig. Ll1ʳ)

But as this example shows, the comfort of which he speaks comes, not from the poem alone, but from his consciousness of poetic power. Wither like all the Spenserians is a Platonist in his attitude to inspiration; that is, he believes in the *furor poeticus* brought upon him by the Muse, 'a light and winged and holy thing', as Plato called her. All the Spenserians were, we may say, possessed by this idea, as well as by the Muse herself. The *idea* of poetic transcendence excites them; they write *about* and not merely *in* a state of rapture. But none does this so often, so eloquently, or with such a close approach to the Romantic position as Wither. He does not always use the Muse to convey his feelings in this matter, for it is the reality of the experience, rather than the reality of the Muse, that excites him, and she accordingly becomes dispensable. His poems *Faire-Virtue* and *The Shepheards Hunting* are both full of passages expressive, and convincingly expressive, of his sense that poetry's concern is with the ineffable. In *Faire-Virtue* he returns again and again to his 'mounting thoughts'. In *The Shepheards Hunting* he modestly reserves this experience for his friend Willie (William Browne), urging him to go on with his poem, despite envious carpings:

> If thy Verse doe bravely tower
> As shee makes wing, she gets power:
> Yet the higher she doth sore,
> Shee's affronted still the more:
> Till shee to the high'st hath past,
> Then she rests with fame at last,

> Let nought therefore, thee affright:
> But make forward in thy flight:
> For if I could match thy Rime,
> To the very Starres I'de clime
> There begin again, and flye,
> Till I reach'd Æternity.   (*S.H.*, sig. Ll8ᵛ)

But his own Muse takes wing as he writes, and soon he is celebrating again the comfort she has brought him, in lines which Émile Legouis describes as 'an outburst of gratitude to Nature . . . which at this date is surprising, one which contains all Wordsworth in germ':[5]

> In my former dayes of blisse,
> Her divine skill taught me this,
> That from every thing I saw,
> I could some invention draw:
> And raise pleasure to her height,
> Through the meanest obiects sight.
> By the murmure of a spring,
> Or the least boughes rusteling.
> By a Dazie whose leaves spred,
> Shut when *Tytan* goes to bed:
> Or a shady bush or tree,
> She could more infuse in mee,
> Then all Natures beauties can
> In some other wiser man.   (sig. Mm1ᵛ)

Elsewhere, the 'germ' seems that of Shelley rather than of Wordsworth, as in this remarkable passage from *Faire-Virtue*:

> And yet soft, (I feare) in vaine,
> I have boasted such a *Straine*.
> *Apprehensions* ever are
> Greater, then expression farre.
> And, my stryving to disclose
> What I know; hath made me lose
> My *Inventions* better part:
> And, my *Hopes* exceed my *Art*.

---

[5] Émile Legouis and Louis Cazamian, *A History of English Literature* (1947 edn.), 324.

> Speake I can; yet think I more,
> *Words* compar'd with *Thoughts*, are poore.
> And I find, had I begun,
> Such a *Straine;* it would be done,
> When we number all the sands,
> Washt ore periur'd *Goodwins* lands,
> For, of things, I should indite;
> Which, I know, are infinite.
> I doe yeeld, my *Thoughts* did clime,
> Far above the powre of *Ryme:*
> And no wonder, it is so;
> Since, there is no *Art* can show;
> Red in Roses, white in Snow;
> Nor expresse how they doe grow. (*F.V.*, sig. M1ᵛ)

In its awareness that the poet's apprehension of things ultimately defies expression, this recalls Marlowe's Tamburlaine ('What is Beauty? saith my sufferings then'), but it also anticipates Shelley's argument that 'the most glorious poetry that has ever been communicated to the world is probably a feeble shadow of the original conceptions of the poet.' Indeed, the whole poem is an affirmation of the faith Shelley was to hold:

What were virtue, love, patriotism, friendship – what were the scenery of this beautiful universe which we inhabit; what were our consolations on this side of the grave – and what were our aspirations beyond it, if poetry did not ascend to bring light and fire from those eternal regions where the owl-winged faculty of calculation dare not ever soar?[6]

In *Faire-Virtue*, Wither's 'airy' Muse, far from being 'owl-winged', has the wings of Shelley's skylark: 'as she makes wing, she gets power.'

Later, Wither's 'apprehensions' increasingly took on a religious and Christian character. Even in *Abuses Stript and Whipt* he had seen himself as inspired by God to 'make these Observations', and 'mounted aloft on Contemplation's wings' had surveyed the sins and follies of his fellows. By the time he came to write *Britain's Remembrancer* (1628), his conviction that he was God's chosen prophet was complete:

[6] *A Defence of Poetry*, in *English Critical Essays (Nineteenth Century)*, ed. Edmund D. Jones (1916), 156.

> Oh! what am I, and what my parentage?
> That Thou of all the Children of this Age
> Didst chuse out me, so highly to prefer,
> As of thy *Acts*, to be a *Register*?   (*Sp.Soc.*(1880), 208)

> What should we do but speak, when we are willed?
> What can we doe but speake when we are filled?
>   (*ibid.*, 282)

The change is regrettable, yet even now he can still produce eloquent, and even convincing, descriptions of those moments of rapture when his

> towring *Soule* is winged up, as if
> She over-flew the top of *Tenariffe*.   (*ibid.*, 91)

All the Spenserians, as I have said, are excited by the idea of poetic transcendence. Browne's declarations on the matter need not perhaps be taken too seriously. Despite the evidence of certain of his love sonnets, he is not very Platonically minded, and exclamations like

> O what a rapture have I gotten now!

seem in him no more than a happy playing at being inspired, and another way of expressing pleasure at his literary exploits. But for all the rest the belief in the divinity of poetry is central. Drayton, for instance, well deserves Professor Tillotson's description of him as 'perhaps above all, a religious poet – not so much in his biblical poems as in his view of poetry'.[7] Exclamations concerning the divine origin and power of poetry break from him frequently: poetry is 'the purest of the purest arts' and 'onely heavenly and divine'; the poet is 'a god, compar'd with ordinary men'; poets are 'Those rare PROMETHII, fetching fire from Heaven'. Drayton both admires 'brave translunary things' in others and seeks to achieve them himself. And as C. S. Lewis says, the line 'Ravish'd a World beyond the farthest Thought' 'sums up the essence of Drayton's best poetry.'[8] Drayton's celebration of the poet's raptures, though much less self-regarding than Wither's, is just as heart-felt and immediate.

[7] K. Tillotson, Hebel, V, 'Introduction', xiv.
[8] Lewis, *English Literature in the Sixteenth Century* (1954), 496.

The most rhapsodic of the Spenserians is, however, the one who is least rhapsodic about poetry itself. In his address 'To the Reader' before *Christs Victorie, and Triumph* Giles Fletcher states the case for religious poetry, and makes plain his literary loyalties and enthusiasms. In the poem itself, however, he does not often intrude. When he does so, his association of poetry with the ineffable is as marked as in any of the others. He addresses the personified Heavenly Mercy of his first book as the source of all eloquence:

> He that his pen but in that fountaine dipps,
>   How nimbly will the golden phrases flie,
>   And shed forth streames of choycest rhetorie,
>   Welling celestiall torrents out of poësie?   (*C.V.T.*, I, 48)

but at the same time laments his inability to tap such a source. The final stanza of the poem sums up his feeling that in seeking to convey 'the beatificall vision of God' his reach has inevitably exceeded his grasp:

> Impotent words, weake sides, that strive in vaine,
> In vaine, alas, to tell so heav'nly sight,
> So heav'nly sight, as none can greater feigne,
> Feigne what he can, that seemes of greatest might,
>   Might any yet compare with Infinite?
>   Infinite sure those joyes, my words but light,
> Light is the pallace whear she dwells. O blessed wight!
>   (IV, 51)

Most of the Spenserians, having learned well Sidney's lesson that poetry is 'feigning', make some reference to the doctrine in their verse. Fletcher is here recalling it to emphasise that his vision of the truth surpasses the rarest of poet's fictions. This straining after an *o altitudo* in which poetry will dissolve into a vision of reality, at the same time becoming an embodiment of it, is characteristic of both the Fletchers, of Wither, and of Drayton. The flight of the poet (or of his Muse) merges for them into the flight of the soul. Both Drayton in *Endimion and Phœbe* and Wither in *Britain's Remembrancer* describe the ascent, familiar in Platonic and Hermetic tradition, 'through ayre, and fire, and Moone, and Sun, and Planets, and Firmament, to that place which we conceive to be Heaven'.[9] Wither, as ever, writes of himself. Drayton makes Endimion a type at once of the astronomer, or, more generally, of the philosopher, seeking knowledge of the kind that Virgil in *Georgics* II, 475 *sq.*, begged the Muses to give him; of the soul of the lover, following the path described by Plato in the *Phaedrus*; and of the poet.[10] At other times the image of the Muse as a bird becomes one with the image of the winged soul, pulled back from its flight by the clogs of its coarser nature. We see this in Wither's beautiful lines,

> But oh! I feele the fumes of flesh and bloud,
> To clogg those Spirits in me, and like mudd,
> They sinke againe. More dimly burne my fires;
> To her low pitch, my *Muse* againe retires:
> And as her heavenly flames extinguisht be,
> The more I finde my Cares to burthen Me.
>
> (*W.M.*, sig. F1ʳ)

It is also implied in Giles Fletcher's allusion to his 'weake sides', as elsewhere (I,43,44) to his 'corse', his sluggish hearse', his soul's 'thicke lome'. But generally what these writers choose to stress is not the downward pull, but the 'towering', the mounting upwards, and failure to make permanent or to give adequate expression to the experience is seen less as a failure of flesh than as a failure in words themselves, as in Wither's

> Apprehensions in my mind,
> Of more sweetnes then all Art,
> Or inventions can impart.
> Thoughts, too deepe to be exprest,
> And too strong to be supprest. (*F.V.*, sig. F6ᵛ)

In all these poets there is an eager, restless striving to find and to 'digest' into words that 'one thought, one grace, one wonder at the least' of which Tamburlaine spoke. Tennyson's comment on Shelley's 'Life of Life': 'He seems to go up into the air and burst'[11] fits them

---

[9] The quotation is from Donne, Sermon LXVI. For an account of the tradition of the Soul's Journey, see Morton W. Bloomfield, *The Seven Deadly Sins* (Michigan, 1952), 16 *sq.*, 47.

[10] See my article, 'Brave Translunary Things', *Modern Language Review* (1964), LIX, 501–10.

[11] Quoted by A. C. Bradley, *op. cit.*, 161.

C

also very well, at least when they are writing of their poetic aspirations and experiences. Carried to its ultimate, as in Phineas Fletcher's
friend and follower Edward Benlowes this attempt surely is:

> Could I but coin a word beyond all sweets! 'Twere that!

> Immense ETERNITY! What mystic art
>   Of THEE may copy any part,
> Since THOU an indeterminable CIRCLE art!

> ... Oh, swallow me, ABYSS![12]

it may even seem oddly to be approaching the poetic ideals of
Mallarmé.

One very obvious difference between the school of Spenser and that
of Donne lies in the addiction of the former to the long poem, particularly the narrative poem, and its almost total abandonment by the
latter. Donne's break with tradition and with the tastes of his immediate
predecessors is nowhere illustrated more clearly than in his lack of
interest in narrative, for this involved also a disregard for much of the
cherished poetic of the Renaissance. Thus whatever weight we put
upon his oft-quoted statement to Sir Robert Carr that 'I did best when
I had least truth for my subjects', it remains clear that the doctrine of
poetry as fiction expounded in Sidney's *Apology* has only a limited
relevance to Donne's creations. Although Donne may be proving
himself a 'right poet' by presenting in his lyrics idealised pictures of a
lover's moods,[13] he is nevertheless not the rightest of 'right poets',

---

[12] Benlowes, *Theophila*, Saintsbury, *Minor Poets of the Caroline Period* (1905), I, 380, 382, 389.
[13] Since Donne is a familiar example of the 'strong-lined' poet, it is worth noting that
Phineas Fletcher at one point equates 'strong lines' with hyperbole, and both with
'feigning'. He writes of his 'choice Nymph', Parthenia (*P.I.*, X., 30):
> It is a strong verse here to write but true:
> Hyperboles in others are but half thy due.
In 'A reply upon the fair M.S.' (*Works*, II, 240], he even produces a poem that might
fairly be called Metaphysical, by agreeing that he *was* no poet in a former poem censuring
woman's levity, since he then spoke the truth.

for that, in Sidney's eyes, is clearly the narrative poet. Nor, though he may make things 'better than Nature bringeth forth', does he fulfil that other function of the 'right poet', in making things 'quite anew, forms such as never were in Nature, as the Heroes, Demigods, Cyclops, Chimeras, Furies, and such like'. The Spenserian poets, on the other hand, do all these things. 'Who says that fictions only and false hair Become a verse?' asks George Herbert. And, though they might have objected to the way the question was phrased, they could only have answered: 'We do.'

Their choice of subject itself shows how nearly synonymous for the Spenserians were making and make-believe. They love the golden worlds of pastoral, of mythology, and of fairy. They love them for their idealisation of ordinary experience, and for the means of escape they offer from it. But they also love them, and the long poems that usually embody them, for the opportunities they afford the poet of exercising his creative skills. It is the spaciousness, the roominess, that attracts. The Spenserians like a poem that gives them a place, a space to move about in, as in *Poly-Olbion*, *Britannia's Pastorals*, *The Purple Island*. There they can experience the 'golden hours' of creating that Browne writes of in a sonnet, hours

> Wherein my Ffancy led me to the woods
> And tun'd soft layes of rurall merriment.
>
> (Lans. 777, f. 16ᵛ)

Significantly, they like to employ the image of the poem as a garden to describe this pleasure. This image is in itself a commonplace, but not always as they use it. As a rule the ideas associated with the poem-as-garden are orderliness ('well-keptedness'); variety (from the flowers); and of course, beauty.[14] Orderliness implies cultivation and hence, in a poem, Art as opposed to Nature. Wither, who professes to care nothing for Art, several times uses the image to establish what his poem is *not*, as well as what it is. Thus he offers his *Juvenilia* to his readers, knowing that 'though some may dislike, some will approve':

---

[14] See, for example, Sir William Alexander, *Anacrasis* (1634), in *Critical Essays of the Seventeenth Century*, ed. Spingarn (1908), I. 182: 'I compare a Poem to a Garden, the disposing of the Parts of the one to the several Walks of the other . . . and the Variety of Invention to the Diversity of the Flowers thereof.'

> For, many men will leave a pruned Grove,
> And curious Garden Allies, to goe see,
> What pleasures in untilled Mountaines be:
> And much delight in Woods to take the shade,
> Of Artlesse Arbors, by rude Nature made.

He repeats the image in the Dedication of his *Emblemes*, Book III, again contrasting the pleasures of walking in 'Artlesse Groves' with those offered by 'well-trim'd *garden-bowrs*'.[15] In assuming this attitude of 'the Mower against Gardens', however (the parallel with Marvell's figure is worth noting), Wither is not representative of the Spenserians. His fellows value the garden image primarily, it is true, for its stress upon variety, but also because of the apt emblem it provides of Art *combining* with Nature.[16] Thus Drayton in the Preface to *Poly-Olbion*, invites the reader to 'walke forth into the *Tempe* and Feelds of the Muses' (this is England seen, not as a wilderness, but as a garden – 'the Garden of the World erewhile'; it is also, of course, the poem). Through 'most delightfull Groves', he promises him, he will be led 'to the top of an easie hill',

where in artificiall caves, cut out of the most naturall Rock, thou shalt see the ancient people of this Ile delivered thee in their lively images.

Here Drayton nicely makes the point that, though his method may be Art's, his material is Nature.

The rest of Drayton's statement stresses the delights of variety which the poem will afford, and this, as I have already suggested, is the Spenserians' usual emphasis. Characteristically, however, the delight they have in mind is primarily self-delight. William Browne develops a very long and elaborate garden-image as an apology and justification for his own poetic grasshopper-mindedness. Here variety of invention is signified by all parts of the garden, not simply by the flowers. The planning of the garden is appreciated, but primarily for the variety of the pleasures it affords:

[15] *cf.* Addison's comparison (*Spectator*, No. 417) between the *Aeneid* and the *Iliad*, representing the *Aeneid* as a 'well-ordered garden', the *Iliad* as 'a Country uninhabited', offering 'savage prospects of vast deserts, uncultivated marshes, huge forests, mishapen rocks and precipices'.

[16] Vauquelin de la Fresnaye in his *L'Art Poétique* (published 1605; written c.1574–89), develops the analogy between God, 'iardinier de la terre', and the artist, precisely to emphasise this point.

> Where here the curious cutting of a hedge,
> There, by a pond, the trimming of the sedge;
> Here the fine setting of well shading trees,
> The walkes there mounting up by small degrees ...
>
> (*B.P.*, II, sig. I4^v)

The visitor to such a garden is overwhelmed by the diversity of its attractions:

> Then to the arbours walke, then to the bowres,
> Thence to the walkes againe, thence to the flowres,
> Then to the Birds, and to the cleare spring thence,
> Now pleasing one, and then another sence.   (sig. K1^r)

'Pardon! that I have run astray so long,' the passage begins. 'Blame me not then ...' it ends. The reader is left to work out the parallel between garden and poem for himself.

The Spenserians' affinity with Keats on this matter too is strongly marked. One remembers Keats's pleasure, when beginning *Endymion*, at the prospect of having to 'make 4,000 Lines of one bare circumstance and fill them with Poetry', or his answer to his own question, 'Why endeavour after a long Poem?',

Do not the Lovers of Poetry like to have a little Region to wander in where they may pick and choose, and in which the images are so numerous that many are forgotten and found new in a second Reading: which may be food for a Week's stroll in the Summer?[17]

Yeats too tells us that in his youth he thought of a long poem 'as a region into which one should wander from the cares of life'.[18] 'Ever let the Fancy roam.' There are poets, it seems, particularly young poets, for whom this is the most delightful of precepts, and best fulfilled in the long poem. The Spenserians, and most of the Romantics, are this kind of poet.

Browne's garden simile, which is really a digression in praise of digressions, anticipates the opinion of someone else, however, besides Keats. Tristram Shandy in his fourteenth chapter was to expatiate on the difficulties of a man's getting to his journey's end:

---

[17] *The Letters of John Keats*, ed. Maurice Buxton Forman (1952 edn.), 52.
[18] Norman Jeffares, *W. B. Yeats, Man and Poet* (1962 edn.) 23.

For if he is a man of the least spirit, he will have fifty deviations from a straight line to make with this or that party as he goes along, which he can no ways avoid. He will have views and prospects to himself perpetually soliciting his eye, which he can no more help standing still to look at than he can fly.

Comparison between this passage and Browne's makes Browne appear Shandean, not just through the fact of his digression, but through its content also. The impulse being celebrated and confessed to by both writers is something rather different from a simple Keatsian delight in the opportunity to make endless poetry: rather, they are giving a welcome to the opportunity literature offers for simple garrulity, for self-indulgence and self-portraiture. Elsewhere (B.P., II, sig. F1^{v}) Browne compares himself in his digressions to a maiden gathering a nosegay, and wandering off after the prettiest flowers, a comparison which Wither also uses in *Britain's Remembrancer*.[19] Browne and Wither, in fact, provide extreme examples among the Spenserians of what we might call their libertinism in verse. All the Spenserians, even Drayton, the most decorum-conscious, and Phineas Fletcher, the most controlled, tend to be self-indulgent in matters of structure, thus making of their long poems 'loose baggy monsters', but only Browne and Wither make a principle of this. And Browne, who sometimes seems an unconscious impersonator rather than an imitator, was probably following Wither, for his protestations about his 'free-born Muse' all occur in the second book of the *Pastorals*, and quite possibly when he wrote the first book he did not yet know either Wither or his poetry. Wither constantly – in *Faire-Virtue*, *Wither's Motto*, *Britain's Remembrancer* – uses the claims of *self* to excuse a lack of method and of art. He frequently takes note of the critics who have complained that his songs 'exceed the fiddler's last', but only to scorn them:

> I disdaine to make my Song,
> For their pleasures short or long.
> If I please Ile end it here:
> If I list Ile sing this yeere.   (*F.V.*, sig. C3^{r})

In the Preface to *Wither's Motto* he comes very close to Sterne:

The *Method* is none at all: for I was loath to make businesse of a recreation. And

---

[19] Sylvester also uses this comparison in *D.W.W.*, beginning of 'The Vocation' (1611 edn., sig.Cc7^{r}). This may have provided the model for both Browne and Wither.

we know, he that rides abroad for his pleasure, is not tyed so strictly to keepe
High-wayes, as hee that takes a Iourney.   (sig. A3ʳ)

In *Britain's Remembrancer*, his many 'justifications' of his 'Method' have
become formidable. When he begins to write, he declares,

> *Mogul* doth know
> As well as I, what path my *Muse* will goe. . . .
>
> And though my matter, when I first begin,
> Will hardly fill one page, yet being in,
> Methinks, if neither faintnesse, friends, nor night,
> Disturbed me, for ever I could write.   (*Sp.Soc.*, 276)

Later, in *Campo-Musae, or The Field-Musings of Captain George Wither*
(1643), he was to claim that the war made such writing necessary:

> Destructive times, distractive muzings yeeld,
> Expect not therefore method now of me.
>   (*Sp.Soc., Misc. Works*, I, 7)

But by this time no-one can have expected it.

Sir John Harington in his *Briefe Apologie of Poetrie* (1591) had
defended Ariosto's habit of 'speaking so much in his own person by
digression', and it might seem that Ariosto provided the Spenserians
with their chief model and justification in this respect. But Ariosto's
digressions are, as Robert M. Durling has shown,[20] controlled and
purposeful, and the *Orlando Furioso* is as 'well-wrought' as any urn.
Like Spenser, Ariosto has a 'compass course' from which he never
really deviates. Of the Spenserians, only Phineas Fletcher, within of
course much smaller limits, has anything like this narrative drive.
Browne's 'course' in particular seems to exist only to be deviated from.
Thus although the love of variety exemplified in the long poems of
these poets suggests a continuity of taste and feeling with that of the
romantic epic, their discursiveness is not, I think, to be wholly identified
with the 'chatty discursive strain' which Mr. Durling has noted as a
characteristic of that form.[21] Rather, it is to be attributed to an

[20] Robert M. Durling, *The Figure of the poet in Renaissance Epic* (Cambridge, Mass., 1965),
111–181.
[21] *ibid.*, 10.

indisposition to submit to the disciplines of narrative, and to a desire for quick poetic returns. It also owes something to the new impulse towards self-revelation that characterises the early seventeenth century, but which we are more accustomed to notice in its prose. Phineas Fletcher was probably using the word 'essay' in a very literal sense when he described *The Purple Island* as 'these raw *Essayes* of my very unripe yeares, and almost childehood', but undoubtedly Wither in calling *Abuses Stript and Whipt* 'satyricall essayes' was using the term in its new literary sense. Wither also liked to describe his poems as 'musings'. The fondness of the Spenserians for the Epistle is also worth noting here. If we are reminded by them of the Romantics, it is partly because of their preference for reflective, semi-lyrical forms in which they can relax and 'be themselves'.

At this point, we should also recall the importance to the Spenserians of a poem I mentioned earlier, the *Divine Weeks and Works* of Du Bartas, as translated by Sylvester. Undoubtedly it was Du Bartas's example that encouraged poets like Browne and Wither and Giles Fletcher to turn narrative into discourse. Du Bartas himself uses the Old Testament material that forms the basis of his narrative to expatiate freely on the still-continuing wonders of creation. By frequent comment and exclamation he makes his presence felt in the poem; he is our guide and lecturer, and quite self-consciously so. He is often at his most digressive in his similes, which are long and elaborate. His subject itself, or so he would argue, justifies his method: if variety, as Tasso had argued, is permissible in the little world of the poem since it reflects the variety of the great world itself, how much more must that be so when the variety of the great world forms the very subject of the little one? If the world is the Book of God's works –

> The World's a Book in *Folio*, printed all
> With God's great Works in letters Capitall, . . .[22]

then his poem is the book of the Book. Again, if

> The World's a School, where (in a general Story)
> God alwayes reads dumb Lectures of his Glory, . . .[23]

---

[22] Joshua Sylvester, *Du Bartas his Devine Weekes and Workes* (1611 edn.) sig.C3^v.
[23] *ibid.*, sig. C3^r.

then the poet will become his interpreter and turn those lectures into words. In this way the habit of seeing the long poem as above all an opportunity to talk of many things can be considered to have divine sanction. Du Bartas also has many invocations and prayers to God for assistance to his Muse, which are written in the tone of mingled rapture and humility we have noticed in the Spenserians. The treatment of the Muse in the poems of the Fletchers, and in Drayton's religious poems, where she is like his the Heavenly Muse, is very close to Du Bartas's. In this respect he must be seen as a very potent influence in the development of the Spenserians' rhapsodic attitudes to poetry, as well as on their handling of narrative.

It is not to be supposed that because these poets were so self-seeking and so self-delighted in their verse, they were therefore indifferent to the reactions of their audience. They are, in fact, extremely audience-conscious. But to be audience-conscious is in their case also to be self-conscious, for each is his own first and most admiring audience. This is particularly clear in the case of Browne, Wither, and Phineas Fletcher. The reader of their poems feels himself to be, if not actually an eavesdropper, certainly on the outer ring of observers, for all three use imaginary audiences to enlarge their self-praises and, even more, to enhance their sense of *performance*. More will be said of these audiences, in so far as they are pastoral audiences, in the next chapter. Actually, they can take many forms. Wither when he feels most rapt can cry

Hemme me, *Angels*, in a Ring,   (*F.V.*, sig. H7^{r})

but of course this is only a way of indicating that such is the only audience that could really do him justice. Phineas Fletcher numbers the Muses themselves among his audience – '*Muses* by soft *Chamus* sitting'. The mention of 'Chamus' localises the performance, and is a reminder of the friends who in actual life must have been Fletcher's immediate audience. Similarly in the work of Browne and Wither, whatever the imaginary setting, we are made to feel by scattered references to the banks of Thames that this was where the poems were first read and enjoyed. Between the imaginary audience, that is, and the actual audience (ourselves), we are aware of the presence in these poems of a third audience, the living friends and acquaintances of the poet. In familiar epistle and lyric this is only to be expected; the unusual thing is that it should occur in narrative also.

This 'real-life' audience is rather strikingly feminine in character. The Spenserian poets are distinctly aware of their women-readers, and of their own duties and responsibilities towards them. Quite often they assert the purity of their lines: their Muses are 'maiden', and the maiden can read their poems without fear of corruption.[24] The difference between them and Donne in this respect underlines the admiration of Donne's followers for his 'masculine expression'. Drayton too was praised as 'masculine',[25] and very properly, but the other Spenserians seem neither to have received nor merited the epithet. And even Drayton shares their concern for their women-readers: in the Preface to *Poly-Olbion*, for example, he expresses his fear that the work's 'unusuall tract may perhaps seem difficult, to the female Sex'. Phineas Fletcher's shorter poems frequently celebrate the 'Kentish' Nymphs to whom he 'often pipes and often sings': he addresses poems 'to the fair *M.S.*' and to Lady Culpepper; he bids farewell to 'ye *Norfolk* maids, and *Ida* crue'. The poems make it clear that he enjoys the company of women and enjoys writing for them. Wither's *Faire-Virtue* has for audience

> a troupe of Beauties knowne well nigh
> Through all the Plaines of happy *Britany*.   (sig. B3^r)

They could, of course, be fictitious, but I rather think they are not, and that in the lines quoted Wither is hinting at their identity. In *The Shepheards Hunting* Wither also mentions Browne as one who

> with his Musicke, (to his greater fame)
> Hath late made proud the fairest *Nymphs* of Thame.
> (sig. Mm5^v)

This is puzzling, in that we do not know its precise reference, but is

---

[24] *Cf.* Du Bartas's assurance that he has written only 'Verse that a Virgine without blush may read' (sig. D5^r).
[25] E. Heyward, 'To his Friend the Authour', before *The Barons Warres*, Hebel, II, 7.

confirmed by many allusions by Browne himself to his female
audience, such as his eulogy of the

> All-beauteous Ladies, love-alluring Dames,
> That on the banckes of *Isca*, *Humber*, *Thames*,
> By your incouragement can make a Swaine
> Climbe by his song where none but soules attaine:
> And by the gracefull reading of our lines
> Renew our heate to further brave designes,
>
> (*B.P.*, II, sig. I4^r)

with its conclusion that, since Nature is now so prodigal of such
beauties, his song

> hath beene tun'd and heard by beauties more
> Then all the *Poets* that have liv'd before.

The attitude of the poets to this audience is in part sexual, in part
narcissistic. Basically the audience serves to recapture and prolong the
poet's own delight. They are to savour the verse to the full, to *linger*
over it:

> Let her linger, on each straine,
> As if shee would heare't againe.   (*F.V.*, sig. C1^v)

At the same time, the sensuousness of the verse will receive its most
effective realisation by their participation:

> Charme her quicke senses! and with raptures sweet
> Make her affection with your cadence meet!
>
> (*B.P.*, II, sig. B3^r)

In Phineas Fletcher's poem 'To Mr. Jo. Tomkins' the Muses themselves
are represented as experiencing what is tantamount to a sexual thrill
at Tomkins's 'strains' (since Tomkins was organist at King's College,
these could be either musical or poetic):

> There sitting they admire thy dainty strains
> And while thy sadder accent sweetly plains,
> Feel thousand sugred joyes creep in their melting veins.
>
> (*Works*, II, 233)

Similarly in *Faire-Virtue* Wither wishes for his mistress that his rhymes will 'with ravishings so ceaze her She may feele the height of pleasure'.

The Spenserians are keenly aware of the 'charms', the 'enchanting sweetness', of poetry. That it is a rhetorical, persuasive art is thus one of their basic assumptions. As such, they demand that it should be smooth and musical. This is more than a principle with them, however; it is a passion. The 'sense of musical delight' which they all possess makes them firm on the need for smoothness, and passionately devoted to rhyme. Their principles and practice in this matter are in accord with Puttenham's teachings on 'English measure': they 'use as much as may be the most flowing words and slippery sillables' that they can pick out, and seek 'tunable consents in the latter end' of their verses.[26] Even Drayton sees this harmony that he loves in terms of the love relationship: in his Ode 'To the New Yeere', he promises that

> in my choise Composures,
> The soft and easie Closures,
> So amorously shall meet;
> That ev'ry lively Ceasure
> Shall tread a perfect Measure,
> Set on so equall feet. (37–42)

Similarly Browne's request to the Muses to 'cause every coupling cadence flow in blisses' conveys the deep satisfaction he derives from the heroic couplet. This preference for smoothness, softness, and sweetness separates the Spenserians sharply not only from Donne and his followers, but, to a lesser degree, from Jonson also. Drayton's attack in *Poly-Olbion*, Song XXI, upon those

> Whose Verses hobling run, as with disjoynted bones,
> And make a viler noyse then carts upon the stones,

is thought to be directed against Donne and his school. The other Spenserians do not provide explicit criticisms of the new poetry, but their omission of Donne's name from their various surveys of praiseworthy poets is significant, for they must have known at least his satires and the *Anniversaries*. Jonson was to parody the 'soft ambling verse' of Wither in his masque, *Time Vindicated*, and his 'darling

[26] Puttenham, *The Arte of English Poesie*, ed. G. D. Willcock and Alice Walker (1936), 77.

measure' was in the next century to receive further ridicule for its effeminacy when employed by the 'namby-pamby' Ambrose Philips. Yet many writers in their own period and after, as George Saintsbury says, found 'the sliding, slipping flow of Wither and Browne' 'most alluring'.[27]

The Spenserians must therefore be numbered among the 'superstitious fools' whom Carew in his 'Elegy on the Death of Dr. Donne' mocks for their continued worship of 'old Orpheus'. They see poetry in Orphic terms, as a ravishing of soul and sense through the music and power of words. Thus poetry persuades, even if only to pleasure. Not that any of them would in theory accept the 'pleasure principle' as a sufficient justification of their art: Drayton, Wither, and the Fletchers all hold firmly to a moral and didactic view of poetry, and Browne, like the young Keats, looks forward to the time when he will teach through his poetry. It is because he believes wholeheartedly in the educative function of the poet that Drayton deplores the contemporary habit of circulating poems privately instead of publishing them, verses being 'wholly deduc't to Chambers, and nothing esteem'd in this lunatique Age, but what is kept in Cabinets, and must only passe by Transcription'.[28] Here too, as in his complaints concerning roughness and obscurity, it is assumed that he has Donne and his friends in mind.

Drayton, as his Elegies particularly make plain, saw the decay of poetry – what to him was poetry – in his own day as a national disaster. In verses before Sir John Beaumont's *Bosworth Field* he warned of

> The Plagues that must upon this Nation be
> By whom the Muses have neglected bin.

His Elegy 'To My Noble Friend Mr. William Browne' is 'of the evil times', and Browne repeats the theme in his verses before *Poly-Olbion* (1622), lamenting that 'the *Times* refuse Both *Meanes* to live, and *Matter* for a *Muse*'. The sense of alienation seems particularly strong in these two poets, and may have formed an increasing bond between them as the years passed. But all the Spenserians are alike in seeing the poetry they write as at once something intensely personal and intensely

[27] Saintsbury, *op. cit.*, I, vi.
[28] Hebel, IV, v*.

public. They need a setting and background for it, first the poet's own particular locality – 'Thames' sweet bank', 'learned *Chame*' (rivers figure largely, presumably as local variants of Helicon) – then the wider one of the country at large. Not only do they write poems for and about Britain – *Britannia's Pastorals*, *Britain's Remembrancer*, *Brittain's Ida*, *Poly-Olbion*, *Englands Heroicall Epistles*; the country exists also in their consciousness, almost as an actual presence, as they write – 'our sweet Isle', 'our pleasant Isle' (Browne), 'this our poets' isle' (Wither). Titles like *Britannia's Pastorals* and *Brittain's Ida* illustrate their continuing enthusiasm for the humanistic programme of the sixteenth century: in such poems they sought to put their country poetically on a level with Greece and Rome and Italy. Thus despite its self-delighting character, their verse is not self-sufficient; it is informed with a sense of tradition and of the community. Ultimately it seeks the world, and not itself. It chooses for theme 'traditional sanctity and loveliness'. It is not the way Donne chose to write, but it is a way to which poets often come back, even poets within the 'Donne tradition' – Marvell, for example.

Carew, writing Donne's epitaph, described him as 'Apollo's first, at last, the true Gods Priest'. Donne, however, unlike Spenser, Drayton, and the rest of the Spenserians, was never consciously 'Apollo's Priest'; he never saw himself in that rôle, either in the sense of celebrating Apollo or in the more general sense of emphasising his own place in the poetic order. Whatever his indebtedness to earlier poets, he writes without reference to them. Poetry is to him neither a cult nor a mystery, but simply one of the activities of life. He does not, in writing, watch himself being a poet; what he is saying absorbs him rather than what he is doing or being. He has as little interest in the Muse as in Apollo: he mentions her occasionally, mostly in the *Epistles*, but the references are clearly perfunctory, a mere figure of speech, and like the pavement artist he could have written by his poems 'All my own work' and have added 'No outside help from the Muse'.[29] This indifference to the very notion of tradition and rejection of all bardic ceremonial and insignia separate Donne and his followers very sharply from Spenser and *his* followers. The Spenserians, as we have seen, carry over into the seventeenth century Spenser's sense of the poet's high office as something destined and inspired. The Muse really matters to them; and if

[29] I have borrowed this comparison from James Reeves, *Selected Poems of Emily Dickinson* (1959), xli.

they write less reverently of her, and more familiarly, than Spenser had done, this is partly because their whole manner of writing is more familiar. (The Muse is their 'darling' and they hers.)[30] Like Spenser, they accept the notion of the poet's public responsibility. Drayton is most clearly and immediately Spenser's successor in this respect: he sees it as the poet's function to foster heroism and virtue, by means of

> Wise pollicie, Morallity, or Story,
> Well purtraying the Ancients and their glory.
>
> *(Moone-Calfe*, 407–8)

Thus poetry for him, as for Spenser, exists essentially for 'the great'. (An interesting passage in his *Peirs Gaveston* (1593–4) describes the ideal conditions existing at the court of Edward Longshanks, where 'the learned were accounted little Gods', in terms that would have pleased Spenser or any courtly humanist.) Wither, equally devoted to the idea of poetry as instructress of the young, thinks not of 'learned impes' but of 'the common people'. He converts Spenser's poetic ideal from an aristocratic to a democratic one; his own popularity and the increasing licentiousness of the Stuart court together lead him to a complete dissociation of poetry and virtue on the one hand and 'Princes pallace' on the other, so that in his *Haleluiah* (1641), he has moved so far from Spenser's position as to write (p. 386), '*Courtiers* are so frequently vitious, that some thinke it impossible they should be virtuous.'[31] Wither represents an extreme development. The other Spenserians, the Fletchers especially, would have liked to have made of James I a male Gloriana, and by their own connections they do in part keep up the association of poetry with the great houses. Nevertheless, in their work too we see poetry moving out from the court to the market-place, though seeking at the same time to preserve its old hierarchic function and dignities.

---

[30] Like so many characteristics of the Spenserians, this familiar, intimate way of addressing the Muse probably derives from Du Bartas. *Cf.*, for example, *D.W.W.*, sig, L1ʳ, 'Com, com (my Darling) let us haste to land.'

[31] Spenser, of course, recognised the viciousness of some courtiers, but the whole scheme of *The Faerie Queene* depended on the existence of some who were capable of virtue.

Pastoral Poetry

The most interesting and in many ways the best part of the Spenserians' work, considered collectively, is their pastoral poetry. It is through pastoral that they present themselves as a group, or rather as two separate groups, possessing so many common characteristics that they can often be considered as one. The two groups are: Drayton, Browne, Wither, and their associates on the one hand; the Fletchers and theirs on the other. Their pastoral writing is quite varied in character: Drayton, Browne, Wither, and Phineas Fletcher all wrote eclogues (Fletcher's are piscatories), but Drayton over the years developed his own special type of eclogue, and the other three all carried the pastoral over into other forms, Wither and Phineas Fletcher, in *Faire-Virtue* and *The Purple Island* respectively, giving a pastoral frame-work to non-pastoral themes, and Browne, in *Britannia's Pastorals*, producing the most ambitious pastoral verse-narrative in existence. Their writings show a knowledge of earlier pastoral, chiefly of course, though not exclusively, of Spenser's. They are thoroughly at home in the convention, but they are not mere imitators, and it is because of this that their work has value. Their eclogues, as H. E. Cory long ago noted, show a genuine development of the methods of *The Shepheardes Calender*.[1] Looking at their pastoral as a whole, however, one is struck not so much by the ways in which they have carried on and developed the convention, as by the quality of their personal response to pastoral, the value they set upon it. They can and do imitate, but that is comparatively superficial, not the heart of the matter; their knowledge of pastoral is so intimate that they do not require models – they are merely ladders to be kicked away. They move with ease in the

[1] H. E. Cory, 'The Golden Age of Spenserian Pastoral', *Publications of the Modern Language Association*, XXV (1910), 241–67.

form, as though in their working clothes; they think and feel in it.
Earlier pastoral may have given their thoughts and feelings their
direction, but it is not controlling them now. 'It was the peculiarly
combined satisfaction of freedom and formalism which attracted so
many Elizabethans to pastoral.' writes Kathleen Tillotson.[2] This is true,
but for the later generation of Elizabethans represented by the younger
Spenserians, the freedom counted for more than the formalism. There
was for them, in addition, a 'peculiarly combined satisfaction' of a
different kind – the satisfaction of being at once personal and im-
personal, of depicting simultaneously a brazen and a golden world, the
actual and the ideal. The pastoral enabled them both to tell their
dreams, and to write of life as it was. It is in their pastoral that the
Spenserians 'give themselves away', both intentionally and uninten-
tionally. This chapter is concerned with the ways in which they do it.

There is nothing surprising in the Spenserians' choosing to write
pastoral. Considering their tastes and loyalties, it was an inevitable
choice. It placed them at once in the great tradition, as they saw it.
It did not at the same time make them reactionaries, for, unlike the
sonnet-sequence, pastoral did not go out with the Elizabethan period.
The 'Shakespearian moment', after all, was the moment of *The
Winter's Tale* as well as of *Hamlet* and *King Lear*. And though Donne
personally banished nymphs and shepherds from his poetry, his
disciples, with the exception of George Herbert, did not. The seventeenth century, with its cult of the *Arcadia*, its devotion to French
romances, and its court masques, was as committed to the pastoral as
any. Nevertheless, although the Spenserians had no need to feel that
they were being old-fashioned in writing pastoral, they used the form
to express, quite vehemently, their loyalty to the old fashions. Worn by
them, the shepherd's cloak became a party uniform, and the pastoral
itself – not so much its content as its *use* – acquired symbolic value.
What they did was to appropriate the pastoral, to make of it the
embodiment of the true faith (in poetry) and themselves the inheritors
or preservers of that faith. Their pastoral embodies their poetic. This
does indeed distinguish it from other seventeenth-century pastoral,
which on the whole – in the lyrics of the Cavaliers, for example – is
more a matter simply of the polite disguise. Thus not the fact of their
using pastoral, but their manner of using it, serves, once more, to
emphasise their isolation.

[2] Hebel, V,4.

Briefly, what attracted them was the shepherd-persona, the persona standing, of course, for the poet. The shepherd has seldom any other rôle in their poetry. For Phineas Fletcher he is occasionally a clergyman (though first a poet) and for Drayton he is also, in the person of Rowland, a lover. But for the most part, writ large over all their work is the equation, 'Shepherd = Poet', or, more accurately, 'Shepherd = Right Poet'. And the 'right poet', as we saw in the last chapter, is for them the professional poet, for whom the writing of poetry is a professional act, for which the help of the Muse is necessary. In the shepherd-persona they found this professionalism acknowledged and underlined. The very assumption of a pastoral name set the poet apart from the man; to put on a shepherd's cloak was to put on singing-robes. The great exemplars were, of course, Colin Clout and Astrophel. In *Poets on Fortune's Hill*, John Danby describes Spenser as 'the poet poeticising in public', in contrast with Sidney, who simply wrote for himself. His argument makes Spenser a professional, Sidney a gentleman-amateur. For the Spenserians, however, they were both professionals, not because of their attitude to their public, which is what Professor Danby is concerned with, but because of their attitude to their poetry, their deliberate acceptance of the rôle of poet, as acknowledged in their pastoral pseudonyms.

To write pastoral *was*, as I suggested when discussing *The Shepheardes Calender*, to 'poeticise': that was what the Spenserians liked about it. As Spenser is the poets' poet, so pastoral is poets' poetry. It offers ample scope for 'making' and for craftsmanship, as well as for talking about poetry. Above all, it provides the poet with a mirror in which he may contemplate his own image, as a poet. The Spenserians exploit these opportunities to the full. Their pastorals are, predominantly, poems about poetry. This is true even of Drayton. His *Idea The Shepheards Garland* (1593) is constructed along more orthodox lines than later pastorals are, either his own or those of the other Spenserians, yet its sub-title, *Rowlands Sacrifice to the nine Muses*, accurately indicates its bias. Its pre-occupation with poetry is more marked even than that of *The Shepheardes Calender*. Browne's *Britannia's Pastorals*, although a narrative poem, abounds in portraits of the artist as a young shepherd. The first comes in the opening lines, where, by combining an imitation of the formula with which Spenser introduces *The Faerie Queene* and Virgil the *Aeneid* with echoes of *The Shepheardes Calender*, Browne manages to suggest, correctly though perhaps not entirely deliberately, that he is about to write, not pastoral epic certainly, but the epic of pastoral, national in character and monumental in form:

> I that whileare neere *Tavies* stragling spring,
> Unto my seely Sheepe did use to sing,
> And plaid to please my selfe, on rusticke Reede,
> Nor sought for *Baye*, (the learned Shepheards meede),
> But as a Swayne unkent fed on the plaines,
> And made the *Eccho* umpire of my straines:
> Am drawne by time, (although the weakst of many)
> To sing those Layes as yet unsung of any. . . .
>
> My *Muse* for lofty pitches shall not rome,
> But homely pipen of her native home:
> And to the Swaynes, Love rurall Minstralsie,
> Thus deare *Britannia* will I sing of thee.
>
> (*B.P.*, I, sig., BIʳ)

But being a pastoral poet rather than an epic one, and lacking Homer's capacity for self-effacement, he does not now withdraw. Rather, he remains at our elbow, commenting on his own performance, the omnipresent rather than the omniscient author. He goes further, and presents an image of himself, the shepherd-poet, addressing, not us, the readers, but an audience of shepherd-swains. These pictures usually come when, eclogue-wise, he breaks off the narrative. Some are rather delightful, for example:

> But shepheards I have wrong'd you, 'tis now late
> For see our Maid stands hollowing on yond gate,
> 'Tis supper-time, with all, and we had need
> Make haste away, unlesse we meane to speed
> With those that *kisse the Haresfoot: Rhumes** are bred
> Some say by going supperlesse to bed,
> And those I love not; therefore cease my rime,
> And put my Pipes up till another time.   (II, sig. H2ʳ)

Still not content with this, he goes through the looking-glass into his own story, where he appears as Willy, one of the shepherd-poets who

* i.e. rheums.

entertain the goddess Thetis on her tour of Britain. His long tale of the loves of Tavy and Walla forms the climax of the entertainment. In Book III he again finds a place in the story, this time quite consciously as its author. Meeting his hero, Celadyne, he tells him

> with my voice
> I have recorded thine.

Finally, having placed Celadyne where he may overhear a fairy's song, he insinuates himself into that song too. The fairy, singing of the loves of Cupid and Psyche, tells how Venus, searching for her son, found him with 'a shepherd that was born by west', whom 'the little Cupid' loved for his verse. The shepherd is easily identified.

The pastoral elements in Phineas Fletcher's *The Purple Island* and Wither's *Faire-Virtue* reflect a similar 'self-seeking'. These two narrative poems both have pastoral frameworks, which put the poet, in his shepherd rôle, in the forefront of the poem, and turn his narration into a dramatic performance. *The Purple Island* is a moral epic of the *psychomachia* type, yet so prominent is the pastoral setting that Quarles could salute Fletcher as 'the Ingenious Composer of This Pastorall'. Thirsil, the narrator (i.e. Fletcher himself), is exalted in various ways, first by being chosen may-lord, which is the occasion for his story; then by being placed on high,

> on a gentle rising hill
> (Where all his flock he round might feeding view),

and where also he was

> circled with a lovely crue
> Of Nymphs & shepherd-boyes.
>
> (*P.I.*, II, 1)

(This perhaps owes something to Spenser's description of Colin on Mount Acidale); and finally by being led off in a triumph greater, if anything, than that which in the story has just been accorded the union of Christ and his Church:

> So up they rose, while all the shepherds throng
> With their loud pipes a countrey triumph blew,

And led their *Thirsil* home with joyfull song:
Meantime the lovely Nymphs with garlands new
   His locks in Bay and honour'd Palm-tree bound,
   With Lilies set, and Hyacinths around;
And Lord of all the yeare, and their May-sportings crown'd.

(XII, 89)

The use of a pastoral introduction of this kind for the type of story
Fletcher has to tell is, so far as I have been able to discover, unique.
Its nearest equivalent is the induction, with its May-morning setting,
of the mediaeval dream-poem. Here, however, it is the induction rather
than the story that constitutes the dream, the poet's own dream of
poetic fame and glory. All the Spenserians used pastoral to indulge in
that dream, although Drayton, as we might expect, subordinates his
self-praises, in the person of Rowland, to the blazon of Idea.

To be a pastoral poet was therefore to *be* a poet. The two activities
go so closely together that in the Spenserian poet's mind they seem at
times to become identical. If a shepherd, then a poet, but also, if a poet,
then a shepherd, seems to be the natural assumption. Not all poets
qualify, however; only the 'right poets'. Within their pastoral, the
Spenserians develop a special language in which they write of poetry,
and in this language 'shepherd' stands for poets of their own type, and
pastoral itself becomes an image of the old Elizabethan type of poetry.
The Elizabethan period itself becomes the Golden Age. So Wither,
characteristically enclosing his epithalamion for the Princess Elizabeth
within a rather lengthier account of himself (still as a shepherd)
concludes that, if she will accept his lay, he

> Will ioyfull turne unto my *flocke* again:
> And there unto my fellow *shepheards* tell,
> Why *you* are lov'd; wherein *you* doe excell.
> And when we drive our *flocks* a field to graze them,
> So chaunt your praises, that it shall amaze them;
> And thinke that *Fate* hath new recald from death
> Their still-lamented, sweete *Elizabeth*.

(*Epithalamia*, sig. Gg7ᵛ)

The 'English shepherds' who entertain Thetis in *Britannia's Pastorals*
comprise Colin Clout, Astrophel, Chapman, Drayton, Jonson, Daniel,

Brooke, Davies, and Wither – not all pastoral poets, but all, except Wither, elderly writers, and all representative of the old order.

How deeply and nostalgically the idea of the poet as shepherd was associated in the minds of these writers with the old-fashioned, traditional values, is best seen, however, in the poetry of Drayton. It is a way of thinking and feeling that the younger Spenserians could have derived from him. When he re-shaped his eclogues, in 1606 and later, calling them now simply 'Eglogs' or *Pastorals*, he poured into them much of the bitterness he felt at the changed literary and social climate of the new reign. The idea of the shepherd now became virtually synonymous for him with the old Elizabethan type of poet. A good example is eclogue VI, which is a much revised version of the fourth eclogue of *The Shepheards Garland*. Its central passage is a lament by the old shepherd, Winken, for Elphin, who represents Sidney. This lament is altered in the later version so as to make Sidney's death signify also the death of the old order. The change in mood affects many parts of the poem. Thus in Gorbo's request for a story,

> Or else some Romant unto us areed,
> > Which good old *Godfrey* taught thee in thy youth,
> Of noble Lords and Ladies gentle deede,
> > Or of thy love, or of thy lasses truth,   (S.G., IV, 37–40)

the words 'Which good old *Godfrey*' are altered to 'By former Shepheards', which, in combination with the echo of Spenser in the third line, helps to suggest the Elizabethan age that has gone. Winken's reply carries on the suggestion:

> Shepheard, no, no, that World with me is past,
> Merry was it, when we those Toyes might tell:
> But 'tis not now as when thou saw'st me last,
> A great mischance me since that time befell.
> > > > (*Pastorals*, VI, 41–4)

Nothing corresponding to this occurs in the earlier version. In the lament itself the word 'shepherd' is used repeatedly to signify the type of poet of whom Sidney was both patron and prime exemplar, and with whom are contrasted the 'clowns' of the present day:

When his fayre Flocks he fed upon the Downes,
The poorest Shepheard suffered not annoy:
Now are we subject to those beastly Clownes,
That all our mirth would utterly destroy.   (65–8)

and

The Groves, the Mountaynes, and the pleasant Heath,
That wonted were with Roundelayes to ring,
Are blasted now with the cold Northerne breath,
That not a Shepheard takes delight to sing.   (85–8)

Those shepherds living yet who have inherited his virtues are urged
to continue their piping; under their pastoral names they are easily
identified as the 'old-fashioned' poets, Daniel, Alexander, and Drayton
himself. They are contrasted with those who are so 'puff'd and blowne
with Worldly vanitie that they 'scorn well-neere a Shepheards simple
Name'.

This is a theme to which Drayton often returns, and nearly always
in the same terms.[3] The most moving example comes in his commendatory poem to *Britannia's Pastorals*, Book I (1613). In Browne and his
kind he sees a hope for poetry:

Drive forth thy Flocke, young Pastor, to that Plaine,
Where our old Shepheards wont their flocks to feed;
To those cleare walkes, where many a skilfull Swaine
To'ards the calme ev'ning, tun'd his pleasant Reede.
Those, to the *Muses* once so sacred, Downes,
As no rude foote might there presume to stand:
(Now made the way of the unworthiest Clownes,
Dig'd and plow'd up with each unhallowed hand)
If possible thou canst, redeeme those places,
Where, by the brim of many a silver Spring,
The learned Maydens, and delightfull Graces
Often have sate to heare our Shepheards sing:
Where on those *Pines* the neighb'ring Groves among,

---

[3] See, for example, *Pastorals*, VIII, 72–8, and *The Man in the Moone*, 22–30. Similar
criticisms occur in Drayton's satires, *The Owle* and *The Moone-Calfe*, and in his Elegies
(see next chapter).

(Now utterly neglected in these dayes)
Our Garlands, Pipes, and Cornamutes were hong
The monuments of our deserved praise.
So may thy Sheepe like, so thy Lambes increase,
And from the Wolfe feede ever safe and free!
So maist thou thrive, among the learned prease,
As thou young Shepheard, art belov'd of mee.

Here the pastoral world, the vanished world of Elizabeth, and the
world of art, or poetry, have become one and the same.

The situation Drayton describes in the above lines forms the background of the two 'communal' poems, *The Shepheards Pipe* (1614) and
The Shepheards Hunting (1615). The former consists of seven eclogues
by Browne, followed by 'Other Eclogues' by 'Mr. Brooke, Mr.
Wither, and Mr. Davies', and 'An Other Eclogue' by 'Mr. Wither'.
The Shepheards Hunting includes three eclogues dramatising Wither's
imprisonment in the Marshalsea, and describing the events that led to
it, and the two eclogues already published in *The Shepheards Pipe*.
Browne's poem includes some characters who cannot now be identified – Jockie, Philos, Hobbinol – and who may or may not represent
actual persons, but its central characters are Willie (Browne), Roget
(Wither) and Cuttie (Brooke). These characters reappear in the
additional eclogues, along with 'old Wernock' (Davies) and Alexis
(William Ferrar, a brother of Nicholas). *The Shepheards Hunting*
consists entirely of dialogues between Willie, Roget, Cuttie, and
Alexis.[4] The subject for discussion between these 'shepherds' is always
their own poetry, with, in Wither's case, some discussion of his
experiences in prison. Thus it is in these poems that the Spenserians
present themselves most clearly as a group, the poems themselve.
being at once a dramatic representation of the group and its manifestos
There is a remarkable unity of tone. Friends write speeches for friends –

[4] Alexis appears in the fifth eclogue, reprinted from *The Shepheards Pipe*. Ferrar himself
does not contribute to either poem. In *S.P.* his interlocutor was named Thirsis. The name
was changed to Roget in the first edition of *The Shepheards Hunting*, and in later editions
to Philarete, Wither's pseudonym in *Faire-Virtue*.

Browne for Wither, Wither for Browne, Brooke for Browne, Browne
for Brooke, and so on – and it is sometimes difficult to remember
afterwards whether a poet actually said something, or simply had it
attributed to him by another. Yet so convincing is the impression that
these pastoral portraits are done 'from the life' that this does not seem
to matter. The self-portraits we considered earlier were something of
a shepherd's pipe-dream, in which the poet saw himself honoured and
acclaimed by all (even goddesses). They represented the ideal, the
imaginary. The poems now under consideration, on the other hand,
are expressions of their authors' actual poetic life. The writers are not
here projecting themselves into an imaginary pastoral world; rather,
they are realising their own lives in pastoral terms.

Poetic friendship, real or imaginary, has always been a major theme
of pastoral. E.K. had stressed this element in *The Shepheardes Calender*,
identifying Hobbinol as 'the person of some his very speciall and most
familiar freend, whome he entirely and extraordinarily beloved', and
Thomalin (in 'March') as 'some secrete freend'. But the 'very speciall
and familiar' nature of the friendship, which we have to be told about
in *The Shepheardes Calender*, is something we recognise immediately in
these poems. The Spenserians achieve effects of intimacy and actuality
that are unusual and even, I would suggest, original. This is partly
because the work (*The Shepheards Pipe*, at any rate) is a joint production;
this makes the literary exchanges seem more authentic than those which
are entirely the creation of one writer. But it is also because the
element of pure fiction is less, and the translation of the actual into
pastoral terms greater and more detailed, than is customary. The
poetic discussion in 'October' of *The Shepheardes Calender*, for instance,
which those in the work of Spenser's followers imitate, takes place
between two apparently fictitious characters,[5] possibly, as Hallett
Smith suggests, dramatising Spenser's inner debate with himself. But
when Willie, Roget, Wernock, and Cuttie talk about their poetry,
there is no doubt that both the poetry and people are 'real'; the personal
references – pleas to Browne to get on with *Britannia's Pastorals*, for
example (the second book was not published until 1616), allusions to
Wither's sufferings over *Abuses Stript and Whipt* – make that plain.
Similarly in 'June' although the 'pleasaunt syte' and the mountains
Colin has quitted probably, as E. K. intimates, represent actual places,

---

[5] Paul E. McLane, *Spenser's 'Shepheardes Calender'* (Notre Dame, Indiana, 1961), suggests
that Cuddie is Dyer, but the evidence is slight.

these nevertheless remain vague. In *The Shepheards Hunting*, however, the setting, with its rock and its 'outlaws in their caves half pined', is the Marshalsea prison, and we are kept constantly aware of that, and of the reality of the 'hills and groves and plains' which Roget is denied, not to mention the reality of the friends who visit him to console him in his thraldom. To some extent, what this means is that the relationship between the symbol and the thing symbolised is more subtle and delicate in Spenser, and it might be inferred that this would make the pastoral disguise of his followers even more obviously a fancy-dress, and therefore less justified in terms of function, than it usually is. In fact this is not so. Instead, the pastoral disguise seems less artificial here than elsewhere. This is due partly to the relaxed, natural manner of the dialogue, but even more, perhaps, to the way in which the writers join to create, consistently, the illusion of a pastoral society. It is as if there were a natural affinity or correspondence between their position and that of the shepherd – the shepherd as he appears in literature especially – which makes the finding of pastoral equivalents an easy matter. Some of the situations of pastoral do in fact exist ready-made for them. 'Old *Wernock*' giving advice to 'yong *Willy*' provides a contrast between age and youth that is not only conventional but true. Similarly the respect that Browne shows to Brooke in his fifth eclogue is due naturally to Brooke's seniority in years and position, and to the kind of poet he tried to be, though not, in our estimation, to the poet he actually was. It is sad too to find Alexis (Ferrar), who plays such an active part in *The Shepheards Pipe* and *The Shepheards Hunting*, mourned in an elegy in *Britannia's Pastorals*, Book II, though it also gives the dead Alexis a substantiality greater than that of Daphnis or Lycidas. We *know* that these shepherds 'fed the same flock, by fountain, shade, and rill'. We have seen them do it.

This pastoral is thus peculiarly close to life – the 'real' life of its subjects. It is felt as something lived; once the initial premiss is granted, the rest follows naturally, and is understood without translation or interpretation. There is, to borrow a phrase of T. S. Eliot's, 'a kind of doubleness' in the action, which is not allegory, but is not actual life either.[6] In some ways, the effect is closer to the make-believe of Pirandello's *Henry IV* than to the allegory of *The Faerie Queene*.

These two poems exist primarily as an expression of literary friend-

[6] T. S. Eliot, *Selected Essays*, (1948 edn.), 229.

ship. (Friendship here entirely replaces love as the characteristic pastoral affection.) The *camaraderie* of the writers, and the affection between them, are striking; the eclogues are, in a sense, familiar epistles dramatised (and of course in pastoral form) and in this respect may suggest to a modern reader some of the coterie poetry of the 1930s. (Tennyson's 'Audley Court', even *The Princess*, are also comparable.) Poetry, especially their own poetry, is, as we have already noticed, the chief topic discussed. But not only do the eclogues portray a series of literary friendships; they also vividly suggest the existence of a particular homogeneous community, within which the friendships are carried on. They do this by repeated allusions to a common background – 'our common', 'our daisied downes', 'our revels', 'our Whitson-ale', 'our parish-flocks', 'our May-lord', 'our fellow-swains', and so forth. This possessive formula is repeated too often to be merely a casual and incidental piece of verisimilitude; consciously or unconsciously, a particular effect is being sought, and is achieved. Some of the evidence suggests that what is represented here is the social and literary life of the Inns of Court, or at any rate of that section of it comprising these writers and their friends. Browne, Brooke, Wither, and Ferrar were all members of the Society, the three younger ones being students at the time their poems were written. The dedications of the eclogues of *The Shepheards Pipe* all stress this fact, with the exception of Davies's eclogue. Browne seems particularly concerned to advertise his membership of the Inner Temple. His verses 'To the Reader' before Book I of *Britannia's Pastorals* are dated 'From the Inner Temple, *Iune* the 18. 1613'; and one of his love-poems has the touching postscript, 'From an inner temple than ye Inner Temple'. A large number of law-men, among them Selden, wrote commendatory poems for *Britannia's Pastorals*, both parts. Several sign their poems 'e So. Int. Templ.' or similarly, and all write in appropriately pastoral terms. Perhaps these were the 'fellow-swains' who make up the (off-stage) 'crowd' in the eclogues of Browne and Wither. Some support for the idea that the life of the Inns of Court is being represented comes from Davies's eclogue, which refers (in pastoral terms) to Browne's law-studies, even achieving a pun on 'law' and 'lore'. Wither's eclogue addressed 'To Master William Ferrar of the *Middle Temple*' also points to this conclusion. Roget* is making Alexis's acquaintance:

* The name is changed to Philarete in the 1622 edition, from which I quote, but for convenience's sake I have retained 'Roget', the name used in *S.P.* and early editions of *S.H.*

> here my neighbouring Sheepe
> Upon the border of these Downes I keepe:
> Where often thou at Pastorals and Playes,
> Have grac'd our Wakes on Summer Holy-dayes:
> And many a time with thee at this cold spring
> Met I, to heare your learned shepheards sing,
> Saw them disporting in the shady Groves,
> And in chaste Sonnets wooe their chaster Loves.
>
> (*S.H.*, sig. Mm4^v)

Before entering Lincoln's Inn in 1615 Wither was apparently at one of the smaller Inns, though we do not know which. 'My neighbouring sheepe' is surely a reference to this, and the whole passage, it would appear, describes some of the social exchanges between it and the Middle Temple. In both poems the shepherds quite frequently promise each other new poems to be performed 'next holiday', or look back to those heard 'at our last year's revelling'. The Inns of Court certainly had their revels days. On one of them, January 13th, 1615, Browne's Inner Temple Masque was presented.

The 'cold spring' mentioned by Wither suggests a rather abstemious gathering. Browne, however, mentions not only whitsun-ales but the ale-house. Nor were Wither's springs always so cold. In the fourth eclogue of *The Shepheards Hunting* he informs Browne:

> It is knowne what thou canst doe,
> For it is not long agoe,
> When that *Cuddy*, *Thou*, and *I*
> Each the others skill to try,
> At Saint *Dunstanes* charmed well,
> (As some present there can tell)
> Sang upon a sudden Theame,
> Sitting by the Crimson streame.
> Where, if thou didst well or no,
> Yet remaines the Song to show.   (sig. Ll7^r)

'Saint *Dunstanes* charmed Well' is the Devil and St. Dunstan tavern in Fleet Street, scene of Ben Jonson's Apollo meetings. Brooke, and possibly Drayton, are the only Spenserians of whose membership of

Jonson's 'Club' there is any evidence, but that *The Shepheards Pipe* and *The Shepheards Hunting* contain references to similar literary gatherings, formal or informal, seems probable.[7]

This pastoral thus provides, for their own diversion and that of any of the general public who may be interested, a picture of the Spenserian poets entertaining themselves. It is a lively and sometimes a happy picture, but it is also a serious one. Disappointment, resentment, anxiety, are often the feelings expressed. Shepherds frequently 'droop' and have to be exhorted by others to continue their singing. This is the theme, or at least the starting-point, of almost every eclogue in which the poets themselves appear – of Browne's first and fifth eclogues, and of those Wither, Brooke and Davies addressed to Browne. The repetition is the result, not of poverty of invention, but of the writers' common response to the literary situation. With Drayton, they see the true poetry which they represent as threatened with destruction in the new age. But more than Drayton – Drayton in the *Pastorals*, that is, and the poem before *Britannia's Pastorals* – they represent this destruction as a personal attack upon themselves. Frequent reference is made to their enemies, to carpers and detractors. Thus Willie, sympathising with Roget, declares:

> Welladay! such churlish Swaynes
> Now and then lurke on our plaines:
> That I feare, a time, ere long
> Shall not heare a Sheepheards song,
> Nor a Swayne shall take in taske
> Any wrong, nor once unmaske
> Such as do with vices rife
> Soyle the Sheepheards happy life:
> Except he meanes his Sheepe shall bee
> A prey to all their iniury.   (*S.P.*, I, sig. B2ᵛ-B3ʳ)

The immediate occasion of this was no doubt Wither's imprisonment, but Browne deliberately generalises from it. Wither's fine eclogue

---

[7] Even if the Mermaid club never existed, as I. A. Shapiro argues (*Modern Language Review*, XLV (1950), 1–17), there is still documentary evidence that Brooke was one of the 'Sirenaics' who held regular meetings at the Mitre tavern, at about the time we are considering. These meetings also had a strong Inns of Court colouring. The Apollo room at the Devil tavern was not built until 1624, and Percy Simpson suggests that Jonson's '*Legis Convivium*. in the APOLLO of the Old Devil Tavern' was written after that date.

addressed to Browne represents Browne as refusing to renew his 'song' because he has been accused of plagiarism. To Roget's question,

> *Willy*, What may those men be,
> Are so ill to malice thee?

he answers

> Some are worthy-well esteem'd,
> Some without worth are so deem'd.
> Others of so base a spirit,
> They have nor esteeme, nor merit.
>
> (*S.H.*, sig. Ll6ʳ)

That this alludes to some actual criticism of *Britannia's Pastorals* seems clear. Complaints about the treatment of poets are an accepted feature of Renaissance pastoral and familiar from Mantuan, but again the Spenserians are notable for their extremely personal application of the convention.

Furthermore, in *The Shepheards Sirena* Drayton portrays a situation as particular as those presented in the poems of Browne and Wither. This poem is, in its concluding section, his companion-piece to *The Shepheards Pipe* and *The Shepheards Hunting*.[8] (We notice, for instance, the same use of possessive adjectives – 'our flocks', 'our downes'.) Drayton's statement is obscure, yet precise. He sees the swineherds massing for attack:

> Rougish Swinheards that repine
> At our Flocks, like beastly Clownes,
> Sweare that they will bring their Swine,
> And will wroote up all our Downes.   (*S.S.*, 356–9)

He takes comfort, however, in the assurance,

> And we here have got us Dogges,
> Best of all the Westerne breed:
> Which though Whelps shall lug their Hogges,
> Till they make their eares to bleed.   (376–9)

The 'dogges' are probably Browne and Wither.

---

[8] See K. Tillotson, Hebel, V, 207, for a discussion of the parallels.

Browne's second eclogue also concerns a swineherd, whose swine have been damaging the shepherds' property:

> I wonder he hath suffred been
>   Upon our Common heere,
> His Hogges doe root our yonger treen
>   And spoyle the smelling breere.
> Our purest welles they wallow in,
>   All over-spred with durt,
> Nor will they from our Arbours lin,
>   But all our pleasures hurt.
>   (*S.P.*, sig. D1ᵛ–D2ʳ)

This swineherd, unlike Drayton's, makes overtures of friendship to the shepherds and wishes to become one of them. The idea is received with snobbish scorn (the impression that the shepherds represent a set that at any rate fancies itself to be exclusive is strong) and with a promise to

> make him from our plaines depart
> With all his durty herd.   (sig. D1ᵛ)

As a group, the Spenserians appear in this part of their work both isolated and ingrown. The final impression is less of exclusiveness than of a closing of the ranks, a banding together in the face of a common danger. Pastoral itself has become for them a kind of ark in which they take refuge against what they would doubtless have agreed to call 'this filthy modern tide'. And they provide their own entertainment on board. The idea that they must find their satisfaction in a 'fit audience, though few' is epitomised in Willie's answer to Roget:

> For a Song I doe not passe,
> Mong'st my friends, but what (alas)
> Should I have to doe with them
> That my Musicke doe contemne?
>   (*S.H.*, sig. Ll6ʳ)

It would be helpful to know what the particular grievances of these writers were, and who were their enemies. Some of the latter, at any rate, had connections with the court – Drayton s swineherds, for example: 'Angry *Olcon* sets them on.' 'Olcon' was Drayton's name for King James. Davies represents Browne as complaining of neglect at court:

> Ah, who (with lavish draughts of *Aganip*)
> Can swill their soule to frolick; so, their Muse,
> Whan Courts and Camps, that erst the muse did clip,
> Do now forlore her; nay, her most abuse?
> Now, with their witlesse, causelesse surquedry
> They have transpos'd fro what of yore they were,
> That Swaines, who but to looser luxurie
> Can shew the way, are now most cherisht there.
>
> (S.P., sig. G4ʳ)

Again, this is in line with the complaints of Mantuan or Spenser's Cuddie concerning the decay of patronage, but again, very probably, has something specific behind it. The existence of some special tensions between these poets and some members – possibly also poets – of the court, is suggested by the poetry of Wither, particularly by *Faire-Virtue*. Here the familiar Renaissance contrast between the felicities of the shepherd's life and the cares of the court becomes a contrast between the virtues of the shepherd-poet, as represented by Philarete (Wither) and the philistinism of the court, with considerable emphasis on the superiority of the shepherd's poetic gifts. Wither's obsession suggests something of a love-hate relationship. Thus he repeatedly claims equality in worth with the 'learned bards and poets' of the king:

> See, if any *Palace* yeelds
> Ought more glorious, then the *Fields*,
> And consider well, if we
> May not as high-flying be
> In our thoughts, as you that sing
> In the Chambers of a King.   (F.V., sig. B8ᵛ)

He is only a shepherd 'in russet homespun clad', yet such is the power of his verse that the ladies who form his audience surmise

> That *Hee* a greater man was, so disguis'd.   (sig. N4ʳ)

And when he finally quits the scene, he does so in the company of

> Three men that by their *Habits* courtiers seem'd;
> For (though obscure) by some he is esteemd
> Among the greatest: who do not contemne
> In his retyred walkes to visit him.
> And there they tast those pleasures of the mind,
> Which they can nor in *Court*, nor *Citie* find.   (*ibid.*)

Probably this records some actual friendship, of which Wither is proud, and is not simply another example of the kind of wishful thinking discussed earlier, though the poem as a whole is certainly an example of it.

Wither's *Epithalamion* for Princess Elizabeth employs similar contrasts. He begs the princess to

> thinke your Country *Shepheard* loves as deare,
> As if he were a *Courtier*, or a *Peere*,

and assures her, concerning himself and his fellows,

> though they see the *Court* but now and then,
> They know *desert* as well as *Greater* men.   (sig. Gg7^v)

Browne too in *Britannia's Pastorals* expresses, less aggressively and with at any rate a better simulated humility, his consciousness of the distance between the 'courtly swains' and the shepherds. Altogether, it seems reasonable to suppose that the feeling is common to the Spenserians, and not peculiar to Wither, though how far the contrast is based on literary, how far on social, considerations, it is difficult to say. Browne and Wither, as we have seen, sought and found patronage in high places, both among the members of His Majesty's Privy Council, and, in Wither's case, in the royal family itself. And though, like most writers, they had economic problems, their social position was quite respectable.

So far we have been considering literary and social relationships. But the pastoral idiom, it is interesting to note, is also used in these eclogues to represent the economic situation of the writers, and again in rather a personal fashion. At times the shepherd-persona, without ceasing to stand for the poet as poet, comes to stand also for his

D

calling. For though the writing of poetry is the most enjoyable activity of these 'shepherds', it is not their only one. They have also their flocks to care for, or, in 'real-life' terms, a living to earn. In *The Shepheards Hunting*, V, Alexis, urged by Roget to write poetry, answers,

> Yea, but if I appli'd me to those straines,
> Who should drive forth my Flockes unto the plaines,
> Which, whilst the *Muses* rest, and leasure crave,
> Must watering, folding and attendance have?
> For if I leave with wonted care to cherish
> Those tender *heards*: both I and they should perish.
>
> (sig. Mm7^r)

Roget assures him in reply that he does not wish Alexis to neglect his calling for the Muse:

> But, let these two, so of each other borrow,
> That they may season mirth, and lessen sorrow.
> Thy Flocke will helpe thy charges to defray,
> Thy *Muse* to passe the long and teadious day.
>
> (sig. Mm7^v)

The reference evidently is to Ferrar's pursuit of the law. Wither's allusions to the shepherd's flock nearly always have economic implications, and convey a considerable amount of *angst*, at variance with the notion of the shepherd's 'heaven-bred, happy life'. His second eclogue is particularly notable for this, as for example Roget's pronouncement:

> My Friends I will; You know I am a *Swaine*,
> That kept a poor Flocke on a barren *Plaine*,   (sig. I17^r)

or the assurance that he gives Willie and Cuttie:

> Not for both your Flocks, I sweare,
> And the gaine they yeeld you yeerely . . .   (sig. Kk3^r)

We may not *see* the flocks mentioned in *The Shepheards Hunting* so clearly as we see Colin Clout's,

Whose hanging heads did seeme his carefull case to weepe,

but they *mean* more.

Drayton too had used the idea of the flock in complaining of his poverty:

> Such are exalted basely that can faine,
>   And none regards just ROWLAND *of the Rocke*.
>   To those fat Pastures, which Flocks healthfull keepe,
>   Malice denyes me entrance with my Sheepe.
>
> (Pastorals, I, 51–4)

But though his theme is similar to Wither's, his flock is closer to Colin Clout's; part, that is, of the composite picture of the shepherd, not a separate metaphor for his livelihood. The reason seems to be that Drayton does not think of the poet as having any other means of livelihood, whereas Wither, Browne and Ferrar do. All three use the traditional leisure of the shepherd to suggest that the writing of poetry is the product of leisure-hours. Ferrar's poem before *Britannia's Pastorals*, Book I, shows that Wither drew Alexis from the life, for there Ferrar tells Browne:

> Well hast thou then past o'er all other rhime,
> And in a *Pastorall* spent thy leasures time.

The effect of this and similar statements is not to convey an impression of gentlemanly *sprezzatura*, but rather to suggest that, at the time of writing at any rate, these authors did not wish or expect to depend solely on their poetry for a living. They were like poets of today who are also university lecturers: they wrote poetry in their leisure-time, but were not gentlemen of leisure. If the background to the eclogues really is the Inns of Court, then this means that they took their law studies seriously. There is a curious passage in Davies's Eclogue which, though in almost impenetrable rustic language, presents a picture of Browne, torn between love and duty. Willy speaks:

> I am by kind so inly pulde
> To these delices; that when I betake
> My selfe to other lore I more am dul'd;

And therefro, keenely set, I fall to make.
But, well-away, thy nis the way to thriven;
And, my neer kith, for that wol sore me shend:
Who little reck how I by kind am given;
But hur wold force to swinck for thriftier end,
Hence forward then I must assay, and con
My leere in leefull lore, to pleasen them
That, sib to mee, would my promotion,
And carke for that to prancke our common Stemme.

                                          (*S.P.*, sig. G6ʳ)

Perhaps Browne and his 'kith' were both right, for whereas it was no doubt his poetry that won him the patronage of the Herberts, he may also be the William Browne who in April 1615 was appointed pursuivant to the Court of Wards and Liveries. His first office with the Herberts was that of tutor to Montgomery's ward, Robert Dormer.

With a brief glance at the Fletchers, we may leave this subject. The impression that they too live a make-believe pastoral life in or through their poetry comes mainly from Phineas, who by employing, in part, the same dramatis personae and the same setting in *The Purple Island*, *The Piscatorie Eclogs*, and many of the shorter poems, establishes the image of a distinct pastoral community, having Thirsil and his brother at its centre. Giles Fletcher is not a pastoralist, yet the brief contrast he introduces at the end of *Christs Victorie, and Triumph* between his own 'green Muse' and that of 'the Kentish lad . . . young Thyrsilis' suggests that he was willing to play his brother's game and to be a shepherd *because* he is a poet. Phineas has the peculiar habit of changing his pastoral name, and even his rôle, being Myrtilus in his Latin eclogues, Thirsil in his English ones (and, briefly, Algon), and, as Thirsil, appearing in *The Purple Island* and the shorter poems as a shepherd, but in *The Piscatorie Eclogs* as a fisherman. The model and prototype for his piscatories was the Latin *Piscatoria* of Sannazaro, first published in 1526, of which Fletcher's eclogues are the first English imitation. Admiration for Sannazaro and a desire for novelty may have determined Fletcher's choice, but perhaps also considerations of scene-setting gave him the idea. For both the Fletchers, but Phineas particularly, located their poetry in Cambridge: they are the poets of Cam (or, as they prefer it, Chame). As a shepherd, Phineas sits most often 'by yellow *Chame*'; as a fisherman, he thus has an appropriate setting ready to hand. Sannazaro's fishermen fish in the sea (actually the Bay of Naples); Fletcher's *talk* about the sea, but are always found by rivers, Chame mainly, but also Medway (the Fletchers' home was in Kent) and Trent (in an eclogue celebrating Fletcher's removal to Derbyshire and his betrothal there). They are found by, rather than on, rivers, for it is the peculiarity of these fishermen (copied from Sanna-zaro's) to stay on shore in bad weather and sing: 'In calms you fish; in roughs use songs and dances' (*P.E.*, VII, 32). In this way, the idyllic character of the formal pastoral is maintained, and the perils of the sea are suitably distanced. Fletcher is almost invariably more formal in his pastoral (and piscatory) than the other Spenserians – these eclogues are a blend of Sannazaro, Virgil, and Spenser – but it is interesting to notice him nevertheless using it for personal statement in a manner similar to theirs. The second eclogue is the most significant in this respect. Most of it consists of Thirsil's complaint to Thomalin of the treatment he and his father (Thelgon) have received from 'ungrateful *Chame*'. The actual biographical facts that form the basis of the complaint are obscure, but the action itself appears to take place on the eve of Fletcher's departure from Cambridge to become chaplain to Sir Henry Willoughby. Fletcher uses the particulars of the fisher's trade to convey his sense of injury:

> Not I my *Chame*, but me proud *Chame* refuses.

His fish ('the guerdon of my toil and pain') have been seized, rather awkwardly, by the river, and his nets broken:

> My boat lies broke; my oares crackt, and gone:
> Nought has he left me, but my pipe alone,
> Which with his sadder notes may help his master moan.
>
> (*P.E.*, II, 7)

This is not very effective as figure, but it shows Fletcher making the same sort of extension to the meaning of the fisher-persona through the attributes of his trade (singing fisherman = poet, working fisherman = aspiring scholar) as that we noticed the Inns-of-Court Spenserians making to the persona of the shepherd.

So far we have been considering the Spenserians' pastoral symbolism. But pastoral, even the 'drawing-room pastoral' so disliked by Mr. Graves, involves some description of shepherd-life *as* shepherd-life. There is a world to be created, Golden or otherwise. And the Spenserians' pastoral, however much it may intrigue us through its symbolism, delights us principally through its fiction. Once more Fletcher, the more classical and conventional, stands apart, but the others, Drayton, Browne and Wither, produced work distinguished for its native English character and its naturalness. 'Drayton and his group,' as H. E. Cory noted, brought these elements of Spenser's pastoral 'to their climax of development.'[9] Each did so, however, in his own characteristic and individual way. Their pastoral worlds have much in common, but are not identical. I shall examine, briefly, the differences as well as the resemblances between them.

Drayton's eclogues, by which I mean *The Shepheards Garland*, in its original and revised versions, most obviously invite comparison with Spenser's. Structurally the resemblances are of sufficient consequence to suggest that *The Shepheardes Calender* has been his model, but if there is one passage in that poem which he has taken especially to heart, it is that in which Spenser acknowledges Chaucer as his master:

> The God of shepheards *Tityrus* is dead,
> Who taught me homely, as I can, to make.

Drayton well understood that in 'that same framing of his style to an old rustic language' Spenser was invoking an authority dearer to him than either Theocritus, Virgil, or Sannazaro, namely that of our own 'most excellent Authors and most famous Poetes', and 'having the sound of those auncient Poetes still ringing in his eares', was endeavouring to achieve continuity with them. By a more discreet use of this language, Drayton linked himself to the same tradition. But he also learned from Spenser the art of establishing continuity with the past not only for his poem but for his pastoral world itself, by allowing his shepherds to use their old-fashioned speech to tell old tales, remembered from past times. So Motto introduces his story of Dowsabell as

> A pretie Tale, which when I was a boy,
> my toothles Grandame oft hath tolde to me.
>
> (*S.G.*, VIII, 119–20)

---

[9] Cory, *op. cit.*, 266.

Actually Drayton uses this device more often than Spenser. 'Old *Wynkin de word*', for instance, is stocked with similar tales

> of *Gawen* or *Sir Guy*,
> Of *Robin Hood*, or of good *Clem a Clough*,   (IV, 35–6)

as well as with 'Romants' taught him by 'good olde *Godfrey*' in his youth. The balance between old age and youth is not so well maintained in Drayton's pastoral as it is in Spenser's. The old predominate, and, whether consciously or unconsciously, Drayton uses them, their memories, and their speech to root his pastoral in the past – the English past. It is in this way that he makes it 'homely'.

The homeliness of Drayton's pastoral, however, should not be overstressed. His touches of realism – lines like

> Yon little elvish moping Lamb of mine,
> Is all betangled in yon crawling Brier,
>
> (*S.G.*, IV, 154–5)

occur mainly at the end of the eclogue, which is the conventional place for them, where even Barnabe Googe could achieve some success.[10] Essentially he was not interested in creating a 'real' world. His pastoral world is a world of art; like that of *The Shepheardes Calender*, it is of the earth but not on it. Again, though homely, it is not undignified. Drayton's natural tendency to loftiness rather than lowliness ensures that. His central character, Rowland, is a figure of more tragic dignity than Colin Clout, as 'with stone-colde hart' he 'stalketh towards his flock'. His opening eclogue includes a prayer to Pan, 'Creator of the starrie light'; in such a context the humbleness of 'A Shepeheards boye (no better doe him call)' would be unfitting. Drayton's pastoral, in fact, constantly aspires to the condition of the heroic, and the struggle between that aspiration and Drayton's strong sense of decorum has left its mark upon his work. His shepherds, in their extreme self-awareness, their constant care that their speech should be limited by

---

[10] As, for example, the end of his eighth eclogue:
> Looke how the beastes begin to fling
> and cast theys heades on hye,
> The Hearonshaw mountes above the clouds
> ye Crowes ech wher do cry
> All this showes rayn, tyme byds us go,
> com *Coridon* awaye . . .

rules of decorum binding on them as characters in a pastoral, are expressing their creator's own consciousness of his temptations. When in 1606 Drayton published his revised version of the *Garland*, he openly acknowledged this tendency in himself. Rowland's blazon of Idea in the fifth eclogue, for example, is now recognised by Motto as 'much disagreeing from a shepherd's vein', and changes in the conversation between him and Rowland make this clearer. In 1619, when he added the 'Address to the Reader', Drayton described his pastorals as having 'almost nothing pastoral . . . but the name'. Doubtless he was thinking of their unusual loftiness of tone.

In 1606, moreover, Drayton added yet another 'new strain' to his pastoral, when he cast a glamour not only over the natural world, but over the pastoral world itself. Within his massive talent there had been from the start a dainty Ariel struggling to get out; there are hints of this in the song for Beta and in 'Dowsabell', but not until the ninth eclogue of 1606 were his wings entirely freed.[11] Here at last, in the description of the shepherds' feast, on Cotswold soil and within the formal bounds of the eclogue, he achieves satisfying expression for his intuition of the ideal, which shines for him in everything beautiful and noble, in the natural world, in heroes, in women, and in poetry itself. Cotswold field is Drayton's Mount Acidale. There his pastoral tributes to Anne Goodere reach their climax, and the reader, like Sir Calidore, sees the Graces dance to the poet's melody.

Something of the same magical quality appears in *The Shepheards Sirena* and the mysterious *Quest of Cynthia*. And at the end of his life Drayton produced in the unique and matchless *Muses Elizium* (1630) a world in which both pastoral and poetry are transfigured. The poem is a serene vision of a poet's paradise:

> There in perpetuall Summers shade,
> *Apolloes* Prophets sit
> Among the flowres that never fade,
> But flowrish like their wit.
>
> ('The Description of Elizium', 85–8)

The recollections of Theocritus are there, faintly, in the endless loving poetical debates and contests, to make it authentic pastoral, but it is a Theocritus aetherialised. An element of 'country clownage' and country

[11]The two songs of this eclogue had, however, already appeared in *Englands Helicon* (1600).

humour colours its rustic festivals, but on the whole the scale the poem
works on is that of the dainty, the diminutive, the ineffable. Though
Elizium is not fairy-land, it is not far removed from it: when a wedding
occurs, it is between a Fay and a girl who has fairy ancestors. This is the
most golden of all golden worlds. Everything that happens on its
'Elyzian plaines' seems effortless, not least the poetry itself, that pours
out, fluent as bird-song, pure as spring-water. The lightness and ease of
the verse are remarkable in themselves, but doubly so when one remembers the clumsiness and the struggles with syntax too often
encountered in Drayton's earlier work. And the content matches the
form. Quotation is difficult from a work the effect of which depends so
much more on the whole than on the part, but perhaps we could note
as typical such lines as

> With full-leav'd Lillies I will stick
> Thy braded hayre all o'r so thick,
> That from it a Light shall throw
> Like the Sunnes upon the Snow,
> 　　　　　(M.E., 'The second Nimphall', 199–202)

or

> Naiis:　Behold the Rosye Dawne,
> 　　　　Rises in Tinsild Lawne,
> 　　　　And smiling seemes to fawne,
> 　　　　Upon the mountaines.
>
> Cloe:　Awaked from her Dreames
> 　　　　Shooting foorth goulden Beames
> 　　　　Dansing upon the Streames
> 　　　　Courting the Fountaines,　　　　(III, 153–60)

or

> Cleere had the day bin from the dawne,
> All chequerd was the Skye,
> Thin Clouds like Scarfs of Cobweb Lawne
> Vayld Heaven's most glorious eye.
> The Winde had no more strength then this,
> That leasurely it blew,
> To make one leafe the next to kisse,
> That closly by it grew.　　　　(VI, 1–8)

D*

What the poem finally demonstrates is Drayton's instinctive assumption that the essence of poetry is to be found in pastoral. For the poem is an attempt to capture in verse the 'purest of purest, most refined fine' essence of poetry itself; and the form is pastoral. Not realism, but the light that never was, on sea or land, is the distinguishing characteristic of Drayton's pastoral verse.

It is, rather, to Browne and Wither that we must turn, if we wish for the light of common day. Not that theirs is exactly the world of the *Lyrical Ballads*, but it is palpably nearer to it. Browne, having learned the lesson of homeliness from both Spenser and Drayton, has applied it more literally than either. (These remarks apply only to *The Shepheards Pipe*; consideration of *Britannia's Pastorals* must be deferred till Chapter VII.) There is some incidental idealisation, but on the whole it is a credible picture of the life of the English countryside that he gives us, comparable both in character and in authenticity with Clare's 'Village Minstrel' or his *Shepherd's Calendar*. It is buoyant and unpretentious. Even a trivial incident like that of Philos's dog stealing his dinner is acceptable for its naturalism, suggesting as it does the illustrations in a Book of Hours, or the details in a Dutch painting. It is in fact a working English village that Browne depicts, not an isolated and artificial community. The opening of eclogue V is typical:

> Morne had got the start of night,
> Lab'ring men were ready dight
> With their shovels and their spades
> For the field, and (as their trades)
> Or at hedging wrought, or ditching
> For their food more then enritching.

(Clare would have appreciated that.) Like the villages of Hardy, moreover, this one has its dramas: 'old Neddy', for instance, in the third eclogue, is a kind of village Timon, cheated by his servants:

> Hee had milch-goates without peeres,
> Well-hung kine, and fatned steers
>   Many hundred head.
> WILKINS cote his Dairy was,
> For a dwelling it may passe
>   With the best in towne,   (*S.P.*, sig. D3ᵛ)

but now,

> That is gone, and all beside,
> (Well-a-day, alacke the tide)
> In a hollow den,
> Underneath yond gloomy wood
> Wons he now, and wails the brood
>   Of ingrateful men.   (sig. D5ʳ)

Neddy's tale is told by Thomalin, as he and Piers watch him coming through the morning mist, a figure like Wordsworth's leech-gatherer:

> Good old man! see how he walkes
> Painfull and among the balkes
>   Picking lockes of wull.   (sig. D3ᵛ)

The situation of Browne's seventh eclogue also would have had much to commend it to Hardy (or Clare): it records Palinode's consternation at discovering that his friend Hobbinol is to marry Phillis:

> Remember when I met her last alone
> As wee to yonder Grove for filberds straid,
> Like to a new-strook *Doe* from out the bushes,
> Lacing herselfe, and red with gamesome blushes
>   Made towards the greene,
>   Loth to be seene:
> And after in the grove the goatheard met.   (sig. E8ᵛ)

This may owe something to D'Urfé's *L'Astrée*, which Browne had probably read, and the account there of Olimpe's rendez-vous with Lycidas, 'dans le plus retiré du bois de Bon-Lieu'. But I doubt it; Browne hardly needed to go to literature for a knowledge of such 'country-matters'. He is much too literary to be, or even to affect to be, a 'peasant poet', but in these eclogues he has kept any literary aids to invention well out of sight, so that Nature only seems to reign. Their naturalness brings them nearer to Theocritus than the pastoral of Spenser, or perhaps that of any of the followers of Virgil and Mantuan, had been. As in Theocritus, work and play are integrated into a single picture. Fontenelle, who thought that pastoral should be an image of our laziness, would not have approved of Browne.

Wither's pastoral, like Browne's, is strikingly English. The scene of his *Faire-Virtue*, indeed, is more localised than that of Browne's eclogues, for it is his own part of Hampshire: had it only had more rivers, he tells us, 'honest' even in this,

> *Arcadia* had not seene
> A sweeter plot of Earth then this had beene.

The pastoral has become truly homely in this poem: Wither describes his own home, and does it in a homely way. 'Homeliness' was a moral, not just a literary, ideal for Wither. His regard for the pastoral form itself and its traditions is less than that of the other Spenserians. He thought of himself, indeed, as a satirist rather than as a pastoralist; as he says in eclogue II of *The Shepheards Hunting*,

> I was not noted out for *Shepheards layes*
> Nor feeding Flocks, as, you know, others be:
> For the delight that most possessed me
> Was hunting *Foxes*, *Wolves*, and *Beasts* of *Prey*
> That spoyle our *Foulds*, and beare our *Lambs* away.
>
> (sig. I17ᵛ)

'It is not unlikely some will think I have in divers places been more wanton, as they take it, than befits a satirist,' he admits in 'A Postscript' to the poem. Professor Kathleen Tillotson has drawn attention to the 'satyr doubly armed with scourge and shepherd's pipe' on the title-page of Wither's *Vices Executioner*, adding 'an interesting comment on contemporary pastoral'.[12] In fact, both the satyr and the shepherd tend to merge in Wither's verse into a single persona, that of the plain, honest countryman, a more astringent, and more poetical, Thomas Tusser. This is the image of himself that he projects in the shepherd's boy of *Faire-Virtue*, in his 'country habit', expressing his 'untaught country art'. So *Abuses Stript and Whipt* is presented as a 'country dance' of satyrs. In this sense, Wither's was always a 'rurall Pen', his work always 'a Countrie dish'; even the newsletter he wrote during the civil war was *Mercurius Rusticus: or A Countrey Messenger*. How successfully he projected this image of himself, with some readers at least, is seen from Richard Baxter's comment in 1681:

12 Hebel, V, 220, footnote.

Honest George Withers, though a rustic poet, hath been very acceptable, as to some for his prophecies, so to others for his plain country honesty.[13]

Despite this rather sober colouring, Wither wrote some of the freshest and gayest of English pastoral verse. His descriptions of rural sports, outdoors and (in 'A Christmas Carol') indoors, have great exuberance.

Phineas Fletcher's pastoral is for the most part in direct contrast with that of the other Spenserians. His few references to May-games and May-lords are merely perfunctory; he has no interest in the life of the English countryside. Spenser has not taught *him* 'homely, as I can, to make'; what he has responded to in the *Calender* is, rather, the image of the shepherd as 'one who complains' (the phrase is John Arthos's), and the elegance of Spenser's rhetoric, the 'pretty epanorthoses', and the use of pathetic fallacy. Unlike the other Spenserians, he adapts and transposes, rather than develops. His eclogues, though piscatory, are closer in form to Spenser's than are those of the others: they are *The Shepheardes Calender* in fisher's garb. And what is not Spenserian is Virgilian, or Sannazarian – and Sannazaro's fishermen have themselves been called 'des Sannazars parlant Virgile'.[14] Fletcher twice speaks of his humble aspiration merely to 'lackey' Colin Clout and the Virgil of the *Eclogues*; the wish itself echoes Spenser's desire, expressed at the end of the *Calender*, 'to followe farre off' Chaucer and the poet of *Piers Plowman*. Fletcher is so steeped in Spenser's verse, he falls naturally into his phrases and formulae. Even his pipe is Spenserian:

> Go little pipe; for ever I must leave thee,
> My little little pipe, but sweetest ever;
>
> *(Works, II, 235)*

> Was never little pipe more soft, more sweetly plained.
> *(P.E., VII, 36)*

That is Thirsil, shepherd and fisherman, speaking. And this is Colin:

> Goe little booke . . .

> Goe lyttle Calender . . .

---

[13] Quoted by Frank Sidgwick, *The Poetry of George Wither*, I (1902), xli.
[14] A. de Tréverret, quoted W. P. Mustard, *The Piscatory Eclogues of Jacopo Sannazaro* (Baltimore, 1914), 26.

> Gather ye together my little flocke,
> My little flock, that was to me so liefe . . .,

and, of course,

> Here will I hang my pype upon this tree,
> Was never pype of reede did better sounde.

On the whole, the appeal of *The Shepheardes Calender* for Fletcher is stylistic rather than imaginative. He does not respond to its pastoral *world* as the others do. This seems to be true of his response to Sannazaro's eclogues also. Fletcher's fishing-world is not very vividly recreated: it lacks salt. His few stage-properties of boats, oars, nets, waves, and 'whistling winds 'gainst rocks their voices tearing' (a line that – with reason – he liked so much, he used it several times) provide the rather scanty setting. He does not give us the detailed seascapes that Sannazaro does; instead, he uses 'water' imagery more for figure than description. This is in keeping with the precise allegorical intention of much of the work, but it is also symptomatic of his addiction to rhetoric and the decorative style.

The Purple Island, however, shows that there is one pastoral world that appeals to Fletcher by its beauty, and that is the world created by Virgil. Thirsil's story takes seven days, and Fletcher achieves many Virgilian effects in indicating the pauses in it, particularly those caused by the coming on of evening, where he can imitate Virgil's eclogue-closures. He is fond of recalling Virgil's,

> ite domum saturae, venit Hesperus, ite capellae,

as in

> Home then my full-fed lambes; the night comes, home apace.

But this whole stanza is Virgilian in character, with reminiscences of the first eclogue as well as the last:

> But see, the smoak mounting in village nigh,
> With folded wreaths steals throught the quiet aire;
> And mixt with duskie shades in Eastern skie,
> Begins the night, and warns us home repair:
>   Bright *Vesper* now hath chang'd his name and place,

And twinkles in the heav'n with doubtfull face:
Home then my full-fed lambes; the night comes, home apace.

(P.I., IV, 33)

Elsewhere, in the shorter poems, Fletcher creates a Virgilian world in
Cambridge, a world of male friendships (though not exclusively):

Here for my *Thenot* I a garland made
With purple violets, and lovely myrtil shade,

(Works, II, 232)

and a world where

Light Fawns & Nymphs dance in the woodie spaces.

(ibid., 234)

Cutting across the exoticism of this pastoral scene, Fletcher occasionally gives us another image of the shepherd, in which he appears as the
embodiment of domestic content:

His bed of wool yeelds safe and quiet sleeps,
While by his side his faithfull spouse hath place:
His little sonne into his bosome creeps,
The lively picture of his fathers face:
  Never his humble house or state torment him;
  Lesse he could like, if lesse his God had sent him:
  And when he dies, green turfs with grassie tombe content him.

(P.I., XII, 6)

This is the passage Isaac Walton quoted, when he praised Fletcher as
'an excellent divine and an excellent angler'. It is the nearest Fletcher
gets to homeliness. (No room for Amaryllis here.) The picture seems
compounded of Golden Age literature, Horace, and Spenser's Meliboeus, the whole quickened by personal feeling. It is the image of a
state that Fletcher, like George Herbert, had to train himself to be
content with – that of the life, not of a shepherd, but of a country
parson. For him too, as for the other Spenserians, the contrast between
the humble shepherd's life and that of the court was proved upon the
pulses, as his epistle 'To Mr. Jo. *Tomkins*' testifies.

Fletcher uses the pastoral occasionally for criticism of the church, and is more conscious than the other Spenserians of the identification of the shepherd with the religious singer and with the pastor. When his pastoral becomes piscatory, the 'lazy fisher' affords an equivalent for the lazy shepherds of Spenser and Mantuan:

> Their floating boats with waves have leave to play,
> Their rusty hooks all yeare keep holy-day.

> (P.E., IV, 14)

The luxurious life of the 'princely fishers' by the Tiber is described. In this connexion, it is worth noting that Fletcher maintains the piscatory image in *The Apollyonists*, addressing God as 'Thou world's sole Pilot' and alluding to himself as 'me poor ship boy'. In the third canto an allusion to

> Those Fisher Swaynes, whome by full Jordans wave
> The Seas great Soveraigne his art had taught,   (III, 21)

introduces a long description of the Roman Church and the papacy in piscatory terms. Fletcher evidently knew the traditional appellation for the papacy, 'the chair of the fisherman'.

Fletcher's play *Sicilides* is also entitled 'A Piscatory'. It is a tedious, complicated 'entertainment', following Italian example by providing a 'fishy' equivalent of such pastoral dramas as Guarini's *Il Pastor Fido*. It has a Prologue spoken by 'Chamus', and in general confirms the impression that Fletcher sought to establish for himself a special 'line' as a Piscator.

Most of these characteristics separate him, as a pastoralist, from the other Spenserians. His work is less English than theirs. His taste is for the voluptuous and the florid, rather than for the simplicities of the shepherd image.

The Spenserianism of the Spenserians' pastoral is not in doubt. Phineas Fletcher, as we have seen, 'lackeyed' two masters – Virgil and Spenser – but the rest of them, despite the admiration they express for Sidney, have essentially only one. However different the final product, the frame of reference within which they work is basically that provided by

Spenser. Their elegies invite comparison with his, especially Browne's elegy for Thomas Manwood, in *The Shepheards Pipe*, eclogue IV. Their discussions of poetry are a perpetual 'dreaming-back', an attempt to recapture in their own persons the spirit of the master. Most of all, perhaps, *The Shepheardes Calender* was to them a blueprint for the creation of a poet; that is, for the creation in verse of the image of a poet. That is why the 'June' and 'October' eclogues mean so much to them, 'June' for its humility, 'October' for its ambition. A line from 'June', 'Enough is me to paint out my unrest', expressive of the pastoral humility, haunts them as much as do the other lines, already referred to, in which Colin speaks of the homeliness he has learned from Tityrus. (Fletcher's version, 'Enough for thee in heav'n to build thy nest', addressed to his muse [*P.I.*, I, 25] is revealing in its fusion – or confusion – of attitudes.) Browne follows Drayton in making a moderate use of the archaisms and rusticities by which Spenser had achieved his homeliness of style. Wither uses very few; he prefers a real to an affected plainness. Of course homeliness is also a matter of content and attitude, and in this respect the Spenserians have 'overgone' their master, for whereas the homeliness of his shepherds is only an apparent homeliness, theirs is often genuine. Their 'rural Minstralsie' does not shadow weighty matters; it celebrates the country life (and their own). Its affinities in this respect are with the pastoral song which in the years since *The Shepheardes Calender* had made 'pastoral' almost synonymous with 'lyric'. (*Englands Helicon* (1600), to which Drayton contributed, is, of course, the prime example.) But Spenser's pastoral does not lack this element, and any account of his followers' 'debt' to him must take note of Perigot's song in 'August'. This in itself could have given their lyricism and homely gaiety all the stimulus they required. Its inspiration is clearly marked in Drayton's 'Dowsabell' and 'Daffadil' songs; and directly or indirectly (through Drayton), it probably helped to form the song-like speech Browne and Wither cultivated in their 'tripping' septasyllabics and other light measures. Another eclogue which (according to E. K.'s divison) is also 'recreative', the March one, deals in a kind of pastoral chit-chat which has its counterpart in the eclogues of the Spenserians. Thus in general it is the lighter parts of Spenser's pastoral – those in which indeed it is most 'pure' and Theocritean – that appeal to his followers. Compared with his, their work lacks weight and density. (Even Drayton's moral ardour cannot quite give him equality in this respect.) One part of Spenser's pastoral that they do not even attempt to emulate is his use of a symbolic structure, by which the pastoral becomes an image not only of men living but of the life of man. Although the titles of their poems (*The Shepheards Garland*, *The Shepheards Pipe*) accurately reflect their character, this emblematic significance does not go beyond the title.

Colin Clouts Come Home Againe has yet to be mentioned. Their preference on the whole for the more relaxed kind of eclogue must have made this poem attractive to the Spenserians, and the personal and literary discussions of *The Shepheards Pipe* and *The Shepheards Hunting* probably owe much to it.

Despite their strong Elizabethan loyalties, however, and their particular debt to Spenser, the Spenserians' pastoral is moving perceptibly away from the Renaissance. In so far as they seek, like Spenser, to establish continuity with Chaucer and the middle ages, theirs is a backward movement, but in so far as they have reduced the distance between the persona and the person to a thin transparency, it is a forward one. The pastoral poet in their work is in process of metamorphosis into the country poet. Yet their sense of identification with the country, their sympathy with its life, is more complete than that we find in succeeding poets of their own century, like Randolph in his 'Ode to Mr. Anthony Stafford to hasten him into the Country' or Cotton in 'The Retirement', who, though they speak directly, dispensing with the pastoral idiom, still remain apart from the delights they celebrate, *gentlemen* enjoying the opportunity afforded in the country 'To read, and meditate, and write'. Comparison with these poets or for that matter with Herrick serves to emphasise the Englishness, the un-classical, un-Horatian character of the Spenserians, Phineas Fletcher excepted. The country is for them not a place of retirement or retreat, but a natural habitat. Their true successor in the seventeenth century is Dorothy Osborne, writing of the real life of Chicksands:

. . . about six or seven o'clock I walk out into a common that lies hard by the house, where a great many young wenches keep sheep and cows, and sit in the shade singing of ballads. I go to them and compare their voices and beauties to some ancient shepherdesses that I have read of, and find a vast difference there; but, trust me, I think these are as innocent as those could be.[15]

And beyond the seventeenth century, their successors are Thomson, and Wordsworth, and Clare, and William Barnes.

[15] *Letters to Sir William Temple*, ed. E. A. Parry (n.d.), 84–5.

The Poetry of Drayton:
1 The heroic

Micheal Drayton was, as Professor Douglas Bush has called him, Spenser's chief heir. Although he only once (in *The Shepheards Garland*) took Spenser directly as his model, his indebtedness to him throughout the fifteen-nineties was of that fundamental and far-reaching kind that indicates discipleship. His style was largely fashioned under Spenser's influence. Without aiming consciously at a Spenserian effect or (as the later followers were to do) a Spenserian impersonation, he cultivated in his own verse the qualities for which Spenser's verse was noted, and tried to achieve Spenser's characteristic combination of sweetness with loftiness, sensuousness with seriousness. Imaginatively too he was stimulated by Spenser; in particular, his own imaginative delight in pagan myth and British antiquities received encouragement from Spenser's example. His poetry, moreover, echoes Spenser's in a way only that of a receptive and responsive reader could do. But above all Drayton is a Spenserian, and remains one even after 1600, when the signs of direct indebtedness diminish, because he shares Spenser's values and embodies them in his own verse.

Oliver Elton asserts that Spenser

infected Drayton with his lofty and proud conception of what the poet's calling really is, when it is confronted with the brute and bastard ambitions of the world.[1]

The similarity between the two poets in this respect may, however, be more a matter of natural affinity than of direct infection. The love of poetry and the feeling that poetry is ultimately identifiable with the heroic both in life and literature were innate in Drayton. They must have been encouraged, but were not created, by Spenser's example.

[1] Elton, *Michael Drayton* (1905), 30.

But Drayton did inherit (he was the only one of the Spenserians to do so) Spenser's conception of the poet's function as being, not merely to teach, but by celebrating heroes to make heroes. His belief in the divinity of poetry we noticed in chapter III. This belief gave him a special reverence for the 'old Poets', who inevitably stood closer to the divine source, the fountain of light, than later poets. At the same time it led him to see in poetry a great tradition handed down from those same 'old Poets', like an Olympic torch passed from one generation of 'Promethii' to the next. These views too he shared with Spenser. Drayton is the true inheritor of Spenser's heroic ideal.

Drayton's beliefs concerning poetry are epitomised in his tribute to Marlowe:

> Neat *Marlow* bathed in the *Thespian* springs
> Had in him those brave translunary things,
> That the first Poets had, his raptures were,
> All ayre, and fire, which made his verses cleere,
> For that fine madness still he did retaine,
> Which rightly should possesse a Poets braine.
>
> ('To Henry Reynolds', 105–10)

Compared with this, his lines on 'grave morrall *Spencer*' in the same poem seem staid. It is high praise he gives him: Drayton knows no-one since Homer, he says, better fitted for the task which Spenser undertook:

> To set downe boldly, bravely to invent,
> In all high knowledge, surely excellent. (83–4)

The statement is just and generous, but lacks the fire of the lines on Marlowe. And the lack is symptomatic of a difference – essentially a temperamental difference – between the working of the heroic ideal in Spenser's verse and in Drayton's. Drayton is more of an enthusiast than Spenser, more eager to pierce at once to the 'brave translunary things', and therefore in a quite literal sense less 'grave'. He works in a different way towards the same end. To demonstrate this is the purpose of this chapter.

Drayton's enthusiasm is Pindaric. The odes he writes are not Pindaric, but the spirit of his work, taken as a whole, is. His address 'To the Reader' before the *Odes* shows that he understood the nature of Pindar's work:

Some [odes] transcendently loftie, and farre more high then the Epick (commonly called the Heroique Poeme) witnesse those of the inimitable *Pindarus*, consecrated to the glorie and renowne of such as returned in triumph from *Olympus*, *Elis*, *Isthmus*, or the like.[2]

And, though they may formally owe nothing to him, the Ballad of Agincourt,

> O, when shall *English* Men
> With such Acts fill a Pen,
> Or *England* breed againe,
>   Such a King HARRY?   (117-20)

and 'To the Virginian Voyage':

> You brave Heroique Minds,
> Worthy your Countries Name,
>   That Honour still pursue,   (1-3)

are Pindaric in mood and intention. 'In his eyes, the poet and the victor belonged to each other.'[3] He made poetry 'once more into praise of the prowess which is a pattern for posterity.'[4] 'Through his work the heroic spirit and the praise of heroism which were the inspiration of the epic are reborn in lyric form.'[5] All this was said of Pindar; it could also be said of Drayton. Even the last statement may stand, for though Drayton is by genre more a narrative than a lyric poet, emotion in his narrative poems is raised to a higher pitch than is usual in that form, and it is the emotion of the poet, stirred to passionate excitement by the contemplation of the great deeds he is relating. Drayton's Pindaric spirit is clearer in his narrative poems than in his odes.

Like Pindar, and Homer before him, Drayton worships *aretê*, heroic excellence, the great spirit manifesting itself in great deeds. C. M. Bowra refers to Pindar's belief

that there is after all some kinship between men and gods, which is manifest when men realise their powers to the utmost. . . . They cannot become gods, and must

---

[2] Hebel, II, 345.
[3] Werner Jaeger, *Paideia: the Ideals of Greek Culture*, transl. Gilbert Highet (1939), I, 208.
[4] *ibid.*, I, 208.
[5] *ibid.*, I, 209.

not attempt to, but within their mortal limitations they can at times resemble the gods, and this is indeed an end worthy of pursuit.[6]

With this we may compare Drayton's words addressed 'To the Reader' before *Englands Heroicall Epistles:*

And though (Heroicall) be properly understood of Demi-gods, as of HERCULES and ÆNEAS, whose Parents were said to be, the one, Cœlestiall, the other, Mortall; yet is it also transferred to them, who for the greatnesse of Mind come neere to Gods. For to be borne of a cœlestiall *Incubus,* is nothing else, but to have a great and mightie Spirit, farre above the Earthly weakenesse of Men . . .[7]

Drayton never wrote a poem that can be unquestionably classed as epic, nor has he a satisfying epic hero. *Poly-Olbion* (to be discussed in the next chapter), though epic in scope and intention, is chorographical, not heroic, in character. His history poems and legends have occasional epic features and are infused with an epic spirit, but lack the full epic structure and effect. Drayton may have thought of both kinds as types of the brief epic. In his preface to the *Legends* in 1619, he describes the legend as 'a *Species* of an *Epick* or Heroick Poeme', adding,

it eminently describeth the act or acts of some one or other eminent Person; not with too much labour, compasse, or extension, but roundly rather, and by way of Briefe, or *Compendium.*[8]

The description accurately reflects Drayton's own interests. The concentration upon the acts of 'some one eminent Person' it refers to is something Drayton sought instinctively. And beyond the act, he sought the spirit of the act. Because this is so, Drayton's historical poems are in a sense interesting more for their reach than for their grasp. They are charged with a love of the heroic, and a desire to isolate it, to capture its pure essence. This accounts for many of their weaknesses, as well as their strengths: for the undigested lumps of history that can drive a reader like Professor Mario Praz to describe Drayton's poetry as 'in the Elizabethan region . . . certainly the most extensive expanse of flat country'[9] (the description is unjust, however), and for the all-too-frequent lack of organisation and control. Drayton is so impatient to achieve air and fire, he too often leaves earth and water untransmuted.

[6] Bowra, *Pindar* (1964), 96, 97.
[7] Hebel, II, 130.
[8] *ibid.,* 382.
[9] Praz, 'Michael Drayton', *English Studies* XXVIII(1947), 107.

Not all the shortcomings of his historical poems are due, however, to his pre-occupation with the rare and the rarefied. Equally noticeable is a dissipation of interest, which necessarily hinders the achievement of the concentration he desires. In neither *Mortimeriados* nor its later version *The Barons Warres*, which are Drayton's most serious attempts at the heroic poem, are we certain where the centre of interest lies. In the former, judging by its title, it ought to lie with Mortimer, but in fact the questions of 'kingship, succession, and the ethics of civil war' the subject raises are so attractive in themselves to Drayton that he fails to keep them properly subordinate, and Mortimer, as hero, remains far too much 'off-centre'. In *The Barons Warres*, on the other hand although the attempt to make the poem more of a national epic in the manner, above all, of Lucan, is clear, the story of Isabel and Mortimer usurps so much of the interest in the final books that much of this national character is lost. Thus this uncertainty of aim in the two poems is due, partly to Drayton's willingness to pursue multiple objectives, but also to the existence in him of interests in themselves compatible but difficult to reconcile within the subject chosen – interests, namely, in the nation and in the single hero. This further involves a diverse and partly conflicting interest in physical, usually choric action, and in the isolated character or passion. Where, as in *The Battaile of Agincourt*, Drayton is able to treat the first of these interests singly, or, as in the *Legends* and *Heroicall Epistles*, the second, there is, formally, a considerable gain.

Mortimer, the hero of *Mortimeriados* and *The Barons Warres*, is Drayton's most ambitious attempt at portraying a hero. It is a curious choice. Perhaps Drayton saw in the Mortimer of Marlowe's *Edward II* possibilities left undeveloped. Drayton's debt to that play, here and in the earlier *Peirs Gaveston*, is, as Professor Tillotson has shown, considerable. Marlowe's influence upon Drayton's work generally is, in fact, of the first importance, and hardly surpassed by that of Spenser himself. In Marlowe's dramas Drayton found encouragement and stimulus for many of the things he was trying to do, and it was encouragement from a remarkably kindred spirit. Professor Tillotson says happily of the 'strange wild beauty' of the sonnets in *Ideas Mirrour*, 'It is almost as if Marlowe were writing sonnets.'[10] The reason is not hard to find: the poems are full of towering thoughts and images that could have come from Marlowe. Here Drayton too is 'the Over-reacher', to adopt

[10] Hebel, V, 15.

Professor Levin's term. Even in the poems that precede *Mortimeriados*, Drayton's imaginative response to Marlowe's work is clear. In the sweetness and smoothness of their style *Peirs Gaveston* and *Matilda* owe much to Spenser, but in their exuberance, colour, and fire, they are Marlovian, rather. Drayton seems to be writing under the spell of 'Marlowe's mighty line'. There is climbing, rapturous passion in both poems, yet, as in Marlowe, there is also a dense, luxurious physicality. And though the richness is Drayton's own, warmer and even denser than Marlowe's, it clearly owes much to his inspiration. Edward's love makes a kind of small-scale Tamburlaine out of Gaveston:

> My port and personage so magnificent,
> That (as a God) the Commons honored mee.
> And in my pryde, loe thus I could devise,
> To seeme a wonder unto all mens eyes.   (813–16)

This is Gaveston speaking. Edward lavishes upon him the kind of things Tamburlaine had promised Zenocrate:

> In ritchest Purple rode I all alone,
> With Diamonds imbroidered and bedight,
> Which lyke the stars in *Gallixia* shone . . .   (817–19)

> Upon a stately Jennet forth I rode,
> Caparisond with Pearle-enchased plumes,
> Trotting as though the Measures he had trode,
> Breathing Arabian Civit-sweet perfumes.   (823–6)

In *Matilda* King John too becomes a Tamburlaine in his wooing:

> Great troupes of Ladies shall attend my Gerle,
> Thou on thy brave tryumphing Chariot borne,
> Thy drink shall be dissolved orient Pearle,
> Thy princely Cup of rarest Unicorne:
> Then live at ease, and laugh the world to scorne.
>   And if our musick cannot like thine eares,
>   Thy *Jove* shall fetch thee musick from the Spheres.
>   (407–13)

Both poems are full of Marlowesque splendours of this kind.

Drayton's Mortimer is a distinctly Marlovian hero, even closer to Tamburlaine that to his namesake in *Edward II*. He is not well portrayed: much of the time we have to take the promise for the performance: we are told that he is a hero, rather than see it for ourselves. Nevertheless, Drayton is here attempting something highly significant and interesting. Mortimer, he tells us, is 'of the old HEROES great and Godlike Straine'. He has

> A mighty spirit, a minde which did aspire;
> Not of the drossy substance of the earth,
> But of the purest element of fire.
>
> *(Mortimeriados, 65–7)*

Drayton sees him as a 'clear spirit', one whose animal spirits are so purified that he has become god-like:

> The temper of his nobler mooving part,
> Had that true tutch which purified his blood,
> Infusing thoughts of honor in his hart,
> Whose flaggie feathers were not soyld in mud.
>
> (71–4)

He is man at his noblest, the incarnation of *aretê*, and he shows his *aretê* in his aspiration and pride:

> Men looke up to the starres thereby to knowe,
> As they doe progresse heaven, he earth should doe.
>
> (930–31)

This is the gist of Drayton's argument concerning him, in both poems.

Drayton's Mortimer is a Marlovian character alike in his aspiration, his anger ('the angry lion', he is called in *Mortimeriados*), and his amorality. Drayton finds in him, moreover, the 'brave translunary things' of the 'old Poets' which later he was to praise Marlowe for possessing. In other words, he recognises, both in his own hero and in Marlowe's, the type of demi-god or near-demi-god whose relationship to Marlowe's Tamburlaine has been so brilliantly demonstrated by Mr. Eugene M. Waith in his study, *The Herculean Hero*. Indeed, Drayton's work confirms Mr. Waith's findings, even providing specific comparisons between Mortimer and Hercules. Thus the line immediately preceding the last passage quoted ('Men looke up to the starres . . .') is '*Alcides* pitch'd his pillers in the sand', which, when Hercules's stellification is recalled, gives additional point to the reference to the stars. In what is the central episode – indeed until his final capture the only one where he is seen in action – his escape from the Tower, Mortimer is presented in *Mortimeriados* as 'the sonne of *Jove*' (in *The Barons Warres*, 'Alcides'), who

> new toyles must undertake,
> Of walls, of gates, of watches, woods, and streames.
>
> (689–90)

Again, Isabel, lamenting his downfall in the final stanzas of *Mortimeriados*, declares

> In Bookes and Armes consisted thy delight,
> And thy discourse of Campes, and grounds of state, . . .
>
> A *Cato* when in counsell thou didst sit,
> A *Hercules* in executing it.   (2864–70)

The significance of this is brought out by Mr. Waith's remarks on the Stoic tendency, as shown for example in Seneca's *Moral Essays*, to couple Hercules and Cato together as complementary types of stoical wisdom and endurance, Cato being its supreme human exemplar and Hercules its mythic embodiment.[11] The emphasis upon Mortimer's learning and statesmanship makes it clear that he intended to exemplify that nobler type of *aretê* summed up, as Werner Jaeger has shown, in the claim of Phœnix, Achilles' old teacher, that he has brought Achilles up to be both 'a speaker and a man of action' (*Iliad*, IX).[12] It also points once again to the Renaissance doctrine of the 'clear spirit', the man who is perfected in knowledge as well as in physical prowess and endurance.

In the Herculean hero, Mr. Waith assures us, the amorality is to be accepted as the defect of his qualities, and as a small price to pay for his greatness. Drayton seems implicitly to have accepted this position in

---

[1] Waith, *The Herculean Hero* (1962), 30.
[2] Jaeger, *op. cit.*, I, 6.

his portrait of Mortimer, though it is difficult for the reader (who is evidently more detached) to do so. One reason why the two poems fail as epics is the unsuitability of this type of hero for the form. Mortimer, it could be argued, resembles Achilles in his pride and wrath, but even Achilles fought for his country's cause in the end. Mortimer is too much of an individualist to be identified with the nation; his cause is not, or only very limitedly in so far as Edward II was a bad king, the nation's cause. Thus the epic and heroic elements in the poem pull in opposite directions.

The stress in Drayton's chief hero is consequently much more on greatness than on goodness. He does not exemplify the ideal of service set forth in Prince Arthur and Spenser's other heroes. In 'that mighty Malcontent' there are, rather, links with another Elizabethan type, the 'Senecal man'. But, taking Chapman's heroes as representative here, it is Bussy, not Clermont D'Ambois that he resembles. Of Chapman's Senecan portrayals, from *Bussy* to *Byron*, Professor Nicholas Brooke writes,

The pursuit of virtù, however honest, ends inevitably in conflict with plain 'virtue'.[13]

This is something which, I think, Drayton too, with his orthodox Christian (and Spenserian) love of virtue, came to realise. The 'aspiring pride' of a Mortimer risks comparison with the devil, as well as with Hercules. Possibly the slight modifications in his presentation in *The Barons Warres* were due to Drayton's recognition of this. At any rate, his next hero, Robert Duke of Normandy, following very closely on Mortimer (both poems appeared in 1596), seems intended to adjust the balance, and to provide a more truly Christian version of 'the clear spirit'.

This Legend, like its companion pieces, was subsequently much reduced and revised, becoming, like the others, a more shapely but less exuberant work. It has an unusual structure for a Legend: instead of the ghost telling its own story, Robert appears accompanied by the goddesses Fame and Fortune, each of whom tells his story from her own angle and claims it as an example of her power. Fame, however, has the last word and thus virtually wins the contest:

---

[13] N. Brooke, Chapman, *Bussy D'Ambois* (1964), Introduction, xxxiii.

> His body thine, his crosses witnes be,
> His mind is mine, and from thy power is free.   (1245-6)

Fame's discourse offers Drayton the means of making rhapsody *functional*; it is a blazon, an extended victory-ode. This applies especially to the first version of the poem, which is constantly losing itself in an *O altitudo* of praise:

> Eternall sparks of honors purest fire,
> Vertue of vertues, Angels angeld mind,
> Where admiration may it selfe admire,
> Where mans divinest thoughts are more divin'd,
>   Saint sainted spirit, in heavens own shrine enshrind . . .
>   (869-73)

This and many kindred passages disappear in the later version, which concentrates more on the story, although the central purpose, that of presenting Robert, the Crusader, as the perfect 'Christian champion' remains unchanged. The association of him with saints and angels in the lines just quoted suggests a different emphasis from that in the portrayal of Mortimer, and this contrast is everywhere apparent. His courage and fire and 'purity' are as great as Mortimer's:

> When in the Morne his Courser he bestrid,
> He seem'd compos'd essentially of Fire . . .,
>   (1619 version, 820-1)

but they are combined with a proper Christian humility:

> Greatnes he decks in modesties attire,
> Honor he doth by humblenes advance,
> By sufferance he raiseth courage hier,
>   His holy thoughts by patience still aspire . . .
>   (1003-6 (1596))

He leaves Rufus in possession of the throne of England, rightfully his, while he goes to fight in the Holy Land:

> A crown of gold this Christian knight doth scorne,
> So much he lov'd those temples crown'd with thorne.
>   (853-4)

In the later version, this point is further emphasised by his refusal to become king of Jerusalem after its capture:

> So farre it was from his Religious Mind,
> To mixe vile Things, with those of Heav'nly kind.
>
> (832–3)

He refuses all marks of honour:

> No tryumphs doe his victories adorne,
> But in his death who on the Crosse had died,
> No lawrell nor victorious wreath is worne,
> But that red Crosse to tell him crucified,
>
> (1212–15 (1596))

and returns home clad as a 'poore Pilgrim' in Palmer's grey,

> Leaving his Lords to lead his warlick traine,
> Whilst he alone comes sadly on the way.   (1228–9)

In short, he is the embodiment of 'Humble valour, valiant humilitie', and a perfect example of Christian magnanimity.

Drayton's later heroes, in his poems published after 1600, continue to exemplify greatness of spirit, though with some variation in treatment. Cromwell, for instance, who provides, as Drayton himself says, 'the Example of a new Mans fortune, made great by Arts of Court, and reach of a shrewd Wit, upon the advantages of a corrupt Prince',[14] yet has greatness within himself, a 'glorious fire' in his breast, impelling him to rise above his circumstances. In his insistence that true nobility is a matter of 'virtue', not birth, he is a Tamburlaine; in the means he adopts to realise that nobility, however, he is a Macchiavel. On the whole, the 'clear spirit' has been cut to size here; we see a social type rather than a demi-god. The portrait, as Professor Tillotson has shown, is historically a much more faithful one than were the two discussed above.

The two historical poems, *The Battaile of Agincourt* (1627) and *The Miseries of Queen Margarite* (1627) are poems of action and event, and are concerned more with the group – army, nation, or faction – than with a central figure. Henry V is 'that man made out of fire' (after

[14] Hebel, II, 382.

Shakespeare, he could scarcely be less), but it is on the aspiration of the nation, its collective 'clear spirit', that Drayton concentrates. Margaret is described as a 'mighty spirit' tempting Fortune 'till againe she smile', but no real attempt is made to enforce this. Suffolk too is presented as a 'mighty minde', driven by love and ambition, but the ascription of these qualities to him seems automatic and perfunctory, as if the character had become a stock type for Drayton. He shows little interest in Suffolk and disposes of him briskly:

> And when no more they could the Duke deride,
> They cutt his head off on the Cock boate-side.
>
> (399–400)

This is almost anti-heroic. And indeed there is hardly any heroism in this poem. Drayton seems to find small glory in the later combats: Yorkists and Lancastrians are for him 'Equall in envie, as in pride and power' (633).

David in *David and Goliah* and Moses in *Moses his Birth and Miracles* are both clear-spirited heroes. David has

> A valour so invincible and hie,
> As naturally enabled him to flye
> Above all thought of perill.   (595–7)

Moses impresses the daughters of Jethro with his 'beauty, shape, and courage' and 'Exceeding these, the honour of his minde' (I, 653–4). But the need for fidelity to his source and to his model (Sylvester) perhaps prevents Drayton from giving much prominence to this aspect of his theme.

Nimphidia, Drayton's fairy poem, is, we should remember, mock-heroic, written to please those who delight in 'love and armes': its hero is an Oberon Furens, or Furioso. Drayton's sense of the heroic did not desert him after 1600, but on the whole it sought other outlets than that of historical characterisation.

To turn back, however, to the fifteen-nineties. *Peirs Gaveston*, *Matilda*, and *Mortimeriados* all testify to Drayton's fondness for the theme of romantic love. This, indeed, whatever his other purposes, is the real nerve of all three poems. In *Englands Heroicall Epistles*, first published in 1597 and enlarged in 1598 and 1599, Drayton found a form which enabled him to combine into a unity this and the other interests that absorbed him – namely, British history and the heroic. It is a highly successful collection, generally regarded, and with justice, as one of Drayton's best works. The formal obligation to begin 'in mediis rebus' enabled him to go straight to what had always been his main concern, the central passion of his hero, and at the same time obliged him to focus all else upon this passion. History and narrative, which before had often distracted attention from it, had now to be converted into the substance of the passion itself. Although, moreover, chaos – the chaos in the mind – is often the subject of the poem, its presentation involves an ordering of that chaos. Drayton has here accepted the discipline of the closed couplet, and has used it to achieve a movement that is at once formal, and yet, within its formal limits, free. He has found a way of loading every rift with ore without any drastic curbing of magnanimity.

Englands Heroicall Epistles consists of twelve pairs of letters, exchanged between various royal or noble lovers celebrated in English history, from Henry II and Rosamond down to Gilford Dudley and Lady Jane Gray. The model is Ovid's *Heroides*, although, as Professor Tillotson points out, all but the last six of Ovid's poems are monologues, not dialogues. There are recognisable similarities in tone and manner: the heightened emotion, the rhetorical devices, a combination of formality with familiarity in the address, all these immediately establish the connexion for us. Drayton's Epistles, nevertheless, are a development rather than simply an imitation of Ovid. Professor Tillotson in her excellent Introduction to the poems has stressed the greater variety in Drayton. This arises principally from his concern with a relationship, rather than with the emotional state of one person alone, but owes something also to the range of emotional states with which he deals. Drayton presents, for example, the beginning or middle stage of a love affair, rather than its end. The situation of betrayal, which is basic in Ovid, he does not use at all. Separation (sometimes exile, or imprisonment) there has to be, and nowhere are these poems more like Ovid than in their frequent, poignant sense of the 'salt estranging sea', the disappearing sails of the beloved. There are complaints and reproaches, although the complaints are of loss, and of ill-treatment by others, not of desertion, and the reproaches, when they occur (less frequently than in Ovid) tend to be for shame incurred, as in Rosamond's letter to Henry. The sense of physical frustration is less strong than in Ovid; there are not the allusions to pressed grass and empty beds that we meet in him. Indeed, though the passion of Drayton's characters is just as great as that of Ovid's, it is less exclusively a sexual passion. This no doubt is because it is not ultimately the sexual relationship itself so much as the greatness of spirit manifested in that relationship that interests Drayton. These lovers demonstrate their greatness by their manner of responding to a situation, adverse or otherwise. This, as the passage quoted earlier from the address 'to the Reader' indicates, is the significance of the word 'heroicall' in the title. Drayton has written the poems to demonstrate, not simply that England has her *Heroides*, but that she has her heroes too. So we meet again the 'high and turbulent spirit' of Mortimer, uttering even more Tamburlaine-like aspirations and threats:

> A thousand Kingdomes will we seeke from farre,
> As many Nations waste with Civill Warre,
> Where the dishevel'd gastly Sea-Nymph sings,
> Or well-rig'd Ships shall stretch their swelling Wings,
> And drag their Anchors through the sandie Fome,
> About the World in ev'ry Clime to rome,
> And those unchrist'ned Countries call our owne,
> Where scarce the Name of *England* hath been knowne:
> And in the dead Sea sinke our Houses Fame,
> From whose vaste Depth we first deriv'd our Name;
> Before foule blacke-mouth'd Infamie shall sing,
> That MORTIMER ere stoop'd unto a King;
> ('Mortimer to Queene Isabel', 75–86)

the Stoical resolution and defiance of Suffolk:

> Our Faulcons kind cannot the Cage indure,
> Nor Buzzard-like doth stoope to ev'ry Lure;
> ('William De-La-Poole to Queene Margaret', 17–18)

the ambition of Owen Tudor:

My Mind, that thus your Favours dare aspire,
Shewes, that 'tis touch'd with a celestiall fire;
    ('Owen Tudor to Queene Katherine', 153-4)

the courage of Rosamond or Matilda, ready to face death to end, or
to prevent, dishonour; the patience and long-suffering of Jane Gray.
Not all the writers of the epistles are 'fair, and learn'd, and good as she';
but all have the loftiness, intensity, and ardour that, for Drayton,
redeem their faults and make them, like the more perfect Robert,
a 'fit subject for a story'.

Professor Tillotson suggests that a further difference between Ovid
and Drayton is that Ovid's characters are drawn from legend and
Drayton's from history. This is obviously true, but I think that
Drayton also tried to give his characters a legendary quality, largely
by an adaptation of Ovidian techniques. The letter-writers in the
Heroides, for example, often indulge a taste for genealogy, recalling
the distinguished, often divine, ancestry of themselves or their lovers.
'Hermione to Orestes' (*Heroides*, VIII) is an extreme example, but there
are many others. Drayton, well aware of the importance of ancestry
in fashioning a hero, as he shows repeatedly in his history poems,
introduces such references whenever he can, as in Mortimer's expressions of pride in his 'ancient race' and 'ancient house', Queen Katherine's
boast that her ancestry is as good as that of the Lancastrians, and above
all Owen Tudor's claim that the Welsh

  . . . since great BRUTUS first arriv'd, have stood,
 The onely remnant of the *Trojan* Blood.   (*ibid.*, 107-8)

Much of the historical matter, in fact, comes into the poems by way of
these genealogical surveys. In addition, unable, as he acknowledged,
to claim actual divine ancestry for his heroes, Drayton brings them
'near to gods' by frequent use of mythological comparison. Far from
being mere embroidery, Drayton's classical allusions are, as a rule, as
functional as Eliot's or Joyce's. Just as Eliot sees in Sweeney, the
orang-outang and Doris a modern version of Theseus, Ariadne and
Bacchus, so Drayton sees the relationship between Henry II, his wife
Eleanor and Rosamond as corresponding to that between Jove, Juno
and Io. Eliot's purpose, of course, is deflationary, Drayton's inflationary.
Mortimer, comparing himself in his escape from the Tower (and, by

E

implication, in his whole career) to 'Skie-attempting DEDALUS',
is being as 'significant' as Joyce in his choice of 'Stephen Dedalus' as a
pseudonym. There are numerous examples in the *Epistles* of Drayton's
use of this method of association to raise his characters to a heroic and
god-like level. In isolation, they might appear the mere language of
compliment, which, as far as their reception by the *imaginary* reader is
concerned, they are; but their effect is accumulative and taken together
they work to persuade the actual reader that he is in the presence of
something larger than life. There are good examples in the epistle of
William de-la-Poole to Queen Margaret, in a passage beginning

> Had he, which once the Prize to *Greece* did bring,
> (Of whom, th'old Poets long agoe did sing)
> Seene thee for *England* but imbark'd at *Deepe*,   (113–15)

and in Margaret's reply, but still better are those in the exchanges
between Queen Katherine and Owen Tudor. Ancestry is important
here because the Queen is proposing marriage to someone who is
the apparent inferior of her former husband, Henry V, and also because
the union was to mark both the foundation of the Tudor line, from
which Elizabeth sprang, and at the same time (so the 'Tudor legend'
maintained) the return of a truly British sovereignty. Both Katherine
and Tudor are sensitive on this score, and classical comparisons designed
to convey their quality abound. Thus Katherine, comparing herself
with the Lancastrians:

> Nor doe I thinke there is such different ods,
> They should alone be numbred with the Gods:
> Of CADMUS Earthly Issue reck'ning us,
> And they from JOVE, MARS, NEPTUNE, EOLUS;
> Of great LATONA's Off-spring onely they,
> And we the Brats of wofull NIOBE.
> Our famous Grandsires (as their owne) bestrid
> That Horse of Fame, that God-begotten Steed;
> Whose bounding Hoofe plow'd that *Beotian* Spring,
> Where those sweet Maids of Memorie doe sing.   (65–74)

Owen Tudor, besides drawing interesting comparisons between
Henry V and Alcides and himself and Phaeton, expresses the fear of
some new 'rape' of Katherine by the gods:

If you but walke to take the breathing Ayre,
ORITHIA makes me, that I BOREAS feare:
If to the Fire, JOVE once in Lightning came,
And faire EGINA makes me feare the flame . . .   (127–30)

In the poems as first published, such allusions were still more numerous:
Katherine, for example, sees Henry V as wooing her as Jove wooed
Semele, 'Armed with tempests, thunder-boults of fire.' In omitting
much of this, Drayton shows that he recognises that he had weakened
his argument by excess, but the argument itself remains unaltered.

By such means Drayton's English heroes and heroines are raised to
the level of Ovid's demi-goddesses. Drayton has not forgotten, however, that the demi-god is also the demi-human, and his personages are
complex, authentic, individual human beings, differentiated by their
character and circumstances to a degree that surpasses Ovid, and that
undoubtedly owes something to contemporary drama, particularly,
perhaps, the drama of Shakespeare. (The advance on *Mortimeriados*
and the *Legends* is in this respect impressive.) Not all are equally
individualised; sometimes, as in the case of Rosamond, attention is
concentrated on the emotional state, and there is little sense of character
as such. But sometimes, as in King Henry's reply, we are made keenly
aware of a person speaking out of a particular situation. Henry is
manly, tender, restrained, and touching in his loneliness and longing.
King John, by contrast, is hard, cynical, selfish and sacrilegious, a
mediaeval Alec d'Urberville. There is a further contrast to both these
seducers in the womanising of the shallow but attractive Edward IV,
and yet another in the grave courtliness of Edward the Black Prince.
Outstanding among Drayton's women is the portrait of Elinor Cobham
who was imprisoned in the Isle of Man for witchcraft in the reign of
Henry VI. Drayton skilfully builds up the picture of a superstitious,
credulous mind, by the repeated allusions in her letter to omens and
supersititons and, along with them, repeated curses and vain wishes.
Self-pitying, totally lacking in self-knowledge, this is a woman on the
razor's edge of sanity. Her husband, the good Duke Humphrey,
patient, self-controlled, affectionate, is equally well drawn. In these
two epistles the Shakespearian inspiration is unmistakable, but the
characters are, as Professor Tillotson says, re-imagined, and it is this
fact that gives Drayton's characterisation its value. There is no suggestion of his having imposed a set of characteristics from without;

rather, personality is communicated imperceptibly along with the emotion in a way that is truly organic, suggesting a conception of the character that has been discovered, not devised. The delineation seems the product of sympathy, rather than of analysis.

After 1598 much of Drayton's energy must have gone into the preparation and writing of *Poly-Olbion* (begun in that year, according to Meres). He found time, however, constantly to revise his work and to experiment with new forms. Of the richness, variety, and originality of his poems of the 1600s – the odes and elegies especially – I have no room to write. Many of his elegies, like the satires and pastorals written at this period, express his disgust at the ignobility of life under James I. His love of the heroic still possesses him, but in these unheroic days, when values have been so reversed that the world is 'all arsey varsey' and 'nothing is its owne', life presents itself to him in a series of images, as repulsive as his earlier images – in *Peirs Gaveston* or the end of *Mortimeriados* – had been dazzling. After 'the melancholy acuity of vision', as Professor Tillotson finely calls it, of *The Owle*, these images become increasingly crude and coarse: we have the 'monstrous birth' of the androgynous Moon-calf – the embodiment of the sins and vices of both sexes ('a distorted bloodshot vision,' Oliver Elton calls this); the 'bestiall heard', 'a sort of swine' in the Epistles to Sandys and to Jeffreys; and the obscene episode of the devil's purge which produces 'a rude ribauld crew Of base Plebeians', in that to Master William Browne. The humanist in Drayton, for whom Hamlet's 'What a piece of work is man!' could have provided a creed, is affronted by men's repudiation of their humanity. They have become lunatics, beasts. They have forgotten nobility, and with it, virtue and brave deeds. This is the core of his vision: the nobleness gone from life, the moral and social orders collapse together:

> Such are by titles lifted to the sky,
> As wherefore no man knowes, God scarcely why;
> The vertuous man depressed like a stone
> For that dull Sot to raise himselfe upon;
> He who ne're thing yet worthy man durst doe,

Never durst looke upon his countreys foe,
Nor durst attempt that action which might get
Him fame with men: or higher might him set
Then the base begger (rightly if compar'd;)
This Drone yet never brave attempt that dar'd,
Yet dares be knighted, and from thence dares grow
To any title Empire can bestow.

('To Master William Browne', 49–60)

This is the 'Herculean' vision of the early poems turned upside down.

Especially grievous to Drayton was the disesteem, as it seemed to him, into which poetry had fallen. In the satires and satirical Elegies he makes it clear that this is part – again, a central part – of a general social evil. With the collapse of the ideal of nobility, the interdependence between poets and those who should be the leaders of society, the poets inspiring the great men to great deeds, the great men supporting the poets, was inevitably lost. The usurpers of the places of the great, moreover, have by a natural law of opposites a hatred of poetry equal to their own vileness. In key passages in *The Owle* (661–94) and *The Moone-Calfe* (359–426) and variously throughout the *Elegies* Drayton puts these arguments. At the literary level, he is regretting the passing of a state of society that made the writing of epic possible: his pain is part of the growing-pains of the modern world. In this sense, it is more permanent than the similar feelings expressed by Spenser in *The Teares of the Muses*.

Faced with this 'frosty *Boreas*' that 'has nipt our flowery *Tempe*', Drayton shows courage as well as disgust and anger. The *Elegies*, not merely the satirical ones but all of them, are full of a noble stoicism, not the less noble for being hardly won and maintained, as a comparison of the Elegy 'To the Noble Lady, the Lady I. S., of worldly crosses' with Daniel's more tranquil 'Epistle to the Countess of Cumberland' shows. The determination to arm his soul 'with constant patience' is everywhere apparent, and it is the determination of a hero. A vein of biblical imagery runs through these Elegies; Drayton's pessimism requires an assessment of God's position in these matters as persistently as does Hardy's, and sometimes his answer is the same as Hardy's. He suggests at one time that men are 'the Gods fooles', made, not out of love, but 'only as a thing To make them sport with', at another that the world is 'God-forgotten':

As though that God had carelessly left all
That being hath on this terrestiall ball,
To fortunes guiding, nor would have to doe
With man, nor ought that doth belong him to.

(ibid., 85–8)

His most significant suggestion, however, is that God has given more
'Power to the Devill, then he did of yore', permitting him

By his blacke hellish ministers to vexe
All worthy men.   (ibid., 95–6)

On this supposition, such 'worthy men' are in the position of Job, and
in fact the image of Job, that Biblical 'hero', seems often to be in
Drayton's mind, as when for instance he assures 'the Noble Lady, the
Lady I. S.',

God doth not love them least, on whom he layes
The great'st afflictions; but that he will praise
Himselfe most in them, and will make them fit,
Near'st to himselfe who is the Lambe to sit.   (71–4)

'Brave translunary things', it seems, are still possible, even for the
downtrodden poet. Courage is still the one thing needful:

in the extreamest ill,
Apollo's brood must be couragious still,
Let Pies, and Dawes, sit dumb before their death,
Onely the Swan sings at the parting breath.

('To Master George Sandys', 33–6)

In the dearth of other heroes, the poet himself must fill the breach.

But the classical heroes had their Elysium, and it is right that the
poet-hero should have his. Throughout these grim years – at least
until 1622 – the writing of *Poly-Olbion* provided Drayton with a
means of escape from this land of 'savage slaves' into a different Britain.
Then in 1627 in *The Quest of Cynthia* he describes his 'wayless walk'
on the quest, ending with the offer of his mysterious Cynthia's love:
'Here from the hatefull world wee'll live' – a life

> Such as the golden world first sawe,
> Most innocent and free.   (183-4)

Finally, in *The Muses Elizium* the tired old satyr, 'whose ugly shape the Nimphes affrights', climbs the 'craggy by-clift Hill' of Parnassus 'to finde out these more pleasant Fields of rest'. In the 'blessed bowers' of the Muses, 'Free from the rude resort Of beastly people', the poet finds solace. Yet even here he does not forget England, 'that faire Felicia', once Earth's paradise. In the very action of turning his back on it, he expresses the strength of his commitment to it:

> And to Elizium be thou welcome then,
> Untill those base Felicians thou shalt heare,
> By that vile nation captived againe,
> That many a glorious age their captives were.
> ('The tenth Ninphall', 145-8)

The Poetry of Drayton:
2 *Poly-Olbion*

When Part I of *Poly-Olbion* appeared in 1612, the reading public's appetite and energy for digesting a poem of such length on such a subject were already much diminished. Drayton's first words in his address 'To the Generall Reader' are an acknowledgment of this fact – 'this great disadvantage against me.' It is a disadvantage from which the poem has never recovered. Hebel's arguments in his preface to the Shakespeare Head edition, proving that it has had many 'lovers' and been the delight of antiquaries and of readers 'leafing' through it to find some striking passage, only strengthen the impression that, although Drayton's undertaking has been appreciated, the poem as poem, not as a box of delights merely but as an artistic entity, has been little valued. Apart from its length, the main reason for this has been its verse, both the form itself (the alexandrine couplet), and the handling of it. The latter is often clumsy, flat, and prosaic. Even when it is none of these things, it is seldom striking; there are not many lines here the repetition of which would make a man cut himself while shaving. (There are some.) Yet if we consider the whole rather than the part, this is not in itself a disadvantage. A long poem, it may be argued, should be read as *a poem*, not as *poetry*. The material of which it is made may, as Mr. Robert Graves complains, be mere mother-of-pearl; but even from mother-of-pearl a work of art may be fashioned. Drayton's lines at any particular point may be verse rather than poetry when taken in isolation, but this does not prevent them, when taken together, forming a genuine poem. Professor Graham Hough suggests that the novel has now taken the place of the long poem. This observation perhaps might be allowed critically to cut both ways, and we might try comparing the long poem with the novel, rather than with the lyric. *Poly-Olbion* might then, for instance, be seen to be comparable, in the way it subdues a vast and heterogenous mass of material to the shape of a single over-riding vision, with such works as Joyce's *Ulysses* or Proust's *A La Recherche du Temps Perdu*. (Even Proust's title is appropriate.) Like these works, *Poly-Olbion* is a *tour de force*, as Drayton's friends recognised, when they were 'pleased to tearme it' a Herculean labour, an idea which Drayton was pleased to borrow for the poem's last line – 'this strange *Herculean* toyle'. The poet-hero, sustaining this massive work through to its conclusion, like Hercules holding up the world, has become indeed a Herculean hero.

Poly-Olbion is presented on its title-page as 'A *Chorographicall* Description of *Tracts, Rivers, Mountaines, Forests*, and other Parts of this renowned *Isle* of *Great Britaine*, with intermixture of the most Remarquable *Stories, Antiquities, Wonders, Rarityes, Pleasures, and Commodities* of the same.' This establishes the variety and multiplicity of its content. Such variety is an essential characteristic of the poem, stressed by Drayton within the work itself. Yet variety alone is not his aim. Great as is Drayton's debt to Camden, the poem is more than simply a versified *Britannia*. The statement on the title-page adds 'Digested in a Poem', and this is significant. It implies that Drayton has not merely versified his material, but has made something of it, shaped it into a whole. The implication is justified. Faced with a mass of, seemingly, heterogeneous material, Drayton has been surprisingly successful in ordering and imposing unity upon it, without diminishing its variousness. The means that he has employed to do this deter-mine the character of the poem. He fashions them constantly to his purposes.

One characteristic of the poem which the descriptive title fails to stress is its concern with antiquity. This is much more than the mere 'extra' that it appears there. Britain's history is as much the poem's theme as her geography; even more important, it is the sheer ancientness of the land that Drayton wishes to convey. He wants us to see the land – 'this blessed plot, this earth, this realm, this England' – both in its temporal, changing aspects and in those which are eternal. And he wants us to see it all at the same time, and really to *see* it. Wither's epithet for the poem, 'Topo-chrono-graphicall,' is accurate, if clumsy. In inviting 'the Generall Reader' 'to walke forth with the Muses', Drayton offers variety as the paramount attraction. But it is a variety seen first from 'the top of an easie hill ... from whose height thou mai'st behold both the old and later times, as in thy prospect, lying

E*

farre under thee.'[1] This suggests that Drayton himself saw the poem as
a single composite vision in which time and space, past and present, are
united. The word 'prospect' is important; it reinforces 'description' on
the title-page, and is a pointer to the fact that Drayton is not primarily
telling 'our island story' nor writing a poetic guide-book, but is presenting us with a scene, a varied, extensive scene, like the landscape paintings
then coming into vogue, and is asking us, despite its multiplicity, to
grasp it as a whole. Drayton had always been a fine poet-painter, and
this was to be his masterpiece. At the same time, the effects he seeks are
not merely visual. He wants us to see the land and to visualise its
history. But he also wants us to appreciate it down to its roots, physical
and temporal; to understand its soil as soil, and to value its products
rightly. Above all, he wants us to respond to its spirit; to recognise in it
a living thing. He is trying to re-create in verse the very being of his
country. He wishes to teach, but he also has something to express. It
is his own deep sense of these things primarily that he is imparting.
This, presumably, is what Mr. Edmund Blunden had in mind when he
wrote of 'the singular effulgence of the sustaining impulse' of the poem.[2]

Drayton's itinerary in the poem is partly determined by his desire
to conflate history with geography.[3] Thus he begins at the beginning
and establishes the historical as well as the physical dimension of his
subject by introducing the 'God-like' and (according to Drayton and
his authorities) '*Britaine*-founding *Brute*' in the First Song, and by
dealing with Cornwall and Devon, the counties with which he is
associated. He then moves fairly rapidly towards the Welsh border
counties, reaching them and later Wales itself in Song IV. At this point
we hear appropriately of the ancient Britons –

> Then most renowned *Wales*, thou famous ancient place,
> Which still hast been the Nurse of all the *British* race

– of Arthur, and of the early clashes between Britons and Saxons,
Saxons and Normans. Song VIII, dealing with the English border
counties, enlarges the story of the ancient Britons, with an account of
their resistance, first to the Romans, then to the Saxons. When in

---

[1] Hebel, IV, v*.
[2] Edmund Blunden, *Votive Tablets* (1931), 40.
[3] Although it begins like his in the south-west, Drayton's itinerary differs considerably
from Camden's in his *Britannia*. Camden does not reach Wales until much later in the book.

Song XI we finally turn our backs on Wales, it is to receive a long account of the Christianised Saxon kings. Their wars with the Danes follow in Song XII. There is no particular reason, other than that of convenience, for attaching this history to the counties described here. But is will be noticed how thoroughly Drayton has established the antiquity of his subject. The poem also gains in coherence by this method of linking different sections of the island's history to different but appropriate regions, rather than simply recording the historical associations of each place as we come to it (though Drayton often does this too). Other examples of Drayton's care to make the historical narrative fit the place, which thus gains historical depth, occur in Song XVII, where

> Great *Tames*, as King of Rivers, sings
> The Catalogue of th' English Kings,

and in Song XVIII, where the Medway, which 'still had nurst those navies in her Road, Our Armies that had oft to conquest borne abroad', narrates the exploits of our famous soldiers.

Drayton's chorographical procedure is not, or not often, that of a Cobbett. He does not, that is, take us from point to point by a clearly stated route. Rather, he presents us with areas of interest – a whole county, parts of a county, or parts of several counties – which he explores by a variety of methods. He seldom has a fixed base or touring centre. His purpose is to note the chief natural features of the area, and any other interesting landmarks. He plots his itinerary by the landmarks themselves, which means that, above all, he plots it by the rivers. Sometimes he follows a river from source to mouth, noting its tributaries, if any, as he goes. But as well as the movement along the rivers, there is a movement from river to river, which is in fact the chief means by which distances are covered. In his description of Somerset, for example, we slant rapidly south-westwards from the Avon to the Parret, passing the Mendips, '*Ochyes* dreadfull Hole', Avalon, and other places as we go, but with our course determined chiefly by the rivers – Avon, Frome, Chute, Ax, Bry, Gedney, Audry, Brent, and finally 'Cleere *Parret*'. The maps of *Poly-Olbion*, with their wide open spaces and wriggling rivers, looking rather like the snakes on a snakes-and-ladders board, faithfully reflect this characteristic. Each region is for Drayton like an open palm, which he explores not as the crow but rather as the bee flies. Rivers, hills, and forests, but particularly rivers are the flowers with which his 'industrious Muse' busies herself.

By this means Drayton achieves, so to speak, a spatial and not merely a linear advance across the country. By 'advance' I am referring to actual movement within the poem, not simply to the poem's development. For the purposes of this advance, Drayton introduces, naturally enough, a traveller. This traveller, like the hero in an epic poem, is one of the means, indeed the chief means, by which he shapes his material into a unity. The nature of the traveller gives him (or rather, her) unusual powers of unification, for this traveller is principally neither the poet nor the reader, but the Muse. Of course, as we saw in Chapter III, to give the Muse such a rôle can be for the poet a way of commenting on his own performance. But in *Poly-Olbion* it becomes more than that: it becomes part of the performance itself. As the poem proceeds, Drayton's Muse acquires a strange, objective reality, independent of the poet. She becomes the central personage of the poem. It is her journey across the country that we follow, from the moment when first

> The sprightly Muse her wing displaies,
> And the French Ilands first survaies,
>
> (Song I, Argument)

till the final Song, where the poet himself encourages her:

> Yet cheerely on my *Muse*, no whit at all dismay'd,
> But look aloft tow'rds heaven, to him whose powerfull ayd;
> Hath led thee on thus long, & through so sundry soiles,
> Steep Mountains, Forrests rough, deepe Rivers, that thy toyles
> Most sweet refreshings seeme, and still thee comfort sent . . .
>
> (XXX, 1–5)

She travels both on the wing and on foot, becoming a sea-bird in Wales, when she assays

> From *Penmens* craggy height to try her saily wings,   (X, 3)

or experiencing in Lincolnshire the hardships of the foot-traveller:

Through Quicksands, Beach, and Ouze, the *Washes* she must wade.
(XXV, 13)

On one occasion she is so wearied that she

must now,
As Workmen often use, a while sit downe and blow.
(XXII, 1636)

Drayton may have learned this way of writing of the Muse from
Du Bartas, an important influence on this poem as on many other
parts of Drayton's work. Du Bartas's Muse too has her adventures:

But now (deere *Muse*) with *Jonas* let us hie
From the Whale's belly . . .[4]

These, however, remain incidental, not much more than a figure of
speech, and if Drayton has borrowed the device from Du Bartas, he
has also carried it much further.

Around the Muse as his central character Drayton groups the other
personages of his poem. These personages are not human beings (no
human voice is heard in the poem), but rivers, forests, islands, hills,
vales, and plains. Their relationship to the Muse is a curious one. They
owe their voices to her; it is she who endows them with the power of
speech, and they eagerly await the coming (rather than go in search)
of their author. In song XXI, for example, the Muse's aid enables the
Devil's Ditch to become vocal:

That great and ancient Ditch, which us expected long,
Inspired by the Muse, at her arrivall song.   (3-4)

This leads the Vale of Ringdale to complain:

Shall I be silenc'd, when
Rude Hills, and Ditches, digg'd by discontented men,
Are ayded by the Muse; their Mind's at large to speake.
(79-81)

[4] *D.W.W.*, sig.Lɪ^r.

But many of them speak also to as well as through her, and though she may have inspired their speeches, there is no suggestion that she has dictated them. As she moves among these animated hills and rivers, listening to their complaints, being entertained by their singing, witnessing their quarrels, her position is sometimes like that of Alice. St. Michael's Mount, for instance, weeping as he tells his tale ('Then from his rugged top the teares downe trickling fell'), is not unlike the Mock Turtle. Even more than Alice, however, she resembles a monarch, or other dignitary, on progress. Both Drayton and Selden frequently speak of the poem as a progress; 'this my intended progresse', Drayton calls it in his address to the Cambro-Britons. There are progresses and progresses; Drayton, having made his Muse rather than himself undertake this one, perhaps turns it into a royal one without fully realising that he has done so. (We may compare the two swans, king and queen of the Lea and its tributaries, in Vallans's poem *A Tale of Two Swannes*, who make a progress 'Throughout their land to see the boundes thereof'.)[5] The forms of entertainment the Muse receives resemble those enjoyed, or endured, by Elizabeth and James on their progresses: long orations everywhere, often setting forth the merits and history of the place visited; debates and disputations; musical entertainments; elaborate festivals. Although the speeches addressed to her lack the adulation and compliment indispensable in addresses to a human monarch, the Muse's reception is often a royal one; in Dorset, for instance,

> Where *Gillingham* with gifts that for a God were meet
> (Enameld paths, rich wreaths, and every soveraine sweet
> The earth and ayre can yeeld, with many a pleasure mixt)
> Receives her. (II, 133–6)

And when in Song XXVI the Vale of Bever 'receiveth her to Guest' and immediately proceeds to sing her own 'rightfull praise' ('Three Shires there are (quoth she) in me their parts that claime . . .'); when in the ninth Morvinia craves 'especiall audience', to speak of her own character and history; when Itchin, in spite of the other rivers' protests that the Muse has not time for this, insists on narrating the

---

[5] W. Vallans, *A Tale of Two Swannes* (1590). The swans start from the head of the Lea, and pass Whethamstead and Hatfield (with a reference to 'antient Verolam'). Various characters – a swan, an old man, for example – address them and make speeches.

life-story of Bevis of Southampton; and when Weever or Wrekin surveys British history – although their behaviour is at times more informal and unruly than that of the noblemen, scholars and citizens awaiting Elizabeth ever was – they undoubtedly have their counterparts in Mr. John Throgmorton, Recorder of Coventry, enlightening the Queen on the history of 'this antient City', during her visit there in 1565; or in Edward Aglionby, Recorder, who in 1572 undertook to inform her of what 'wee reade in olde writings and auntenticall cronycles' concerning 'the auncient estate of this Towne of Warwik'; or in Mr. Bell of Worcester, in 1575 'brieflie dyvert[ing] to y^r Majesties noble Progenitors, to whom this poor Citie hath byn especially bounde'.[6] And they have a still clearer affinity with that Lady of the Lake who greeted Elizabeth at Killingworth Castle (i.e. Kenilworth) in 1575, when

. . . her Highness all along this Tylt-yard rode unto the inner gate next the base coourt of the Castl: where the Lady of the Lake (famous in King Arthurz book) with two Nymphes waiting uppon her, arrayed all in sylks, attending her Highness comming: from the midst of the pool, whear upon a moovabl Island, bright blazing with torches, she floting to land, met her Majesty with a well-penned meter and matter after this sort: *viz.* First of the auncientee of the Castl, whoo had been ownerz of the same e'en till this day, most allwcyz in the hands of the Earls of Leyceter; hoow shee had kept this Lake sins King Arthurz dayz; and now understanding of her Highness hither cumming, thought it both office and duetie, in humble wize to discover her and her estate . . .[7]

But the Muse has here this advantage over Elizabeth: the kind of encounter that is only make-believe at Kenilworth is 'real' for her.

This character of a royal progress is not maintained at every point of the poem. Drayton's method is too devious for that. It is, however, one of the most important means by which he organises, unifies, and dignifies his subject-matter. Sometimes the Muse seems less a monarch than the representative of a special commission, from whose report good may come. Thus the forests of Hampshire bid her farewell with a speech beginning:

Deere Muse, to plead our right, whom time at last hath brought . . .

[6] Nichols, *Progresses of Queen Elizabeth*, (1788–1821) III, 'The Queen's visit at Coventry', 8; I, 'The Queen's Progress, 1572', 20; IV, 89.
[7] *ibid.*, I, 'The Queen's Entertainment at Killingworth Castle', 7.

At other times her presence at the verbal contests between hills and plains, rivers and forests, is as subordinate as that of a reporter at a football-match, or, when the 'flyting' becomes really personal, of someone overhearing a family quarrel. Essentially, however, she is less a reporter than an omniscient narrator, able to record even the unspoken thoughts of a character, such as those of the river Stour concerning the historical associations of Shaftesbury (II, 149 *sq*.). She records also her own speeches, both what she 'uttereth to herself' (as at I, 133) and what she says aloud, as for example her exclamations of wonder at the sight of London, and of anger at the harm being done to it by the 'upstart Gentry'.

By making frequent, often quite subtle, adjustments in the relationship between the Muse and his subject-matter, or, more accurately perhaps, in the triangular relationship of Muse, author, and subject-matter, Drayton is able to vary his narrative method considerably. This variety is partly offset, however, by a relative monotony in the form given to the material, which for many readers is a major obstacle to enjoyment of the poem. There are too many quarrels, too many love-affairs between one natural object and another. But to admit this is not to admit that Drayton was wrong to employ prosopopœia at all. Without it, he could not have given the poem the unique, authentic life it possesses. Drayton himself in Song VI eloquently defends the practice of blending fact with fiction, as being agreeable 'To man, whose mind doth still varietie pursue'. The meanings of his own fictions, when taken simply as an entertaining method of imparting information, are quite transparent. When 'th' old Heardsman Clent', for instance, pines with unrequited love for the wood-nymph, Feck'nam, whose own heart is set on Salwarp, we know, or a glance at the map will tell us, that this means that the hill overlooks the forest, while the river actually runs through or along-side it. As Selden says of the eighteenth song,

It begins with *Rother*, whose running through the woods, inisling *Oxney*, and such like, poetically here describ'd is plaine enough to any apprehending conceit.[8]

This expository function is, however, the least important aspect of Drayton's fictions. What really justifies their presence in the poem is the strong imaginative life they possess, and the animation they them-

8 Hebel, IV, 383.

selves impart to the subject. By their means Britain becomes the kind of 'other world' Drayton's imagination delights in (a Muses' Elyzium in fact), but without ceasing to be Britain. 'England still waits for the supreme moment of her literature – for the great poet who shall voice her,' Mr. E. M. Forster writes in *Howards End*.[9] But, as Mr. Forster in an earlier allusion to this 'incomparable poem' seems to recognise, Drayton, a good if not a great poet, *has* voiced her, and in a literal sense, through her talking hills and rivers. As beings, these, despite obvious affinities, are essentially neither Greek nor Ovidian in character; Mr. Forster himself is more bewitched by Pan's pipes than Drayton is. Metamorphoses are not characteristic of *Poly-Olbion*; the few that do occur, like the story of the nymph pursued by a satyr and changed into a stream at Giggleswick in Yorkshire, have the air of being fairly self-conscious, as well as pretty, pieces of paganism. (This one is well imagined. Even before her metamorphosis, the nymph already seems half a stream:

> It was a Satyrs chance to see her silver haire
> Flow loosely at her backe, as up a Cliffe she clame.)
>
> (XXVIII, 152–3)

There are few gods in the poem; Neptune is the only one whose presence is really felt. The beings who preside here are not quite the usual tutelary deities. Nymphs, it is true, abound – wood-nymphs, mountain-nymphs, nereids and naiads. But they, on the whole, are subordinate characters, a kind of chorus. The central personages of the poem are not the emanations of the natural objects they represent; rather, they are those objects. In the *Metamorphoses* we read of human beings turning into birds, rivers, and flowers; what we see in *Poly-Olbion* are rivers, hills, and forests apparently turning into human beings. A bifold image is suggested similar to that presented by Bernini's Daphne, caught in a moment of transition, half-girl, half-tree, the face still peering out amid the branching arms. Consider, for example, his description of Lundy:

> This *Lundy* is a Nymph to idle toyes inclin'd;
> And, all on pleasure set, doth whollie give her mind
> To see upon her shores her Fowle and Conies fed,

⁹ E. M. Forster, *Howards End* (Penguin edn., 1960), 249.

And wantonlie to hatch the Birds of *Ganimed*.
Of trafique or returne shee never taketh care:
Not provident of pelfe, as many Ilands are:
A lustie black-brow'd Girle, with forehead broad and hie,
That often had bewitcht the Sea-gods with her eye.
Of all the In-laid Iles her Soveraigne *Severne* keepes,
That bathe their amorous breasts within her secret Deepes . . .

This noblest *British* Nymph yet likes her *Lundy* best . . .

                                    (IV, 11–23)

Lundy at first seems to bear some resemblance to Spenser's Phaedria, in her idleness and her apparent possession of an island, but by the time we reach the end of the description we notice the difference: Phaedria, however truly the embodiment of idle mirth, is first of all a woman, but Lundy, however truly a 'black-brow'd Girle', is first of all an island. Yet there is vigour in the portrait: Lundy remains an island, but one possessing life and personality. *Lustiness* is a quality Drayton frequently attributes to his 'creatures'; it goes with fertility, and the allusion is to the fertility of the soil. Drayton often conveys a sense of this by such characterisation. Thus we see the river Bry rejecting the favours of 'many a plump-thigh'd moore, and fullflanck't marsh', to remain faithful to Avalon. The Vale of Aylesbury, wife of 'old Chiltern' and mother of Tame, appears as a robust matron, 'lustie, frim, and fat', and something of a spendthrift. Somerset, though much thriftier, is equally buxom, 'with her complexion strong, a belly plumpe and full'. In some cases, it will be noticed, the words used apply almost equally well in a literal sense to the object described as they do metaphorically to the object considered as a person. The effect is to increase, rather than to diminish, the sense of the life of the things.

More important, however, than his attribution of human features to inanimate objects is Drayton's attribution to them of human feelings and human speech. Many of his personages speak and act like human beings, while in appearance they 'stay as they are'. It is above all in their relationships with each other that they are made to come alive. Drayton wants us to see the individual natural features of the country as they are, but he also wants us to appreciate them for what they are – part of the living fabric of the country. By endowing parts of the countryside with speech and human feelings, making them love and quarrel, argue and debate, Drayton presents them as a single society, in which not only part with part, but also past with present, is knit into a whole. This society reflects the human one; it involves family and hierarchical relationships. The sense of hierarchy is particularly strong: Salisbury Plain and Stonehenge are introduced as 'Shee, first of *Plaines*; and that, first Wonder of the Land'; Arden, since she was called the sovereign of forests by 'those old Britons', claims therefore 'I needs must be the great'st'; Evesham is 'the Queen Of all the *British* Vales'. and Thames, of course, is 'King of Rivers'. Decorum and consistency of character are as strictly observed as Renaissance theorists insisted they should be: mountains are brave, proud, ambitious, heroic; twisting streams are wanton; old hills venerable and grave. Age is of especial importance in this humanising process, for by making so many of his characters old, Drayton is able to give, in monologue or dialogue, their reminiscences about the past, and thus, by linking event with place, past with present, to achieve the effect of a continuum within a stasis. Mountains, woods, and rivers are everlasting witnesses; they represent the island as it is but also as it was. Even a street may do so, provided it is old enough: one of the most successful passages in the poem is that in which the river Ver and old Watling ('the Ancient Street') discuss the changes they have seen. They lament not only Verulam but the 'goodly fane' of St. Albans, 'which ruind now doth stand', and recall the heroes of the Crusades who lie inurned where only the ruinous heaps of stones with 'burth'nous weight now presse their sacred boanes'. 'Where be those noble spirits for ancient things that stood?' cries Ver. It is a cry from the heart, of Drayton certainly, but also, he wants us to feel, of the land itself. Afterwards Watling at Ver's request ('Right Noble Street, quoth he, thou hast liv'd long, gone farre') reminisces about 'the ancient folk' and the Saxons' various kingdoms. All this is authentic, even moving. By representing natural objects and the creations of men as consciously involved in man's activities, Drayton has brought man and nature into a unity. The familiar processes of 'pathetic fallacy' are reversed: in this passage, and in those many moving passages in which the forests lament the felling of their trees, man, in the person of the reader, sympathises with Nature. At the same time, in the unfailing patriotism of natural objects the metonymy by which 'country' stands for 'nation' is made actual. Hills and rivers throw themselves into the various conflicts between Briton and Saxon and Dane with the fierce partisanship of the Homeric gods, although they are too closely identified with man in the struggle to be equated with the Olympians. If Englishmen have hearts of oak, Drayton's oaks have the hearts of Englishmen. By such means the two halves of his subject, the topographical and the historical, are brought together.

Neither wholly myth nor wholly figurative fancy, the personifications of *Poly-Olbion* are an expression of primal sympathies that are national rather than personal in character. The common ground between man and Nature in the poem is love of this entity which is Britain. Impulses from a vernal wood such as Wordsworth knew do not come within Drayton's experience, and he has nothing to say of the spiritual communion between man and Nature. Yet he has, in his own way, a 'sentiment of being', the kind of sentiment described by Janet Spens as 'a passionate excitement in face of anything which, however momentarily, utterly and exclusively *is* itself'.[10] To capture in words the reality of the thing he is describing is at all times a part of Drayton's purpose. Prosopopœia is only one of the methods he uses. It is combined with direct description; actually the two work together to create for us a country that is solid, substantial, of the earth, earthy, yet at the same time pulsing and brimming over with an authentic life of its own. *Poly-Olbion* has its *Georgics* – its description of Kentish orchards, for example (Song XVIII). It has its Cobbett-like passages:

> What is there that compleat can any Country make,
> That in large measure I, (faire *Lindsey*) not pertake,
> As healthy Heaths, and Woods, faire Dales, and pleasant Hils,
> All watred here and there, with pretty creeping Rills,
> Fat Pasture, mellow Gleabe, and of that kind what can
> Give nourishment to beast, or benefit to man . . .
>
> (XXV, 301–6)

It is with the appraising eye of a Cobbett (rather than with that of a Keats or Wordsworth) that Drayton surveys and judges the land. 'Batful' is a higher term of praise than 'beautiful' though often the one comprehends the other. He can convey a stifling sense of fecundity, as in the Vale of Red Horse's boast:

> As still the Yeere growes on, that *Ceres* once doth load
> The full Earth with her store; my plentious bosome strow'd

10 *Spenser's Faerie Queene* (1934), 46.

With all aboundant sweets: my frim and lustie flanke
Her bravery then displayes, with Meadowes hugely ranke.

(XIII, 395–8)

Often, as here, he seems on the verge of exclaiming, with Milton,
'Enormous bliss!'

Even 'wayless wastes' may teem with life, as in 'cold Cumberland'
goats, deer, and sheep 'the Dales doe over-spread, by them like Motley
made'. Drayton is always alive to such motley. His subject requires
this stress, but his personal excitement in the presence of 'earth's
skeined stained veined variety' ensures that it is a vigorous one. One
of his favourite means of bringing home to us the 'piedness', which
is for him as for Hopkins expressive of the essential being of a region or
natural feature, is by the formal catalogue, used with great freshness
and flexibility. The Trent, for instance, as a result of her recital of the
'thirtie kinds of Fish, that in my Streames doe live', appears a very rivery
river. Similarly in his description of Norfolk Drayton communicates
to us the character of a quite different though equally watery region
by describing the various adornments of its sea-nymphs and river-
nymphs, some of whom 'wore on their flaxen haire Fine Chaplets
made of Flaggs', while others were adorned with 'Water-cans', 'Cat-
tayles', 'Lady-smocks'. By such accumulation of detail he re-creates the
object, making us 'participate in its life', to borrow Arnold's phrase.

What Drayton values in the particular object, however, is not so
much its individuality as such, so much as its perfection of the type.
Self-realisation is, for him, identical with this. Thus the cave in the
Peak known as the *Divels-Arse* is assured that it owes both name and
fame to its perfection of the kind:

O be thou not asham'd,
Nor thinke thy selfe disgrac'd, or hurt thereby at all,
Since from thy horror first men us'd thee so to call:
For as amongst the *Moores*, the Jettiest blacke are deem'd
The beautifulst of them; so are your kind esteem'd,
The more ye gloomy are, more fearefull and obscure,
(That hardly any eye your sternnesse may endure)
The more yee famous are, and what name men can hit,
That best may ye expresse, that best doth yee befit.

(XXVI, 406–14)

The uniqueness of the completely singular exists for Drayton only in those departures from the normal order of Nature which he calls 'wonders' (a 'Sylvestrian' word) – barnacle geese, serpents turned to stone, fish living in the earth. Since, however, God's grandeur is manifested equally in the wonder and in the type, Britain, rich in both, reflects the glory of Creation, and is truly 'a second Eden'.

'My Poeme is genuine, and first in this kinde,' wrote Drayton before the First Part. The claim, as I have tried to show, is justified. *Poly-Olbion* is something better than a 'curiosity' to be ridiculed or patronised. Within the *corpus* of Drayton's work, it stands as his *Faerie Queene*. For although, as Newdigate says, it owes little directly to that poem (the marriage of the Thames and Medway should not, however, be forgotten), it has much in common with it in spirit. Like *The Faerie Queene*, it is inspired by a love of 'brave and ancient things', and takes us back into a remote past which Drayton, like Spenser, sees as the cradle of the heroic. In both poems the world of the poet's imagination becomes one with the Britain he loves, and the poet in portraying it becomes one with the 'old Poets', identified, however, in *Poly-Olbion* not so much with Orpheus and his fellows as with the British bards, whose spirits he 'could have wisht' redoubled in his breast (I, 41). And we have only to look at the poem's frontispiece, where 'through a *Triumphant Arch*' we may 'see *Albion* plas't', to realise that, whatever the relationship between the two poems, Britain itself is Drayton's Faerie Queene.

William Browne of Tavistock

Wlilliam Browne, more completely than any of the other Spenser-ians, is a Romantic born out of his time. He is the Wordsworth, the Clare, the Keats of the Spenserians. The fact is obscured because, whereas he should have written lyrics and short descriptive pieces, instead he put most of his energies into narrative, into the *magnum opus* of *Britannia's Pastorals*, which seems intended to be pastoral on an epic scale. Considered simply as narrative, the poem is largely a failure: his personages are for the most part so flat and artificial and their world is so mreote, that the reader can feel no concern or interest in their experiences. Much in the narrative, moreover, is conventional, or borrowed, or both. Stylistically also Browne is extremely imitative: we may watch him modulate from one author to another like a cinema-organ changing colour – from the dialectic of *Il Pastor Fido* to the sensuous luxury of *Hero and Leander* and its successors, to the exalted 'fustian' of *The Divine Weeks and Works*, to the hearty plainness of Wither. In a protest against the charges of imitation or plagiarism which had evidently been brought against him after the publication of Book 1 of the *Pasrorals*, Browne wrote:

> I never yet but scorn'd a tast to bring
> Out of the Channell when I saw the Spring
> Or like a silent Organ been soe weake
> That others fingers taught me how to speake.
> The sacred Nyne . . .
>
> Were kind in some small measure at my birth . . .
> ('Ffido An Epistle to Ffidelia', Lans. 777, f.34)

The 'sacred Nyne' *were* kind to him, and he did 'see the Spring';

143

nevertheless in *Britannia's Pastorals* he draws too much from 'the Channell':

> I have seene thy worke, and I know thee:
> And, if thou list thy selfe, what thou canst bee,

Ben Jonson wrote in commendatory verses before the Second Book. But Browne never did properly 'list' himself. He *has* something to say, and something rare for his period, but his voice too often comes mingled with the voices of other poets whom he feels impelled to impersonate.

He was, of course, as we saw in chapter III, a very young poet when he began *Britannia's Pastorals*, and undoubtedly he was a very precocious one. Even taking its imitativeness into account, *Britannia's Pastorals* is a remarkable achievement 'for a strength so young'. Elsewhere Browne shows his precocity in briefer compass, in the exquisite 'In Obitum MS x°. Maii 1614', for example:

> May! be thou never grac'd with birds that sing
> > Nor Fflora's pride
> In thee all flowers & Roses spring
> > Myne onely di'de.   (Lans. 777, f. 59)

Or, since this may possibly, although perhaps not very probably, have been written later than the date suggested by its title, to prove his precocity there is the Siren's song in the Inner Temple Masque, 'Steere hither, steere your winged Pines All beaten Mariners'; indeed, there is the masque itself. In this work we see in some completeness the Keatsian Browne, in the sensuousness, the gift for and love of fine phrases, the enchanting music, the haunting cadences (some of which Keats himself was to echo). Browne's song was indeed 'rathe', as Wither calls it. Perhaps this accounts for his talent's failure entirely to fulfil itself. Browne's powers were certainly not spent by 1616, the year in which *Britannia's Pastorals*, Books I and II, was published. Many of his miscellaneous poems, unpublished in his lifetime, were written later, including the celebrated Epitaph on the Countess of Pembroke. Nevertheless, he seems to have given up his poetic ambitions at that date. Personal disappointments, or the decision to devote himself to his career, may account for this. Whatever the reason, Browne's poetic life remains top-heavy, with these two huge, promising books appearing at the beginning of it, and after that only occasional brief spurts of verse, varying in quality and kept hidden in manuscript. (His epitaph on the Countess of Pembroke, however, seems to have been well known.)

Browne's intention in writing the *Pastorals* (apart from the primary one of simply writing poetry) appears to have been two-fold: to enrich Britain with pastorals, and to celebrate Britain by showing that she too is Arcadia. 'Thus deare *Britannia* will I sing of thee.' 'Britannia' may carry a conscious recollection of Camden, but Browne, if he is to be a Camden, is to be a Camden pastoralised. If his intentions are mixed, so are his motives: they combine patriotism with literary ambition. In the opening episodes of the poem, it is the latter which is most in evidence: the promise to sing of Britannia hardly seems to be being fulfilled. These episodes are correctly and fashionably pastoral, in the manner of the best continental models. They employ typical situations of the pastoral drama and romance, fickleness in a lover, attempted suicide, and much sententious debate and haranguing on the nature of love and its problems. The setting is not noticeably British: wild beasts with 'fearefull bellowings' haunt the springs, and a grove contains olive, lotus, and date as well as oak and ash. There are, however, homely references to the shepherd's trade, and a village festival, with song and dance, to give an authentic 'rural' flavour. As the poem progresses, this rural element enlarges, while the element of sophisticated court-pastoral – of pastoral, that is, whose closest links are with the pastoral entertainments, dramatic and narrative, of the Italian and French courts – declines. 'A thousand themes come on,' as Browne himself says. Shepherds and shepherdesses are launched on their careers, like balloons in a balloon race, many of them, like the balloons, never to be seen again. An allegorical tableau on recent British history develops into an allegory of the soul's regeneration. The sea-goddess Thetis begins a cruise around the coast of Britain, and presides at a festival of poets. Familiar Renaissance *topoi* receive extended treatment – the choir of birds, the Golden Age, the siege of Jerusalem, and, naturally enough, the *locus amoenus*. Wild men appear, pursuing innocent maidens: Riot, with his sow-thistle hair and badger legs, pursues Aletheia; 'one like a wilde man over-growne with hayre' chases an unnamed huntress; Limos (Hunger) seizes Marina, the poem's first heroine, and imprisons her in his cave. Thus the poem commodiously expands to include much that is not strictly of a pastoral character. Most notably, Browne's imaginary world expands to become a reflection of *The Faerie Queene*.

Nymphs and shepherdesses are pursued by monsters in pastoral, of course; there is, for instance, the formidable Gorphorost of Montemayor's *Diana*. Polyphemus provides the archetype. But that it is Spenser's 'salvage' men, particularly Malengin and the monstrous aboriginal who makes off with Amoret, who haunt Browne's imagination is clear from the total context and from various descriptive details. From Book I, Song 2 onwards, *Britannia's Pastorals* constantly employs Spenserian motifs. When Marina is carried off in a canoe by a 'cruell Swaine' who

> Intends an act by water, which the land
> Abhorr'd to boulster,   (I, sig. F4ᵛ)

her situation resembles that of Florimel when she finds herself alone in a boat with 'a fisher old and pore'. Browne has already utilised Florimel's rescue by Proteus, along with parts of John Fletcher's *Faithful Shepherdess*, in an earlier episode in which Marina is saved from drowning by a River god, so she cannot on this occasion be saved in this way. Instead, she is deposited on an island (Anglesey), only to fall victim shortly afterwards to the monster Limos, thereby exchanging the misfortunes of Florimel for those of Amoret. The huntress pursued by the wild man (*B.P.*, II, 2), appears to be another working of the Amoret theme, though it is not developed. The huntress herself, however, is modelled on Belphoebe, as, in part, is Aletheia, who represents Truth. The 'two faire columnes' on which Aletheia's 'heavenly body' is raised, for instance, may be the Old and New Testaments, but their description owes something to Belphoebe's 'two faire marble pillours'. Out of Truth's story develops that of Riot, who, looking like Malengin, yet undertakes a pilgrimage like that of the Red Cross Knight. Possibly in his uncouth appearance Browne is remembering Spenser's statement that the Red Cross Knight was at first a 'clownish young man', before he put on Una's armour. Such armour would be inappropriate in a pastoral, so Riot remains clownish, indeed 'salvage', until transformed into Amintas, a 'gallant youth scarce skill'd in twenty yeares', and thereafter united with Aletheia, in an embrace that resembles more than anything the embrace of Scudamour and Amoret in the original ending of *The Faerie Queene*, Book

III. The total neglect of Una in this allegory of Truth and regenerate man is striking. Browne has turned Spenser's sober tale into an Ovidian romance, as much in the manner of *Hero and Leander* as of *The Faerie Queene*. As a religious allegorist, we cannot take him seriously. We can believe in the sincerity of his religious feelings, but in dressing them up in this way Browne is merely playing at being profound, and at being Spenser.

Browne's impersonation of Spenser in the episodes discussed is in part deliberate. Committed to writing narrative and having only slight powers of invention, he naturally turns to Spenser (and others) for help. His poverty of invention is perhaps seen in his repetition of motif – wild man pursues innocent maiden – though I think this is indicative also of the simplicity and innocence of his imagination. But some of his imitation is unconscious rather than deliberate. Browne's *blending* of one Spenserian figure or episode with another has something of the inconsequence of a dream, and must have been unintentional. Because of this, his experience of *The Faerie Queene* determines the character of *Britannia's Pastorals* far more than could be indicated or accounted for by any statement of conscious intention. If the poem, as its opening lines suggest, is an attempt at pastoral epic, then the epic model it follows instinctively is that provided by Spenser. Errant knights are replaced by errant shepherds and shepherdesses, whose travels provide similar 'sweet varietie' for author and reader. There is also, in the first book of the poem, the same vagueness about locality that characterises *The Faerie Queene*. This vagueness is not found in prose pastoral romance, where characters, even when they wander abroad, do so from a fixed, and generally identified, base.

Britannia's Pastorals is thus Browne's *Faerie Queene*, not his *Shepheardes Calender*. (*That* is *The Shepheards Pipe*.) Totally ignoring the knights and their battles, Browne's imagination seizes on the pastoral-mythological parts of Spenser's poem. It is as if he has ears only for the 'oaten reeds', not for the 'trumpets sterne'. For him Colin Clout is indubitably the poem's author. His own aspiration to be a second Colin is underlined for us when, by the mouth of the Tamar, Willy sings for Thetis a song of Tavy and Walla, just as Colin, come home to Ireland, tells a similar tale of Mulla and Bregog.

Thus Browne certainly deserves the description 'Spenserian'. Spenser has gripped and shaped Browne's imagination; his influence over the *Pastorals* is of a formative kind. Other influences were not so: as I have already indicated, Browne was a very imitative poet, but sometimes his imitations are merely occasional, a simple matter of 'borrowing'. One influence comparable with Spenser's, however, and therefore extremely important, is that of Drayton. Browne's reading of *Poly-Olbion*, probably sometime between writing Songs 4 and 5 of Book I, has, I think, changed the character of his poem. In Book II of the *Pastorals* Drayton rivals Spenser as the dominant influence. *Poly-Olbion* was published in 1612, the year before *Britannia's Pastorals*, Book I, appeared. Before Song 5 of the Pastorals, Book I, there is nothing to suggest that Browne has read it. In that song, however, appears Idya, who is a symbolic England. She sits on a marble platform raised on columns, wears a garment of rainbow hues, and holds a cornucopia, from which she dispenses fruit to Aletheia. Although there are differences, she is clearly a verbal counterpart of the beautiful Hole engraving of Albion that appears as frontispiece in the first edition of *Poly-Olbion*, as her 'pastoral name', echoing Drayton's 'Idea', surely acknowledges. Towards the end of the song, Browne compliments Drayton by saying how much better Drayton could have sung the loves of Aletheia and Amintas than he has done.

In Book II Drayton's influence is all-pervasive. So far Browne may have brought the pastoral to Britain: Drayton shows him how to introduce Britain into the pastoral. In Book I, as we saw, the action is unlocalised, but now by line 85 of the first song we find ourselves in Anglesey. Allusions to the richness of the soil and the healthiness of the climate, to bards, to 'mighty *Brute*', quickly follow: it is a *Poly-Olbion* in miniature. By line 817 Thetis has been launched on her cruise, and from then on the poem has, geographically speaking, a direction, as Thetis pursues her journey along the south coast, Cornwall, and Devon, towards the coast of Wales. This gives Browne the opportunity to describe the Britain he set out to celebrate. Drayton's example has, we may say, helped him to find his feet: it has given something resembling a structure to the poem. That it is Drayton's example that has done this is unquestionable, although, as with Browne's imitation of Spenser, the process seems as much unconscious as deliberate. In *Poly-Olbion* 'greene *Thetis* Nymphes' sing the Muse in to her 'wished Bay' from the Western ocean, across 'th' *Armorick* sands' and the French seas. This may have given Browne his idea for Thetis's cruise, which though it has been much more far-flung (touching 'the *new-found World*', 'streit *Hellespont*', and so on) is introduced at a similar point:

> See in haste shee sweepes
> Along the *Celtick* shores, th'*Armorick* deepes
> She now is entring.   (II, sig. E1ʳ)

The interesting thing is to find Thetis, once she arrives in Britain, taking over the function which the Muse had had in *Poly-Olbion*, although with one important variation: whereas in *Poly-Olbion* rivers entertain the Muse, in *Britannia's Pastorals*, the goddess of the sea is entertained by poets. This does not involve the exclusion of rivers from the festivities; for instance,

> At *Ex*, a lovely Nymph with *Thetis* met,
> She singing came, and was all round beset
> With other watry powres, which by her song
> She had allur'd to floate with her along.   (II, sig. K2ʳ)

(Significantly, a marginal note on the rest of this passage refers to Selden's commentary on *Poly-Olbion*.) British history, as well as British topography, is frequently touched on in this book. Thus:

> Now *Thetis* stayes to heare the Shepheards tell
> Where *Arthur* met his death, and *Mordred* fell.
>
>   (II, sig. N2ʳ)

Bards are busy:

> The *Brittish Bards* then were not long time mute . . .   (*ibid*)

> The *Cornish Swaines* and *Brittish Bard*
> *Thetis* hath with attention heard.   (II, sig. M3ʳ)

Not surprisingly, when it is Drayton's turn to sing, it is 'a genuine noate, of all the *Nimphish* traines' that he 'tunes' (II, sig. F3ʳ). 'My Poeme is genuine,' Drayton had himself written in the dedication to *Poly-Olbion*.

Browne's own genuine love of British history and antiquity is attested by the manuscripts he owned, which are still extant – manuscripts of Bede, Malmesbury and Galfridus, for example. His love of British soil is self-evident in his poem. *Poly-Olbion* must have been immensely congenial to him, and its influence on his work was undoubtedly beneficial. His purpose, nevertheless, is parallel to, rather than identical with, that of Drayton. Just as he does not follow Spenser in his pictures of chivalry, so he does not follow Drayton in celebrating 'battles long ago'. It *is* a pastoral Britain, not a heroic one, that he seeks to recreate. Though he seems only half-aware of this himself, the countryside and country life are Browne's true theme. When he can disentangle this from the imported, the artificial, the literary, then he is truly himself, rightly owning one powerful influence, greater than that of either Spenser or Drayton:

> *Tavies* voycefull streame (to whom I owe
> More straines then from my Pipe can ever flowe).
>
> (II, sig. K3^v)

In *Britannia's Pastorals*, mixed up with all the unreal shepherds and their adventures, is a rendering of rural life that is astonishing in its realism and its particularity.

Some particularity, of what we might call the 'curds and clouted cream' variety, was conventional to pastoral. Maypoles, whitsun-ales, fairies, queens-of-the-May, and so on, are the familiar, always delightful 'props'. Through them pastoral realism ('homeliness') and pastoral enchantment are achieved together. Browne revels in this material, as also in that development of it, in which the more sordid, technical aspects of the shepherd's life are recalled – allusions to sheep-rot, for example, such as occur in *The Faithful Shepherdess*. His re-creation of rural life goes far beyond this conventional particularity, however, just as his re-creation of rural landscape far surpasses the generalised picture of 'Vallyes, Rivers, Hils, and Plaines' characteristic of most 'happy *Arcadia*'s. His method is accumulative: by numerous references, in direct statement but more often in simile, he reproduces in his verse the English countryside itself, in impressive fullness and breadth. It is not just a *locus amoenus* that he paints: the

> christall Wels,
> The fertill Meadowes, and their pleasing smels,
> The Woods delightfull, and the scatt'red Groves,
>
> (II, sig. M3^v)

these, as in all pastoral, are his show-piece. But he includes other types of country-side: 'unfrequented wayes',

About the Rivers, Vallies, Holts, and Crags,
Among the Ozyers and the waving Flags;

(II, sig. GI^v)

'Brakes that hide the craggy rockes'; 'furzy tuft, thicke wood, [and]
brake of thornes'; 'marishes', often with evening mists rising from
them; aged rocks, haunted by '*Puffins* (as thicke as *Starlings* in a Fen)'[1];
a creek

Where never gale was longer knowne to stay
Then from the smooth wave it had swept away
The new divorced leaves, that from each side
Left the thicke boughes to dance out with the tyde.

(II, sig. Q2^r)

He finds room for the rough and the rugged, as well as the smooth
and green. Rocks are a frequent feature of his landscape: rocks in rivers,
on the sea-shore, in woods. Dominating everything are his woods, not
all composed of fine, upstanding trees: they have, as well as the tall
trees 'Upon whose tops the *Herneshew* bred her young', fallen oaks, on
whose bare trunks the rain collects in winter; 'short writhen oaks',
with ivy twisting round their bark; aged mossy roots with hollow
trunks in which bees, ants, cuckoos, dormice, have taken up residence;
wild cherries; hollies, ashes, 'everywhere Rob'd of their cloathing by
the browsing Game'; oaks and hazels where

The earely rising *Crow* with clam'rous kawing,
Leaving the greene bough flyes about the Rocke,
Whilst twentie twentie couples to him flocke;

'sharp-hook'd Brambles, Thornes, and tangling bushes'.[2] Browne is
not idealising; he is writing with his eye on the object.

And if Browne's country-side is not always smooth and gentle,
neither is the country life reflected in the poem. There are the maypoles,
and there is the pleasant daily round that Milton too was to celebrate
in 'L'Allegro':

[1] The quotations here are from *B.P.*, II, sig. GI^v; sig. P3^r; sig. DI^r.
[2] *B.P.*, II, sig. Q2^r; sig. DI^v; I, sig. Q4^r; II, sig. C4^v.

> By this had *Chanticlere*, the village-clocke,
> Bidden the good-wife for her Maides to knocke:
> And the swart plow man for his breakfast staid,
> That he might till those lands were follow laid:
> The hills and vallies here and there resound
> With re-ecchoes of the deepe-mouth'd hound.
> Each sheapheards daughter with her cleanly Peale,
> Was come a field to milk the Mornings meale . . .
>
> (I, sig. L2ʳ)

But there are also the 'day-labouring wretch', the '*Labourer* toyling at a *Bay*', the floods sweeping from a yeoman's lands 'His Harvest hope of Wheate, of Rye, or Pease'; the '*Country Gentleman*' who

> from's neighbours hand
> Forceth th'inheritance, ioynes land to land;

the 'griping *Farmer*' who

> hoords the seede of bread,
> Whilst in the streets the poore lye famished;

the 'Clowne' dropping an abortive lamb into a river; the 'hoording huswives', letting food go mouldy while others want.[3] Some of these things Browne records in his satirist's vein; more often, he is simply the observer, re-creating a countryside he has lived in and knows thoroughly. Village life in all its variety unfolds before us as he writes; an actual village life contrasting oddly with the unreal adventures of his characters: maids bringing in water for the night, housewives pounding clothes with their 'washing Beetles', the 'day-lab'ring man' who

> all the morne
> Had from the quarry with his Picke-axe torne
> A large well squared stone, which he would cut
> To serve his stile, or for some water-shut;

the 'swarty *Smith*' spitting in his 'Buckehorne fist' as he prepares to shoe some powerful horse, 'That at the Forge stands snuffing of the ayre'; the

[3] *B.P.*, I, sig. F4ʳ; II, sig. Q1ʳ; I, sig. F4ᵛ; II, sig. D4ʳ (twice); I, sig. D2ʳ; I, sig. E3ʳ.

Angler melancholy standing
Upon a greene bancke yeelding roome for landing;

ballad-mongers on a market-day; a miller letting down his flood-gates; youths wrestling while the people arm-in-arm form a ring about them; another youth 'with wreathed legs' climbing a cherry-tree; a 'little Lad' with his father 'Tracing greene Rushes for a Winter Chayre'; a fowler 'by the floods In winter tyme' creeping softly, going on tip-toe to avoid rotten sticks under-foot or the cracking of the ice, 'As heere and there flutters the wished quarry'; a 'lusty sawyer' moving 'A good sound tree above his sawing pitt'.[4] It is the world of Autolycus enlarged with all the fidelity of a Hardy. (There are hints in the *Pastorals* that Browne was, in fact, prepared to learn from Shakespeare.)[5]

Frederic W. Moorman, in his still valuable study, *William Browne, His Britannia's Pastorals and the Pastoral Poetry of the Elizabethan Age* (Strassburg, 1897), compares Browne's scenes of country life with the similar scenes in Dutch and Flemish paintings of the period.[6] The resemblance is indeed striking. There is the same fidelity of detail, the same relish for the thing as thing, the absence of any desire to see it in terms of something else. This does not mean, however, that Browne actually imitated, or even knew, such painting. Most of it, where the resemblance is most striking, as in the work of Paul Potter, Van de Velde, Cuyp, or Hobbema, for example, is later in date than his poem. Rather, the resemblance is probably to be explained by the fact that Browne shared with these artists a taste for naturalism that is a growing characteristic of the times, of which the clearest development in literature is found in the poetry of rural life written in France during the

---

[4] *Quotations:* B.P., I, sig. L4^r; sig. O1^v; sig. O3^v; II, sig. N3^r; III, *Sarum.*, p.19, p.32.
[5] Browne (probably) remembers *As You Like It* in B.P., I, 5 (sig. M4^r], in his description of school-children:

> when the *Morne* doth looke
> Out of the *Esterne gates*, a Snayle would faster,
> Glide to the Schooles, then they unto their Master;

Love's Labour's Lost in the line, 'And Shepheards Boyes for cold gan blow their nailes' sig. L1^r); *Macbeth* in his 'nightpiece', B.P., II, 4 (sig. O2^v):

> *Rookes* to their Nests in high woods now were flung . . .

> When theeves from thickets to the cross-wayes stir,
> And terrour frights the loanely passenger.

The name Marina perhaps comes from *Pericles.*
[6] Moorman, *op. cit.*, 141.

F

sixteenth century. One French writer who participated in this development was Du Bartas, and if any single artistic influence can account for
this characteristic in Browne's verse, it is his.

Britannia's Pastorals was written under the spell of Du Bartas (or
Sylvester). This is especially clear from Browne's diction, which
frequently includes compounds, either borrowed directly from Sylvester, or formed in imitation of his. Possibly Browne's choice of the
couplet form was influenced by his example. His couplets frequently
sound like Sylvester's; as H. Ashton, in his Du Bartas en Angleterre, says,
some of them reproduce the peculiarities of Sylvester's style so completely that they could have been written by him.[7] Other features too
recall the Divine Weeks: the displays of scientific learning, on the forma-
tion of hail, for instance, or the causes of thunder; the pious apost-
rophes to Aletheia; the occasions when Browne's Muse has to 'wade'
out of a stream or quagmire. (This could come indirectly from Drayton,
but more probably directly from Sylvester.) Browne has passages of
deliberate imitation also: his beautiful description of the rainbow,

> As in the Rainbowes many coloured hewe
> Here see wee watchet deepned with a blewe,
> There a darke tawny with a purple mixt,
> Yealow and flame, with streakes of greene betwixt,
> A bloudy streame into a blushing run
> And ends still with the colour which begun,
> Drawing the deeper to a lighter staine,
> Bringing the lightest to the deep'st againe . . . ,
>
> (II, sig. I3ᵛ)

was probably suggested by Sylvester's, which it surpasses; and as early
as the second song of Book I he introduces an elaborate description of
a landscape painting that is clearly intended to rival, if not to 'over-go',
that of Sylvester (D.W.W., I, vii, 12–59). It is because Sylvester has
done so before him that Browne sometimes sees sheep as a 'fleecy
traine' or 'bleating charge'; fish as 'the scaly train'; beasts as 'this
Forrests Citizens'; the world as 'this spacious round'. And sometimes
when he looks at Nature with the eyes of a Sylvester (more properly
now, a Du Bartas), he sees the same sort of transformation scene:
springs writhing in knots, a river 'amorously clipping' a meadow,

[7] H. Ashton, Du Bartas en Angleterre (Paris 1908), 319–20.

meadows in a 'gowne of greene', mountains in 'frizled coates', earth, in winter, 'in silver sute'. This is the vision of Nature Du Bartas is best remembered (and sometimes ridiculed) for, but, though his most distinctive, it is not his only way of writing of her. He also introduces into his poem many pictures of country life that are prosaic in their homeliness: 'a shoal of Geese on the dry-Summer sand',[8] 'a wild and wanton Colt, got out Of some great Stable',[9] a wall collapsing, a man stumbling and falling down a hill, hawks following a duck, dogs, rabbits, thieves, 'a Playfull Child'. And he introduces them mostly through simile and comparison. *Britannia's Pastorals* is also, as the reader soon recognises, remarkable for its similes. They are extensive and detailed, and it is in them that Browne's pictures of country life mostly occur. Browne may have seen them in part as epic similes, and have been encouraged to use them by Chapman's example, in his original work, as well as in his 'English Homer'. But undoubtedly his main exemplar was *The Divine Weeks*. The following comparison should bring out the nature of the resemblance. This is Sylvester:

> As a blinde man, forsaken of his Guide,
> In some thick Forrest, sad and self-beside,
> Takes now a broad, anon a narrow path:
> His groaping hand his (late) eyes' office hath:
> Here at a stub he stumbles, there the bushes
> Rake-off his cloak; here on a Tree he rushes,
> Strayes in and out, turns, this and that way tries,
> And at the last fals in a Pit, and dies . . .[10]

And this Browne:

> As some way-faring man passing a wood,
> (Whose waving top hath long a Sea-marke stood)
> Goes iogging on, and in his minde nought hath,
> But how the *Primrose* finely strew the path,
> Or sweetest *Violets* lay downe their heads
> At some trees roote on mossie feather-beds,
> Untill his heele receives an Adders sting,
> Whereat hee starts, and backe his head doth fling.
>
> (I, sig. O1r)

[8] *D.W.W.*, 'The Lawe', sig. Hh7r.
[9] *ibid.*, 'The Vocation', sig. Ee1r.
[10] *ibid.*, 'The Captaines', sig. Kk7r.

In both these similes what stands out is the homeliness of the subject (despite the violent climax) and the narrative treatment it receives. Sylvester's is the plainer style here, but the passage from Browne is distinguished by its greater particularity. He really sees the wood, with its 'waving top', its primroses and violets and mossy tree-roots. The Sylvester passage is crude, drab, in comparison. And this is a difference that generally holds good: *The Divine Weeks* may have given Browne the suggestion for his similes, but in his development of them he far exceeds his model in the detail of his descriptions. Having found his strength, he delights in the exercise of it.[11]

Browne's most memorable similes are those concerning children, especially boys – 'little lads' – usually at play. 'But as when children having leave to play . . .' he will begin, or 'as wandring Boyes to gather Nuts', or

> Who so hath seene yong Lads (to sport themselves)
> Run in a lowe ebbe to the sandy shelves:
> Where seriously they worke in digging welles,
> Or building childish forts of Cockle-shels . . .,[12]

> (I, sig. M3^r)

or

> As Children on a play-day leave the Schooles,
> And gladly runne unto the swimming Pooles,
> Or in the thickets, all with nettles stung,
> Rush to dispoile some sweet *Thrush* of her young;
> Or with their hats (for fish) lade in a Brooke . . .

> (I, sig. M4^r)

---

[11] In his description of winter in *B.P.*, I, 4, sig. L1^r, he combines imitation of Sylvester's manner with imitation of Shakespeare:

> When *Hyems* bound the floods in silver chaines,
> And hoary Frosts had candy'd all the Plaines;
> When every Barne rung with the threshing Flailes,
> And Shepheards Boyes for cold gan blow their nailes.

It is a contrast in styles repeated throughout the poem.

[12] Cf. George Chapman, *Homer's Iliads*, The Fifteenth Booke, 329–32:

> And looke how easely any boy upon the sea-ebd shore
> Makes with a litle sand a toy and cares for it no more,
> But as he raisd it childishly so in his wanton vaine
> Both with his hands and feete he puls and spurnes it downe againe.

Chapman uses this type of simile in his original verse too; e.g. in *The Shadow of Night*, he has one beginning 'As when a flock of school-boys. . . .'

F. W. Moorman considered that in his descriptions of country life Browne was 'transmitting to verse the scenes of his boyhood'.[13] I agree with him, and especially, I think, he was remembering his own childhood in those 'wandring Boyes' and 'yong Lads'. *Britannia's Pastorals* is, so to speak, an enlarged 'Boy's Song', more discursive, fuller, and less sentimental than James Hogg's:

> Up the river and over the lea,
> That's the way for [*Willy*] and me.

One even suspects something of a Peter Pan complex in Browne at the time he wrote the *Pastorals*, seen perhaps in his fondness for the 'pretty' (it is one of his favourite epithets) as well as in his similes. For all his desire to become 'our sage and serious poet Browne', he was reluctant to put away childish things.

Once the personal, autobiographical nature of Browne's descriptive writing is recognised, we see what the poem, or that part of it that is truly alive, really is: it is an evocation of the poet's childhood, anticipating Wordsworth's in its intensity and completeness. That Tavy and its environs were to Browne 'a feeling and a love', haunting him 'like a passion', is beyond doubt.

> Haile thou my native soile! thou blessed plot
> Whose equall all the world affordeth not!
>
> > (II, sig. K2^r)

he cries, and although the passage that follows is a proud blazon not at all suggesting Wordsworth, the affection in the apostrophe is as real as in the latter's 'Dear native regions . . .' (also the utterance of a young poet). Nor are Browne's recollections of Tavy and Devonshire limited to his passages of direct reference to them. They are present in his mind at all times, constantly modifying the artificial surface of the poem. The poem is full of the noise of rivers and the rustling of leaves, and throughout, a Clare-like power of observation adds a sharp authenticity: 'speckled *Foxe-gloves*', 'red water plashes', the harebell's 'stainlesse azur'd hue', strawberries changing colour, 'Some greene, some white, some red on them infus'd'; a changing silk compared to the shining of 'yealow flowres and grasse farre off, in one'; 'sleightfull *Otters*', 'The

---

[13] Moorman, *op. cit.*, 140, also 130–5.

F*

little *Sparrowes* which in hedges creepe', and that evocation of the early dawn which Clare himself admired:

> . . . the cattle chew'd the cud
> Low level'd on the grasse; no Flyes quicke sting
> Inforc'd the Stonehorse in a furious ring
> To teare the passive earth, nor lash his taile
> About his buttockes broad; the slimy Snayle
> Might on the wainscot, (by his many mazes
> Winding *Meanders* and selfe-knitting traces)
> Be follow'd, where he stucke, his glittering slime
> Not yet wipt off. It was so earely time
> The carefull *Smith* had in his sooty forge
> Kindled no coale, nor did his hammers urge
> His neighbours patience: *Owles* abroad did flye,
> And day as then might plead his infancy.
>   (II, sig. E3^r – E3^v)[14]

'Dear God, the very houses seem asleep.' It is the same moment of stillness that Browne and Wordsworth have apprehended.

That Browne did not finish *Britannia's Pastorals* is not surprising. It is the sort of work (like the magazine serial, or, still more, the comic strip) of which one scarcely expects a conclusion; it is a continuum of which one supposes merely that it will eventually stop. Although it contains some of his best writing, Browne's attempted continuation in the third book is not very successful. It is put together mainly from verses that appear separately in the Lansdowne manuscript, and that are of a deeply personal nature. I think the real reason why Browne found that he could not go on with the poem was that he now no longer wished nor was able to write narrative, especially of the artificial type he was committed to here. The true hero of Book III is Browne himself, grief-stricken, melancholy, and embittered. Of this later Browne there is no room to write here, but his existence needs to

---

[14] Quotations are from *B.P.*, II, sig. N4^v; I, sig. O4^r; II, sig. I3^r; sig. H3^v; sig. H1^r; sig. O2^v; sig. N4^r.

be recognised. In Book III of the *Pastorals*, and in many of the shorter pieces, Browne writes some of the most directly personal poetry to be found in the Elizabethan period. Some of it is love poetry, some elegiac. In some, love and sorrow combine, for we know that Browne 'loved and lost', possibly more than once. Sometimes the verse is exquisitely tender:

> Sweet Soule thy silent grave
> I give my best Verse, if a Shepheards witt
> Can make a dead hand capable of yt,
>   (*B.P.*, III, *Sarum.*, p. 6)

which seems, oddly, to be approaching Keats's chilling lines to Fanny Brawne; sometimes it is stark in its recognition of the finality of loss:

> Th'art lost for ever! as a drop of Raine
> Ffalne in a River! for as soone I may
> Take up that drop or meet the same at Sea
> And know it there, as ere redeeme thee gone
> Or know thee in the Grave when I have one;
>   ('An Elegye', Lans. 777, f. 50)

sometimes heavily despairing:

> He that at once hath lost his hopes & feares
> Lives not, but only tarryes for more yeares.
> (Much like an aged Tree which moisture lacks,
> And onely standeth to attend the Axe).
> Soe have, and so doe I . . .   (*B.P.*, III, *Sarum*, p. 21)

Although this manuscript material is sufficiently miscellaneous in content to include happy lyrics too

> (For her gate if she be walkinge,
> Be she sittinge I desire her
> For her states sake & admire her
> For her witt if she be talkinge),

the prevailing impression is that here is someone writing *de profundis*.

'Heere needs no fiction,' Browne wrote in one of his sonnets for
'Celia'. That, fundamentally, was always true for him, when he wrote
best as a poet. Although when 'poeticising' he felt obliged (and indeed
wished) to write fiction, poetry for him, when he really wrote it, was
not fiction; it was self-expression.

VIII

The Early Poetry of
George Wither

When we look at Wither's work as a whole, his place in the *Dunciad* among 'the dull of ancient days' seems well earned. Nothing that he published after 1641 – and well over half of his publications are later than that – has value as literature. Even in what he wrote before that date, there is much that is drab and mediocre. He wrote too much and too carelessly ('carelessness' was part of his 'Motto'), and his combination of moral and religious fanaticism with long-windedness too often makes him appear the 'mountebank of wit Self-loving braggart' that Jonson cruelly called him.[1] If he still deserves our attention (as I think he does), it is because there existed in him a genuine poet, and one both sensitive and intelligent; a poet who unfortunately was rapidly stifled by the moral reformer and religious maniac. Wither had the ability to delight, but it deserted him when he decided that his duty was to teach. He is, in a sense, a casualty of Renaissance poetic – as Mr. Allan Pritchard has shown, of the Horatian, Sidneyan, Bartasian notion of the poet's function.[2] His best poems are his pastorals, where his lyricism (rather than, as is usually the case, his moral fervour) is given its head. In addition, the early satires have a rough vitality that keeps them interesting even when their poetic value is slight. Drabness rather than downright dullness is their characteristic failing. Wither's opinions, irritatingly presented though they may be, are often significant and worth having.

Wither is a Spenserian by affinity rather than by imitation. His satires, with which I shall be chiefly occupied in this chapter, are not

[1] Jonson attacked Wither in his masque *Time Vindicated* (1623), representing him as Chronomastix, the Whipper of the Time. Chronomastix woos Fame, telling her 'It is for you I revel so in rhyme', but is rejected as a 'wretched impostor . . ., mountebank, etc.'
[2] Allan Pritchard, 'George Wither: the Poet as Prophet', *Studies in Philology*, LIX (1962), 211–32.

Spenserian at all. Probably even in the pastorals Sidney had more formative influence on him than Spenser: *Faire-Virtue* could be regarded as a lengthy paraphrase of Pyrochles's song in *Arcadia*, book II, 'What tongue can her perfection tell', while the lyric included in it, 'When Philomela with her strains', is Wither's version of Sidney's 'In a grove most rich of shade'. In several respects Wither seems un-Spenserian in his literary tastes and choices. He has no feeling for the heroic, for British history, for mediaeval romance, nor, after the pastorals, for either pagan myth or the English countryside. His stated preference for perspicuity over the 'dark riddles' of allegory looks like a declaration of independence, and his deliberately colourless style is far removed from Spenser's.

These two poets, nevertheless, shared a common passion – for beauty and for virtue. Wither's passion for beauty, suppressed after *Faire-Virtue* or allowed expression only in his praise of the Psalms of David, combines with his passion for virtue to make him, in *Faire-Virtue* at least, true heir to Spenser's philosophy of love. There are Platonic passages in that poem (e.g. 2897–934) that may derive directly from Spenser's 'Hymne in Honour of Beautie', but, more important, the whole is written in the spirit of *Amoretti* and the *Epithalamion*. There are differences: in particular, *Faire-Virtue* is too much a prescription for the perfect woman. Nevertheless, she is an ideal *woman*, not a personified abstraction, and as such her affinity with the bride of the *Epithalamion* is clear.

Moreover, although he would probably have denied this, Wither was markedly mediaeval in his habits of thought. *Faire-Virtue* itself seems to be in some ways – in, for instance, its measure, its apparent interminableness, and its character as a lover's confession – a descendant of works like Gower's *Confessio Amantis* and the *Romaunt of the Rose*. Wither's satire, especially in *Britain's Remembrancer*, has affinities with the mediaeval homily, both in matter and manner. And although he denounced allegory, the allegorical way of thinking was ingrained in him. Examples of psychomachia occur in his satires, including the old debate between Justice and Mercy over man's preservation or destruction. In his handling of the Scriptures, he clings tenaciously to traditional typological interpretations, seeing Mary typified in the burning bush, Christ in the lamb that was sacrificed for Isaac. The completeness of his surrender, in *Britain's Remembrancer*, to the idea that the British are a new Israel and himself their chosen prophet, may even suggest that life itself became something of an allegory for him. Certainly his own life was, according to his own testimony, full of visions. And reading his poems, not simply a prophetic work like *Britain's Remembrancer*, but a collection of hymns such as *Haleluiah*, in which almost every conceivable activity or emotion of man is given a heavenly reference, one becomes aware of how thoroughly the life of a person such as Wither is lived 'sub specie aeternitatis'. Spiritual battles that may be figurative for another are real for him. He sees 'armies of Angels and Devils, night and day, fighting for us, and round about us.'[3] For Wither the threat from the Beast and the Scarlet Whore became increasingly a present reality. There is therefore a sense in which Spenser's allegories are contained in him: he is his own St. George, fighting the dragon of unrighteousness:

> For, this day to stand
> 'Gainst *Princes*, Priests, and People of this *Land*,
> Thou art appointed; and they shall in vaine
> Contend. For thou the conquest shalt obtaine.
>
> (*B.R.*, p. 313)

St. George of Braggadochia was Taylor the Water-poet's name for him.

The habitual self-dramatisation which we meet in Wither's work has, however, important non-Spenserian characteristics and alignments, and it is to these that I now turn.

Abuses Stript and Whipt, with which the *Juvenilia* of 1622 opens, may be taken as Wither's first published work of note. Wither, that is, first appeared before the world as a satirist. In doing so he was employing a form which, especially as practised and understood by the Elizabethans, lent itself readily to personal or pseudo-personal statement: 'speaking his mind' was accepted, almost by definition, as the satirist's activity. The personality that emerges from such speaking – that of a blunt, unpolished, but honest fellow – is not, as Mr. Alvin Kernan has demonstrated in his study, *The Cankered Muse*, to be naively identified with the personality of the author. It is, rather, a convention, a persona adopted by all practitioners of the genre. Wither, in this poem, knows this as well as anyone. Moved by a 'Fury' –

---

[3] *Hymnes and Songs of the Church*, 'St Michael and all his Angels', Introduction, 188.

> Something there is swels in my troubled brest,
> Till it be utter'd I expect no rest (sig. C5^r)

– that recalls, and is surely intended to recall, Juvenal's, he determines to turn himself 'into a *Satyrist*'. He takes up his whip and scourge, the satirist's proper instruments, and announces his programme of chastisement:

> Freely I will discover what I spy ... (sig. C7^v)

> None will I spare, for favour or degree ... (sig. C8^r)

Throughout the poem, the first-person pronoun is constantly in use: 'I see ...', 'I espy ...', 'I know ...', 'I protest'. But the habit of presenting everything in the form of personal experience and observation, does not in itself make the poem a personal poem. Often the 'I' is simply a generalised 'I', the 'I' of the Satirist-figure; or rather, he may be both the Satirist-figure and the poet, but there is nothing to distinguish him specifically as the poet. The moral superiority, chiding voice, and grittiness of tone are all part of the convention, and may or may not be characteristic of Wither himself. In estimating the self-portraiture of this poem, that is, we have to allow for its framework of satiric convention.

Too much emphasis on the conventional elements could, however, lead us into the opposite error of overlooking the extreme self--centredness, and hence the novelty, of the poem. This self-centredness is apparent, firstly, in a quality already discussed in chapter III, the poet's delight in his 'making'. 'For my owne sake I first made it, and therefore certaine I am my selfe have most right unto it,' he states in his 'Epistle Dedicatory'. The poem confirms this self-regarding attitude by making plain the author's extreme self-consciousness, *as* author. Not only are we the readers made aware in it of the importance of the relationship of the teller to his tale; we realise also that this double awareness on our part derives primarily from his. He does not, as Mr. Kernan says of the satirist, 'make every effort to repudiate the Muse'; while emphasising in the orthodox way the 'down-to-earth quality of himself and his work', he still sees the poem as Muse-inspired.[4] Furthermore, Wither does talk about himself a great deal in the poem, in ways that are demonstrably not conventional but frankly autobio-

---

[4] See Alvin Kernan, *The Cankered Muse* (New Haven, 1959), 3-4.

graphical. In 'Revenge', he tells a long story of how while he was out of England, 'a stranger, in another *Clime*' (probably Ireland), he was slandered by an erstwhile friend, and of how, on his return, he magnanimously took no revenge. He stresses that this is fact, not fiction:

> Yet cause perhaps there's some may thinke I faine,
> Or speak a matter fram'd out of my braine:
> Know; This *back-bitter lives*, and may doe long
> To do me more, and many others wrong.   (sig. F6)

Of 'Envy' he tells us,

> I have known it shake the bush belowe,
> And move the leafe that's *Wither'd* long agoe.   (sig. E6ʳ)

Most significant of all is the long autobiographical sketch that opens the poem. Called 'The Occasion of this Worke', it is a miniature *Prelude*, tracing 'the growth of a satirist's mind'. It is one of our primary sources for Wither's biography, describing the course of his life down to the time when, obliged to leave Oxford through a change in the family fortunes and not caring to pursue a 'meer Country businesse' at home under 'owr *Bentworth* beechy shadowes', he came to London, and was there so disgusted by the things he saw that he was driven to write this satire. At this point, we notice, person merges into persona; although even now it is not quite the normal persona of the satirist. Usually the satirist writes from inside the society he is satirising, as an accepted member of it, plain-spoken and blunt, but fundamentally more 'knowing' as well as wiser than the rest of that society, *more* sophisticated rather than less. This is so with Persius, for example, and, among Wither's contemporaries, with Marston and Hall. Wither, by contrast, portrays himself as from the start an outsider. He is a Meliboeus come to court, a plain countryman moved to laughter by the sights he sees, a traveller amazed at the monsters and *Anthropophagi* he meets. Attempts to corrupt and sophisticate him are resisted:

> Nay, which is more, they would have taught me faine,
> To goe new learne my English tongue againe;
> As if there had been reason to suspect
> Our ancient-used *Hampshire Dialect*.   (sig. C3ʳ)

F**

He goes on to tell us that, finding no preferment or employment, he determined that he would, in spite of Fortune, be employed – by writing this satire. The effect of this autobiographical introduction and of the continuing thread of personal reminiscence that runs through the poem, is to modify considerably the satirical persona, by grafting a good deal of Wither's actual self upon it. In this respect (although in no other) Wither resembles Donne. Only Donne, among Elizabethan formal satirists, expresses in his verse a personality that is recognisable as individual and his own. There is a fullness of dramatic treatment, an element of truly personal narrative, in his satires, that we do not meet elsewhere in Elizabethan satire – except (in a very different form) in Wither.

Wither is fully aware of how much he has talked about himself here. 'Those things which concerne my self,' he tells the reader, 'may seeme childish and nothing pleasing; but you must consider I had a care to please my self as wel as others.' The Dedication addressed to himself ('To him-selfe, G. W. wisheth *all Happinesse*') would suggest that this was in fact his first care. It is a piece of bravado that Wither may have copied from Marston, whose *Scourge of Villanie* opens:

> To his most esteemed, and best beloved Selfe,
>
> DAT DEDICATQUE.

Wither, however, makes it more than a stunt by giving his reasons for the dedication. Principally it is because the poem is a *memorandum*, to put him in mind of the course he must pursue in his combat with the world, the flesh, and the devil:

Read it, weekely, daily, yea, and hourely too. What though it be thine owne? thou knowest mans nature to be so uncertaine and prone to forgetfulnesse, even in the best things, that thou canst not have too many *Memorandums*.   (sig. A4^r)

Wither clung to this idea of poetry as a 'remembrancer': it is repeated in the titles of two of his poems. The idea reflects, I think, an attitude of mind similar to that which produced 'the poetry of meditation'. (Many of Wither's hymns are offered to his readers as meditations, to keep them 'mindful' of the spiritual matters with which they deal.)

But not only will this memorandum remind him of his former observations and of the moral principles he had formulated; it will show him his former self:

Then this may shew thee what once thou wert; touch thee againe, with the feeling of thy miseries; and be unto thee that true *Friend*, which, free from all fayning, shall plainly tell thee, what perhaps should else have never bin brought againe to thy remembrance.   (sig.A5ᵛ)

This is Wither's earliest statement of the notion that was to become increasingly a governing principle of his poetry – that poetry *is* self-portraiture. In an epigram to his father accompanying *Abuses Stript and Whipt* but applicable, he says, to 'any of his Books', he writes 'It is a little *Index* of my minde.' Of *The Shepheards Hunting* he admits that 'it wholly concerns myself.' *Wither's Motto* is, not incidentally but avowedly, a self-portrait:

> No; when this *Motto* first, I mine did make,
> To me I tooke it, not for fashions sake:
> But that it might expresse me as I am;
> And keepe me mindefull to be still the same.   (sig. A5ᵛ)

It is a 'Picture of my Minde':

My intent was, to draw the true Picture of mine own heart; that my friends, who knew mee outwardly, might have some representation of my inside also. (sig.A2ᵛ)

The preservation and publication of his *Juvenilia* are actually justified on these grounds:

> Beside; as there be many men, who long
> To see of what complexion being yong
> Their bodies were; and to that purpose save,
> Unalter'd those their Pictures which they have,
> So, he, thus having drawne (as here you finde)
> In childish yeeres the picture of his *Minde*,
> Unalter'd leaves it; that in time to come
> It may appeare how much he changeth from
> The same he was . . .
>   (*Juvenilia*, 'To the Reader', no sig.)

As Mr. John Buxton has reminded us, pictures were valued in the Elizabethan period as, in Sir John Harington's words, 'good re-membrances of our friends'.[5] Wither's interest extended from mental to physical portraiture, or rather, he used the physical portrait to

[5] John Buxton, *Elizabethan Taste* (1963), 109.

underline his interest. From the early engraving, 'aetatis suae 21', with its motto, 'I grow and wither both together', to the striking, kindly old man clad in armour, his head adorned with laurel, whom we meet in Wither's last work, *Fragmenta Prophetica*, Wither always moralised his picture:

> Part of my *Outside*, hath the *Picture* shown,
> Part of my *Inside*, by these *lines* is known,

he writes in an epigram 'on his owne *Picture*' at the end of *Wither's Motto*. The *Collection of Emblemes* has a long 'Meditation upon sight of his Picture', stressing how much more lasting is a portrait of the mind than these vain '*Lines, and Shadowes*', while underneath the picture is the verse,

> What I WAS, is passed by,
> What I AM, away doth flie;
> What I SHAL BEE, none do see;
> Yet in *that*, my Beauties bee.

This suggests that however irritating Wither's egocentricity may be, it had a quite respectable moral and religious basis, and was not utterly gross and insensitive. There is some awareness of the purposefulness of life and the value of the whole in his concern with these changing portraits of himself.

Such frank insistence on the direct, undisguised personal bias of a poem was not common in Wither's day, least of all in the long poem. Spenser felt the personal character of his *Epithalamion* as an unusual self-indulgence: 'So I unto my selfe alone will sing' – for this time only, he seems to imply. The self-indulgence – sheer laziness, in fact – to which Wither's adoption of this manner of writing is due in part, robs it of some of its interest and significance; he puts his experience raw into his poetry because he has not the patience to transmute it into anything else. Yet it has also literary precedent, and is in its way as much characteristic of the growing individualism of the times as are the poems of Donne.

The literary precedent was provided by Montaigne. He too, as Florio admitted, was 'ever selfe-conceited to write of himselfe out of himselfe'.[6] Montaigne's statement of his aims before the *Essays* is

---

[6] *The Essayes of Michael Lord of Montaigne*, translated by John Florio, Everyman edn., II, 'The Epistle', 4.

similar in several points to Wither's. He has 'vowed' the work, he declares,

to the particular commodity of my kinsfolk and friends: to the end, that losing me (which they are likely to doe ere long) they may therein find some lineaments of my conditions and humours, and by that meanes reserve more whole, and more lively foster the knowledge and acquaintance they have had of me.[7]

'It is myself I paint,' he says, and again, 'Myself am the matter of my book.' Wither does not mention Montaigne, and philosophically and temperamentally as well as in stature there are obviously vast differences between them. Yet there seems little doubt that the personal emphasis of Wither's writing and his justification of it owe much to Montaigne's example. *Abuses Stript and Whipt* is sub-titled, significantly, *Satyricall Essayes*. The essay was at this time a fashionable form, although, following Bacon, it was usually in prose, not verse. Wither's description draws attention to the meditative, informal, moralising character of his poem; his looseness of style, as well as his personal allusions, make it clear that Montaigne rather than Bacon is the essayist he is following. He is a 'libertine' in verse, as Montaigne was in prose. Statements like 'I delight more in Matter, than in *Wordy Flourishes*' (*Emblemes*, I, sig. A1[r]), or his expressed conviction that his talent was given him to use 'both to [God's[glory, and the benefit of others' (*A Preparation to the Psalter*, 1619, sig. B1[r]), suggest, however, that *The Advancement of Learning* may have helped to form, or to confirm, his principles.

Montaigne's self-portraiture was achieved in two ways – by self-analysis and confession on the one hand, and by simple 'musing', a revelation of the quality and character of his mind through the expression of his undirected thoughts, on the other. Wither, as his introduction to *Abuses Stript and Whipt* shows, sets out to produce a similar mixture. This comes out in the poem itself in the form of Montaigne-like reflections, in rambling, easy, unaphoristic comment. The essay on 'Sorrow' for instance, begins,

> Of this sad *Passion* I may knowledge take,
> And well say some-what for acquaintance sake.

Then, a few lines later,

7 *ibid.*, I, 15.

> And yet, me thinks, if man would use his might,
> He may asswage if not out-weare it quite,

and so on to

> And therefore, though I doe not discommend
> The moderate bewailing of a friend;
> I wish the Extreame hereof men might despise,
> Lest their profession they doe Scandalize,

and, later,

> I must confesse, 'twas once a fault of mine
> At every misadventure to repine,   (sig. L7ʳ – L8ʳ)

which launches him into a long passage of personal reminiscence. The moral reflections carry the poet's personal recommendation along with them; they are presented as the fruits of his experience.

Abuses Stript and Whipt is, despite its intimidating title, clearly moral rather than satirical in character. Though Wither begins by referring to the manners of the city, his subject is in fact man in general and his domination by the passions. In Book I he deals with such passions as Lust, Choller, Ambition, Fear, Jealousy, Despair. The satirist's voice, scornful, denunciatory, continues to be heard, but increasingly modulates into the voice of the moralist, analysing the condition and suggesting remedies. (Wither himself acknowledges this altered approach in his 'Conclusion'.) In Book II he attempts to return to satire, in a survey of the 'thousand bad humours' of the various classes of society. As an anatomy of the abuses of his day, this part is quite effective, but the poet is now openly the preacher. The book opens with a prayer to God ('E'ne thou by whose desired inspirations I undertooke to make these Observations' – the Sylvestrian echo is clear), and in the Epilogue addresses Man:

> Heere sinfull man, thou maist behold in part
> Thy miserable state, and what thou art . . .
>
>   learne (oh man) to season
> Thy heart with sacred thoughts, with truth and reason . . . ,

Prevent the Divels baits and his temptations
With earnest Prayers, and good Meditations.

(sig. X5^v, X6^r)

Donne, Hall, and Marston all became divines, while Wither did not,
yet it is impossible to imagine them writing thus in their satires.

As satire, *Abuses Strip and Whipt* is then fairly enough dismissed as, in
John Peter's words, 'a garrulous and tepid affair'.[8] As a collection of
moral essays, it has rather more interest. So considered, its observations on 'the world's mad humours' fall into place with the
Character rather than with the formal satirists. (Wither's awareness of
the Character as a literary form is shown in *The Schollers Purgatory*,
1624, where he contrasts the character of the 'meere stationer' with 'the
definition of an honest stationer'.) In however limited a way, Wither
shares in his period's interest in the psychology of human behaviour.
He insists that his observations are his own, and apologises for not
'gracing' the poem with 'examples of old ages past, And wise mens
sayings'. There are indeed few allusions or sententiae in the poem. Its
matter nevertheless seems to owe something to the classical moralists,
Plutarch, Epictetus, but above all Seneca.

Wither's imprisonment for *Abuses Stript and Whipt* turned him into
a 'Senecal man'. In *The Shepheards Hunting*, written, he says, to recreate
himself during imprisonment, he appears as a shepherd Stoic, content
even in thraldom:

> They may doe much, but when they have done all,
> Onely my *body* they may bring in *thrall*.

> And 'tis not that (my *Willy*) 'tis my *mind*,
> My *mind's* more precious, freedome I so weigh
> A thousand wayes they may my *body* bind,
> In thousand *thrals*, but ne're my mind betray:
> And thence it is that I *contentment* find,
> And beare with *Patience* this my loade away:
>   *I'me still my selfe*, and that I'de rather bee,
>   Then to be Lord of all *these Downes* in fee.   (sig. I12^v)

Earlier, in the *Epigrams* and *Epithalamia*, he had combined the personae
of shepherd and satirist to create a picture of the 'honest homely

---

[8] John Peter, *Complaint and Satire in Early English Literature* (1956), 156.

Rusticke' writer. Then, with shepherd's cloak and satyr's scourge both laid aside, rustic honesty and stoic contentment combined to produce *Wither's Motto* (1621).

The *Motto* is a better poem than *Abuses Stript and Whipt*; it is also shorter. Montaigne may again have been the inspiration for what is in effect a familiar essay. The result, however, is in most repects far removed from Montaigne. There is the occasional picturesque detail which seems not only to recall Montaigne but, as Lamb saw, to anticipate Sir Thomas Browne:

> I *no* Antipathy (as yet) *have* had,
> 'Twixt me, and any Creature, God hath made:
> For if they doe not scratch, nor bite, nor sting,
> Snakes, Serpents, Todes, or Catts, or any thing
> I can endure to touch, or looke upon.   (sig. B4ᵛ)

But in general what his motto, 'Nec habeo, nec Careo, nec Curo', provides is an opportunity at once to assert his contentment and to cock a snook at Fate, Fortune, and his enemies. Like *Abuses*, the poem has elements both of satire and moral essay, but is given shape and a greater incisiveness by employment of the device of the motto, and by the frank concentration now upon the author's opinions. It is a statement of principles, not a series of intimate revelations, and unlike Montaigne's *Essays* or Browne's *Religio Medici*, is clearly didactic in intention. Stoicism has furnished the positive part of the motto, which could be summarised in Seneca's words, 'Quid enim deesse potest extra desiderium omnium posito?' Wither portrays himself as a Christian Stoic; as he says of the emblem illustrating the motto as a frontispiece:

> This litle *Embleme* here, doth represent,
> The blest condition, of a man Content.   (sig. A1ᵛ)

The portrait is idealised, though Wither, one suspects, believes in it. Like Sir Guyon, he 'evermore himselfe with comfort feedes, Of his own vertues', and we can understand the exasperation of Jonson when he read such lines as

> Low place I keepe; yet to a *Greatnesse* borne,
> Which doth the Worlds affected Greatnesse scorne.
>   (sig. C8ʳ)

The Stoical scorn of the last line now often modulates into cynicism, which must have annoyed Jonson even more. In the years since *Abuses Stript and Whipt*, Wither has learned defiance: 'Hah! will they storme? why let them; who needs care?' the poem opens. He dramatises himself constantly, picturing himself as a heroic fighter against the court and all 'great ones'. At times he appears a Bosola, 'the only court-gall', commenting sourly on all the 'Proiectmongers', 'gaudy Upstarts', and 'unworthy *Groomes*', who are

> The foes to Vertue, and the Times disease.   (sig. E1ʳ)

At other times he is, rather, a Bussy D'Ambois, poor, honest, and proud, nobly defying the 'mighty Tyrants' who oppose him:

> But all those threatning *Comets*, I have seene
> Blaze, till their glories quite extinct have beene.
> And I, that crusht, and lost was thought to bee;
> Live yet, to pitty Those, that spighted Me.   (sig. E6ᵛ)

Sometimes his protestations are Job-like; he rises to a passage of sustained eloquence when he declares his willingness to suffer any ill that may be if it is to the glory of God:

> Yea, let me keepe these Thoughts; and let be hurld,
> Upon my backe, the spight of all the world. . . .
>
> Let me become unto my foes a slave; . . .
>
> Let my Religion and my honestie;
> Be counted till my death Hypocrysie.
> And, when I die, let till the generall *Doome*
> My *Name*, each houre into question come,
> For *Sinnes* I never did . . .
>   So that, in Me,
> Those comforts may encrease, that springing be,
> To helpe me beare it. Let that Grace descend,
> Of which I now, some portion apprehend:
> And then, as I already (here-tofore)
> (Upon my *Makers* strength, relying) swore,
> So, now I sweare againe. If ought it could,
> Gods glory further, that I suffer should.   (sig. E7ᵛ)

There is no doubting the sincerity of this. While it would be naive to suppose that this 'continued self-eulogy of two thousand lines', as Lamb called it, is also a completely realistic self-portrait, one thing is certainly real, and that is the moral passion that informs it.

Wither's Motto was one of the 'best-sellers' of its day, going through several editions in the first year of its publication, as *Abuses Stript and Whipt* had also done. 'Quite through this *Iland* hath my *Motto* rung,' Wither wrote in 'A Postscript'. Wither's works were in fact immensely popular from the start. This both confirmed him in his 'careless' literary habits, and gave him a sense of power. In *Britain's Remembrancer* Faith encourages him to stay in London during the Plague, again to be an example of piety:

> The gen'rall notice which men take of thee,
> Will make thy actions more observed be
> Then those of twenty others, who doe seeme
> In their small circuits, men of great esteeme.   (p. 192)

His popularity was, as he admits later in the same poem, with 'the multitude', not with 'the learned':

> A haz the way of making pretty Rimes,
> To fit the apprehension of the times;
> And, him for that the multitude doth favour,   (p. 412)

he reports one of his critics as saying. *Abuses Stript and Whipt* first showed him that he had this 'way', which he then deliberately exploited in *Wither's Motto*. Wither was not, originally, a puritan in the strict sense; he was not, that is, a dissenter, a presbyterian, or a 'precisian'. But, like many other Anglicans, he had a strongly puritan conscience, and his *Motto* is in many ways a classic statement of the middle-class, puritan *credo*. It is devotional, and genuinely moving in its piety; it mocks at the great, the proud, the fashionable, and the ambitious, and exalts poverty and industry:

> Smooth *Wayes* would make me wanton; And my course
> Must lye, where Labor, Industry, and Force,
> Must worke me Passage: or, I shall not keepe
> My *Soule* from dull Securities dead-sleepe.   (sig. E6ʳ)

It is sometimes smug, and at least potentially philistine:

> *I care* for no more knowledge, then to know:
> What I to God, and to my Neighbour owe.
> For outward Beauties *I doe nothing care*,
> So I within, may faire to God appeare.   (sig. C8ᵛ)

> For many Bookes *I care not* . . .   (sig. D1ʳ)

The philosophy of life it expresses was later to be that of Robinson Crusoe, who came to it in the prison of a desert island. It is not surprising to discover that Wither was one of Defoe's favourite authors, actually quoted by him in *Robinson Crusoe*. The two have much in common.

It would be easy to dismiss Wither's next poem, *Britain's Rememb-rancer*, as a mere Jeremiad. Identifying the British people with the new Israelites, Wither sees himself as their prophet, chosen to interpret the dread warning of the Plague (of 1625) to them. Exhaustively and exhaustingly he catalogues their sins, warning them of the destruction that will follow if there is no amendment. But he also describes the actual visitation of the Plague vividly, even racily. (Defoe may have derived some ideas for the opening chapters of his *Journal of the Plague Year* from this poem.)[9] And although it is, with the exception of a few passages, bad poetry, it is quite good journalism. Wither's analysis of the ills of his day and his suggested remedies are sound enough, and one notices the greater involvement now with political affairs, the result, no doubt, of the intensifying political and religious struggle. Throughout, there are long digressions, in which the poet writes about himself. In these passages all suggestion of the persona has disappeared; we have simply Wither, the author, addressing us directly, assuring us that he is not a fool, nor deluded, nor a mere pamphleteer, but is truly a prophet. Occasionally his prophesying justifies itself by its impressiveness:

> The Lord shall call, and whistle from afarre,
> For those thy enemies that fiercest are:

[9] Defoe's account of how he reached the decision to remain in the city (*Journal*, section IV) resembles Wither's in several respects, especially in its emphasis on the guidance he received from Providence. There are also resemblances in his description of the changes in the life of the city (sections VI and IX).

For those thou fearest most; and they shall from
Their Countries, like a whirlewind hither come.
They shall not sleep, nor stumble, nor untie
Their garments, till within thy fields they lye.
Sharp shall their arrowes be, and strong their bow . . .

                                                      (p. 538)

I do not propose to follow Wither further through his poetic career.
Something remains to be said about his 'plain style'. This he adopted,
partly from preference, partly to serve the needs of his audience. His
statement before *Abuses Stript and Whipt*,

. . . for indeed, if I knew how, my desire is to be so plain, that the bluntest
Iobernole might understand me,   (sig. B1v)

may be a retort to Marston's declaration, 'In Lectores prorsus indignos',

> Fye, wilt thou make thy wit a Curtezan
> For every broking hand-crafts artizan?
> Shall brainles Cyterne heads, each iubernole,
> Poket the very *Genius* of thy soule?[10]

It also has a remarkable affinity with the principles and practice of
puritan preachers, as William Haller has described them. Henry Smith's
description of simple preaching may be taken as representative. To
preach simply is

to preach plainly and perspicuously, that the simplest man may understand what
is taught, as if he did hear his name.[11]

It is amusing to find Dryden describing 'wit' in similar terms: it is
most to be admired, he says,

when a great thought comes dressed in words so commonly received that it is
understood by the meanest apprehensions.[12]

[10] Marston, *The Scourge of Villanie*, in *The Poems of John Marston* ed. A. Davenport
(Liverpool, 1961), 96.
[11] Quoted by William Haller, *The Rise of Puritanism* (Columbia Univ., 1938), 30.
[12] Dryden, *An Essay of Dramatic Poesy*, ed. G. Watson, *Of Dramatic Poesy and Other
Critical Essays* (1962), 1,40.

Wither's dislike of conceits, 'clinches', 'flourishes', 'strong lines' and the art of rhetoric in general is indeed Augustan in its vehemence. The common link is probably Bacon. Sharing a platform with Bacon on the one hand and the puritans on the other, Wither's advocacy of plainness must be judged respectable and of its time. At the same time Dryden's comment on Flecknoe, 'He affects plainness, to cover his want of imagination,'[13] fits Wither too. Wither has very little sense of the magic of words. Starved of metaphor, his verse too often provides telling illustration of Pope's celebrated 'And ten low words oft creep in one dull line.'

A suitable retort therefore to Farr's praise of Wither's 'pure Saxon' might be that diction so lacking in sinew and colour is, to adapt Milton's phrase, 'but a blank diction, not a pure'. Yet in some of the hymns of *Haleluiah* it enables Wither to achieve a simplicity and poise reminiscent of George Herbert, who, as his experiments with stanza-form make clear, is Wither's chief model here. 'A Rocking Hymn' is particularly successful:

> Whil't thus thy *Lullabie* I sing,
> For thee, great Blessings ripening be.
> Thine Eldest brother is a King;
> And hath a Kingdome bought for thee.
> *Sweet Babie, then, forbear to weep;*
> *Be still my Babe; sweet Babie, sleep.*   (p. 83)

More often , however, this 'purity' results only in a flatness that brings to mind the less successful of Wordsworth's lyrical ballads, or, at best, treads a knife-edge between this and the Herbertian simplicity, as in these lines from the hymn, 'For one contentedly married':

> Half tir'd, in seeking what I sought,
> I fell into a sleep at last:
> And, GOD for me, my wishes wrought,
> When hope of them, were almost past.
> With *Adam*, I this favour had,
> That out of *Me* my *Wife* was made;
> And, when I waked, I espide
> That, GOD for me had found a *Bride*.   (p. 392)

<hr>

[13] *ibid.*, 22.

The charm of such writing is rather less than its insipidity.

In the couplet, on the other hand, Wither can sometimes approach Wordsworth in his combination of naturalness of expression with essential dignity. On the lines in *Fidelia* in which the heroine allows herself to imagine that her lover has not, after all, deserted her:

> Which if it prove, as yet me thinkes it may,
> Oh, what a burden shall I cast away?
> What cares shall I lay by? and to what height
> Towre in my new ascension to delight   (sig. Q3ᵛ)

Swinburne commented:

There is hardly in all the range of English heroic verse an effect so noble, so majestic a touch of metre as here.[14]

The opening description of *Faire-Virtue* too is unusual for its period in its endeavour to describe a country scene as it really is. This after a brief reference to the 'silver lake' and the 'cold-sweet shadows' of its woods mentions Cynthia, Thetis, and Neptune, it is true, but after that mythology is abandoned and we read:

> Here, you might (through the water) see the lande
> Appeare, strowd o're with white or yellow sand.
> Yonn, deeper was it; and the wind by whiffes
> Would make it rise, and wash the little cliffes,
> On which, oft pluming sate (unfrighted than)
> The gagling Wildgoose, and the snow-white Swan:
> With all those flockes of Fowles, which to this day,
> Upon those quiet waters breed, and play.   (sig. B1ᵛ)

As the description progresses, the reader follows it as a traveller, much as he does in 'Michael':

> The pleasant way, as up those hils you clime,
> Is strewed o're with *Mariarome*, and *Thyme*,
> Which growes unset . . .

---

[14] Swinburne, *Miscellanies* (1886), 71, footnote.

When you into the highest doe attaine;
An intermixture both of Wood and Plaine,
You shall behold: which (though aloft it lye)
Hath downes for sheepe, and fields for husbandry . . .

(sig. B2ᴵ)

Throughout the passage, Wither is endeavouring, like Wordsworth, to look steadily at his subject, and to avoid the interweaving of any 'foreign splendour' of his own in its description.

Lamb praised Wither for his 'kind heart'. Dalrymple, his eighteenth-century editor, maintained that 'Lovers of natural thought and sentiment will be pleased at being brought to acquaintance with *Wither*.'[15] Farr, in the nineteenth century, suggested that 'more frequent development of the delicate filaments of the human heart' than in his writings was scarcely to be found, except in Shakespeare.[16] Although this is an absurd exaggeration, the stress upon the heart is right. There is a generosity of spirit in Wither that keeps his work sweet and wholesome, despite all the poetical prosings and the egocentricity. He was too sensitive, rather than not sensitive enough. He writes eloquently on love – 'the strongest, the commonest, the most pleasing, the most natural, and the most commendable of our affections' – and poignantly on friendship, and the loss of friendship. Speaking of the latter, Faith, in *Britain's Remembrancer*, comments:

These things are very bitter unto such
Whose hearts are sensible to ev'ry touch
Of kindnesse, and unkindnesse.   (p. 185)

Years later, writing his hymn 'for them who are afflicted by the Unkindnesses of their Friends', Wither comments, 'For them who are of a gentle nature this is a very great affliction.' *Haleluiah* has many such touching comments, within the poems and without. It is truly 'homely' in its inculcation of the domestic and family virtues. In the hymn to be sung 'When we ride for pleasure', it expresses a humanitarianism anticipatory of Fielding or Blake:

---

[15] *Extracts from Juvenilia or Poems by George Wither*, ed. Dalrymple (1785), 14.
[16] *Haleluiah*, ed. E. Farr (1857), Introduction, xii.

> For, he that wilfully shall dare
> That Creature, to oppresse or grieve,
> Which GOD to serve him doth prepare,
> Himselfe of mercy doth deprive.   (p. 57)

Much earlier, *Fidelia* had established that humanitarianism by a vehement attack upon forced marriages, as well as by its general sensitiveness to the woman's point of view. The revival of interest in Wither in the late eighteenth and early nineteenth centuries is easily understood. Satirist, fanatic, prophet, he was above all a man of feeling.

Giles and Phineas Fletcher

The relationship between Giles and Phineas Fletcher, in their work as well as in their lives, is a close one: they are brother-poets as well as brothers. The area of agreement between them, in matters of taste, belief, and style, is very great, and the resemblance of each to the other is stronger than the resemblance of either to any other writer. This composite quality, the impression they give of being a kind of seventeenth-century Tweedledum and Tweedledee, is well summed up in Phineas's lines:

> Their nearest bloud from self-same fountains flow,
> Their souls self-same in nearer love did grow:
> So seem'd two joyn'd in one, or one disjoyn'd in two.
>
> (*P.I.*, I, 3)

There are differences between them (Phineas wrote secular as well as religious verse, while Giles did not. Giles is a better poet than Phineas, with more quickening power over words), but they are differences of the 'dum' and 'dee' variety, divergences from a common base. Taken together, as their work invites us to take them, these two poets present an unusually united front.

Perhaps surprisingly, their most striking common quality is neither their religiosity nor their Spenserianism nor any one or more stylistic habits or mannerisms. It is, rather, their sensuousness. That is to say, each, taken separately, is astonishingly sensuous; doubled, as it is when they are taken together, this sensuousness stands out as their major characteristic. Between them, the Fletchers produced some of the most voluptuous verse of their period. As a result, they, who are often described, quite correctly, as 'the chief heirs of Spenser's moral allegory',

181

may also be seen as the chief heirs of his pagan sensuousness. The temperament and sensibility (in each) that have made this possible perhaps explain the further paradox that they, who are violently protestant in sympathy and self-proclaimed followers of Du Bartas as well as of Spenser, also write in a manner strongly suggestive of the baroque art of the counter-Reformation.

It is easy to see the poems of the Fletchers as a classic example of sexual feeling masquerading as religious and moral concern. Book II of *Christs Victorie, and Triumph* 'overgoes' the Song of Songs to produce a notoriously luscious description of Christ:

> His cheekes as snowie apples, sop't in wine,
> Had their red roses quencht with lillies white,
> And like to garden strawberries did shine,
> Wash't in a bowle of milke, or rose-buds bright
> Unbosoming their brests against the light . . . ,
>
> (*C.V.T.*, II, 11)

and later adapts Spenser's episode of the Bower of Bliss to the Temptation in the Wilderness, leading Christ through a garden (where for the bathing nymphs who tempted Guyon is substituted a picture of Pangloretta ('Vaine-Glorie') copulating in a fountain running rosewater) to a house where, in a 'loft' carved in ivory white,

> whiter Ladies naked went,
> Melted in pleasure, and soft languishment,
> And sunke in beds of roses, amourous glaunces sent. (II, 52)

The question whether the poet has himself been seduced by the 'beauties' he describes, whether he in fact writes out of attraction or repulsion, is here even more crucial than in the corresponding episode in Spenser. For Spenser's picture of the Bower of Bliss includes many natural things – 'sweet and holesome' air, 'ioyous birdes shrouded in chearefull shade', 'gentle warbling wind' low answering to all;

> what ever in this worldly state
> Is sweet, and pleasing unto living sense

– as well as the decadent and artificial beauty which C. S. Lewis insists

on so much. In such circumstances, to have mixed feelings seems
perfectly natural, and healthy. But in Pangloretta's domain there are
only decadence, excess, perversion. (It is, in fact, what some critics feel
Acrasia's bower *should* have been.) Physical sensations have a peculiar
intensity here, and include an element of pain mingled with pleasure:
rose leaves lie on the water like burning coals on liquid silver, and
water falls from the breasts of 'gaping mermaides',

> To Lions mouths, from whence it leapt with speede,
> And in the rosie laver seem'd to bleed.   (II, 48)

Fletcher is careful to describe the scene as 'this false Eden', and he does
also introduce a straightforwardly disgusting drinking scene. (Both the
Fletchers always vehemently condemned drink.) Nevertheless, his
attitude remains ambiguous. Was Christ's journey through such a
place really necessary – through *just* such a place?

Similarly with Phineas Fletcher, one wonders, despite the precedent
provided by Spenser's Belphœbe, whether it was really necessary, in
describing Parthenia ('Chastitie in the single'), for example, to dwell
so long upon her 'daintie breasts, like to an Aprill rose', with 'their
little rising heads' and 'silver circlets' (*P.I.*, X, 37). Phineas Fletcher
has also some extremely erotic secular verse. *Venus and Anchises* is
pornographic art, a youthful day-dream of quintessential love-making,
with Anchises seen simply as 'the Boy' and Venus as the Queen of Love.
The Sion College epithalamion is desire climbing with a tongue of fire;
its verve, its richness of expression, and massive and musical stanzaic
structure make it one of Fletcher's finest achievements. The poet's
excitement, as he writes of

> the fort & mayden tower
> Where Hymen yet keepes his unconquered bower
> Folded in daintie leaves of purple gylliflower,   (175–7)

is unmistakable. Both poems are remarkable productions for a clergyman or intending clergyman. In general, Phineas Fletcher seems more
preoccupied with sex than Giles: his treatment of it is at once cruder
and more straightforward. Together they form a family fleshly school
of poetry, its fleshliness so pronounced that H. E. Cory speaks of
them (along with other members of their 'school', such as Joseph

Beaumont), as 'strumpet-minded', 'half-divine, half-diseased poets'.[1]

This, however, is too harsh a judgment. Undoubtedly in part of their work – in the second book of *Christs Victorie, and Triumph* and generally throughout *The Purple Island* – the Fletchers illustrate in a protestant context that reversal of values and state of unbalance which Mlle. Odette de Mourgues finds characteristic of the baroque. 'If,' she writes,

according to Catholic tradition, the senses and imagination contribute to the glory of God, it does not follow that the glory of God and His saints should contribute towards indulging the most intense cravings of the senses and imagination.[2]

It does not; but neither does it follow that such indulgence cannot co-exist with a genuine piety. The rest of *Christs Victorie, and Triumph* with its glowing spiritual fervour, refutes this, in the case of Giles. There is much Christian Platonism in this poem, both in the portrait of Mercy in the first book, and in the picture of Heaven in the last. In *The Purple Island* the uniformly over-emphatic, over-sensualised style makes it difficult for the reader to recognise and respond to the moments of genuine rapture or near-rapture that do occur, such as the description at the end of the poem of the union of Christ and his Church ('Eclecta'), which follows the Canticles, but in a relatively restrained fashion. But Phineas was not naturally a poet of rapture. His talents and interests, as he acknowledges, are more earthbound than Giles's: it is not for his 'lighter skiffe' to 'dare to enter in that boundlesse main' (*P.I.*, VI. 20). He is Martha to Giles's Mary: his Christianity is orientated towards the active rather than the contemplative. The most revealing passage in *The Purple Island* is that in which, in describing the procession of Virtues marching to the combat with the Vices, he distinguishes between Love, meaning Man's love for God (distinguished also from God who is Love itself), and the

> fresh and lovely Swain,
> Vaunting himself *Loves* twin, but younger brother,
>
> (IX, 37)

who is Love of one's neighbour. Fletcher's genuine engagement is shown by the extended treatment the subject receives, and by the nature of

[1] H. E. Cory, *Spenser, the School of the Fletchers, and Milton*, 342, 344.
[2] Odette de Mourgues, *Metaphysical, Baroque, and Précieux Poetry* (1953), 82.

the treatment, which is not emblematical but simply a detailed description of behaviour, of virtue in action. In his prose devotional works, written after he became a parish priest (as indeed the passage just considered may have been), *Joy in Tribulation* and *The Way to Blessedness* (both 1632) and *A Fathers Testament* (1670, posthumous), Fletcher's humanitarian and pastoral care is clear. The last is Fletcher's most mature work. It recommends detachment from a world whose false values he himself has come to recognise through experience. 'Felicity seldom dwelleth with riches,' he tells his sons, 'never is patcht up with raggs of earth.'[3] As for worldly pleasures,

Before we enjoy them, how dearely, how highly do we prize them? What refuse we to do, or suffer that we gain them? we long, we pine for them; we ride, we run for them; sweat and toyl for them; venter limb and life for them; but no sooner do we obtain, but finding their emptiness, our heart goes off from them to some other object . . .[4]

In addressing his sons, he tells them that he leaves them the same legacy his dying father left him – 'nothing but your education'. Such domestic details and intimacies are typical of Fletcher:

> Strange power of home, with how strong-twisted arms
> And Gordian-twined knot dost thou enchain me!
> (*Works*, II, 228)

a poem written from Cambridge, possibly soon after he became a student, begins, going on to tell how his dreams bring back the well-loved place,

> Till the morn bell awakes me; then for spite
> I shut mine eyes again, and wish back such a night.   (*ibid.*)

'Home' always exercised this power over him: he writes with strong, simple feeling of family relationships, particularly in his elegy for Sir Antony Irby, *Elisa*. Among the psalms he chose for paraphrase was number 127, on the theme that 'heirs are God's inheritance':

> That man shall live in blisse and peace,
> Who fills his quiver with such shot.   (*ibid.*, 252)

[3] *A Fathers Testament* (1670), sig. C3ᵛ.
[4] *ibid.*, sig. B5ᵛ.

The wishes he expresses, in *The Purple Island* and elsewhere, for a life of
retirement were perhaps, after all, more than a pose:

> Safe in my humble cottage will I rest;
> And lifting up from my untainted breast
> A quiet spirit to heav'n, securely live, and blest.

(ibid., 234)

Mrs. Craik showed perhaps a true discernment when she made him
virtually the patron saint of her idyll of the industrial Midlands,
John Halifax, Gentleman.[5]

No 'snap judgement' on the Fletchers is therefore possible. They are
both, but especially Phineas, more complicated than at first appears.
And the complexities of their moral make-up are repeated in their
literary make-up. In the models they choose to follow, they are quite
bewilderingly eclectic. Spenser, however, remains the chief one. Apart
from the passages of direct imitation and the numerous verbal echoes,
both poets try to make their verse both look and sound like Spenser's,
by using various simplified adaptations of the Spenserian stanza,
achieving a superficial, deceptive likeness by concluding with an
alexandrine. Syntactically, they share Spenser's clarity, but in matters of
diction, despite the appearance of a few characteristically Spenserian
words and phrases, they tend, like the other Spenserians, to avoid
Spenser's archaisms and thus to sound, generally, much more modern.
They have been attracted to Spenser by his verse, not merely by his
matter. His appeal for them is perhaps, as I have already suggested,
principally a sensuous one. Nevertheless, as protestant allegorists, they
have also gone to him for material, and for instruction on method. As
allegorists, they are his most conspicuous imitators. Their poems abound
in personified abstractions, many of them bearing a strong family
resemblance to figures in Spenser. The main scheme of *The Purple
Island*, a description of the human body in terms of an organised state,
is an expansion of Spenser's description of the same body in terms of an
organised household, in his account of the House of Alma (*F.Q.*, II, ix).
The action which follows this description is a psychomachia culminat-

---

[5] Phineas Fletcher, narrator of the tale, and life-long friend of Halifax, is represented as a
descendant of the poet. Mrs. Craik makes him a Quaker. Her quotation of the passage in
P.I. concerning rural contentment (quoted here, p. 103) suggests that it was this aspect of
Fletcher's work that she valued.

ing in the defeat of the Dragon of the Apocalypse by Christ. Parallels
with *The Faerie Queene*, Book I, naturally occur here. Fletcher's
protestant consciousness is haunted by the images of Book I, particularly
by the foulness of Error and Duessa. They reappear several times, in
association with 'our whore of Rome', in *The Apollyonists*. Both
brothers attempt their own variations (as who did not?) on Spenser's
Despair. Despair's cave even serves in *The Purple Island* as a model for
the spleen, which is characterised as

> Darke, dolefull, deadly-dull, a little hell.   (III, 18)

In *Christs Victorie, and Triumph* Despair is the first of Christ's temptations. Fletcher's figure repeats Spenser's too closely to be called either
plagiarism or pastiche; rather, it is an example of the kind of 'daylight
robbery' practised by T. S. Eliot, as the transference of two lines in their
entirety,

> Darke, dolefull, dreary, like a greedy grave,
> That still for carrion carkasses doth crave,
>
> (*C.V.T.*, II, 23)

makes plain. Christ is led to the cave by Satan in the guise of 'a good
old Hermit', an 'old Palmer', who closely resembles Archimago in his
first encounter with the Red Cross Knight and Una. Later, after
visiting Presumption in her pavilion 'Over the Temple, the bright starres
among', Christ, a Guyon-like figure (as Guyon in the Cave of Mammon
is a Christ-like figure) is led through the garden of Pangloretta, as we
have already noticed. Pangloretta herself blends reminiscences of
Lucifera and Mammon's daughter with the character of Acrasia. Thus
different parts of *The Faerie Queene*, Books I and II, converge and merge
here, to create a successful and quite viable piece of Spenserian imitation.
Although the sensuousness of the description is at times in excess of
what the subject demands, Fletcher's treatment of his material is
carefully worked out thematically. The temptations are an extension,
but an allowable extension, a paraphrase, of those in the Gospels, and
the association of despair and presumption is theologically sound.
Fletcher shows grasp of Spenser's method too by his 'charactering' of
his personages by their place, a point to which his marginal notes draw
attention.

The Fletchers are, among Spenser's followers, the most mediaeval in taste and manner. This in itself makes them appear to stand closer to him. The debate between Justice and Mercy in 'Christs Victorie in Heaven' is Giles Fletcher's version of the popular mediaeval debate between the Four Daughters of God. The subject was still a favourite one in sermons and poetry, so that he was not being uniquely or outrageously old-fashioned in using it. He was, however, reaffirming his sympathy with Spenser. In the Mutabilitie cantos, moreover, Spenser instructs the reader who wishes to know more about Nature's garments to 'Go seek he out that *Alane* where he may be sought.' Giles Fletcher, whether acting on this advice or not, does exactly that. His description of Mercy's dress is based on the Prosa 1 of the *De Planctu Naturae* of Alanus de Insulis. In Phineas Fletcher the mediaeval affinities are even more strongly marked. Tillyard even states that he is more consistently in the mediaeval tradition than Spenser.[6] I doubt whether this is so, however. His psychomachia in which the Soul and the Intellect, king and queen of the body (or Purple Island), are fought over by embattled virtues and vices has many mediaeval counterparts, notably in *Sawles Warde*, the *Cursor Mundi*, and Lydgate's *Assembly of the Gods*. His lengthy catalogue of the virtues and vices, moreover, recalls the prose treatises of the middle ages, works like the early thirteenth-century dialogue of *Vices and Virtues*, or even parts of the *Specula* of Vincent of Beauvais. Nevertheless, in his handling of this material, Fletcher turns to other models, and above all to Du Bartas.

Structurally, *The Purple Island* combines the idea of the House of Alma with that of the Divine Weeks and Works. Thirsil's story, as we noticed in the chapter on pastoral, takes seven days to tell. It does so because it is the story of the microscosm, the 'little world' of man. Fletcher's purpose is to reveal the 'wonders' of this world, as Du Bartas had revealed those of the greater one. So complete is the parallel that this little world has both its Golden Age and its Fall, enabling even Lingua, the tongue, though now seen as a monster, 'curb'd ... with iron bit', and 'pratling wife' to Gustus, to be described as 'lovely once, perfect and glorious being' (*P.I.*, V, 58). Fletcher's material had itself been treated by Du Bartas as part of his larger scheme – in his discourse on the digestive system, for instance, or on the construction of the human frame (*D.W.W.*, III, 6) – so that there are resemblances in content as well as structure between them. Fletcher's exclamations of wonder at the divine Providence are distinctly Bartasian:

[6] E. M. W. Tillyard, *The English Epic and its Background*, 371.

Oh powerfull Wisdome, with what wondrous art
Mad'st thou the best, who thus hast fram'd the vilest part!

(II, 26)

A literary allegiance such as this cannot be classed as mediaeval; it is
very up-to-date.

The Purple Island is carefully and elaborately planned, not only in its
'ingenious' opening anatomical analogy, but in its psychomachia also.
Knights personifying the various virtues and vices parade as in a
tournament. The armour, device, and motto of each are carefully
described. Their appearance is more like that of the knights of Tasso or
Ariosto than of the grotesquely mounted personages of some mediaeval
(and Spenserian) encounters. The opposing qualitites are those listed by
St. Paul in his Epistle to the Galatians V, 17–23, as, respectively, 'the
works of the flesh' and 'the fruit of the Spirit'. (Fletcher follows St.
Paul's order closely.) In portraying them Fletcher has sought aid in
various places. The vices in canto VIII, for example (Over-boldnesse,
Vain-Expence, Feeble-mindednesse, and others) are drawn from the
Nicomachean Ethics. (Fletcher underlines this by giving many of his
characters Greek names, as well as by a marginal reference to Aristotle.)
Another important source is Joseph Hall's Characters of the Vertues and
Vices (1608). Some of Fletcher's Vices plagiarise Hall, for example,
Superstition:

Her onely bible is an Erra Pater;
Her antidote are hallow'd wax and water:
I'th'dark all lights are sprites, all noises chains that clatter.

(VII, 44)

Hall had written 'Of the Superstitious' that he never 'goes without an
Erra Pater in his pocket . . .; every lanterne is a ghost, and every noise
is of chaines'; and, earlier, 'This man dares not stirre forth till his brest
be crossed, and his face sprinkled.'[7] Fletcher treats most of his Vices in
this Theophrastian manner, discovering in himself a real vein of social
satire, much of it contemporary in reference. Aselges (Lasciviousness),
for instance, spends his time at court, in an environment suggestive of
that of Cynthia's Revels:

[7] Hall, Heaven upon Earth, and Characters of the Vertues and Vices, ed. Rudolph Kirk (New
Jersey, 1958), 175.

There oft to rivalls lends the gentle Dor,
Oft takes (his mistresse by) the bitter Bob;
There learns her each daies change of Gules, Verd, Or,
(His sampler) if she pouts, her slave must sob.   (VII, 25)

The criticism of court life is essentially that which Spenser had voiced
in *Colin Clouts Come Home Againe*, but Fletcher is 'of his time' in
preferring this Jonsonian form of expression. Other characters do recall
Spenser (in *The Faerie Queene*), and even De Guilleville. Flattery, for
instance, although the details of his behaviour come mainly from Hall,
still unnaturalistically, in the manner of De Guilleville, carries a sword
in his mouth. Such a mixture of modes makes Fletcher something less
than 'thoroughly' mediaeval (even if it does not make him 'thoroughly'
modern either).

This is still truer of *The Apollyonists*, Fletcher's English enlargement
of his Latin poem, *Locustae*. Its subject is the Gunpowder Plot, treated
apocalyptically as the work of the locusts of *Revelation*, identified with
the Jesuits. The treatment is Spenserian, in that it makes use of personifications, such as Sin ('The Porter to th'infernall gate'), Ignorance, and
Error, and in doing so imitates Spenser's 'nastiness'; and also in its
elaborate description of statues and paintings. But the germ of the idea
comes from Tasso's account of the infernal council meeting in
Gerusalemme Liberata, Book IV, which is fused with contemporary
protestant interpretations of *Revelation*, chiefly perhaps the *Paraphrase*
by James I, the publication of which is made in *The Purple Island* to
signal the Church's victory and to provide the climax of the poem.
Although its theme, and the spirit of hatred in which it is written, make
it unattractive, this is fundamentally a good poem, genuinely and
forcefully imagined. Its combination of protestant legend (the scan-
dalous history of the Papacy, familiar from Foxe and others) and
protestant myth (its rendering of the Apocalypse) give the poem good
right to be considered as a brief, protestant epic. As a brief satirical
epic, using Biblical material for its central myth, it may be seen as a
forerunner of Dryden's *Absalom and Achitophel*. Its nearest contemporary
counterpart, for literary value as well as for tone and treatment, is
Donne's prose pamphlet, *Ignatius His Conclave* (1611), which Fletcher
may be imitating in places.[8]

---

[8] Apollyon, praising the Jesuits for having made new recruits, comments 'If they had
fail'd wee must have sought a coast I'th'Moone (the Florentines new world) to dwell'

More attractive is the unpretentious but moving *Elisa*, the funeral elegy for Sir Antony Irby which Fletcher wrote at the request of his widow. We might have expected from Fletcher a poem like *Daphnaida*, or at least a pastoral elegy of some sort. Instead, with what seems to me considerable originality, he dramatises the death-bed scenes, thereby achieving the kind of pathos we associate with Elizabethan domestic drama, with the last scene of Heywood's *A Woman Killed with Kindness*, for example. From the opening stanzas of the poem, with their image of the dying stag, lying 'in coverts thick' among 'green brakes and primrose sweet', followed immediately by

> So lay a gentle Knight now full of death,
> With clowdie eyes his latest houre expecting, (I, 2)

we are transported to a scene which in its grouping, its dignity, orderliness, and tender family feeling is the verbal equivalent of a seventeenth-century tomb. The death-bed provides a focal point for a number of emotions, attitudes, and experiences. In particular, we are given a picture of the ordered institution which marriage ideally is, and which this marriage has been. This comes out as the husband in his last speech surveys their past life, and commends the care of 'our boyes' and of the whole household, which has hitherto been his, to his 'dearest *Bettie*':

> And now our falling house leans all on thee;
> This little nation to thy care commend them:
> In thee it lies that hence they want not me;
> Themselves yet cannot, thou the more defend them;
> And when green age permits, to goodnesse bend them ...
>
> (I, 35)

The death itself is touching in its peace and piety:

> Thus said, and while the bodie slumbring lay,
> (As *Theseus Ariadne*'s bed forsaking)

(*Ap.*, II, 33). In *Ignatius His Conclave* Lucifer proposes with the aid of the Pope and Galileo to colonise the Moon with Jesuits.

With the allusion of 'Loiol's eldest Sonne' to Henry IV of France,

> Hence love wee that great King so heartily,
>   That but his heart nought can our hearts content, (*Ap.*, IV, 27)

cf. Ignatius, in *His Conclave*, speaking of Princes '. . . whose hearts, wee do not beleeve to be with us, till we see them' (sig. E2ʳ).

His quiet soul stole from her house of clay;
And glorious Angels on their wings it taking,
Swifter then lightning flew, for heaven making.   (I, 41)

In the representation of the wife's anguish and grief that follows, the violence of her feeling is not at all glossed over, nor is it suggested that it can be soon appeased by the consolations of philosophy. Instead, her earlier comparison of herself to a headless trunk becomes violent reality as she visualises it in a state of trance:

A thing impossible too true she found:
The head was gone, and yet the headlesse body sound. (II, 25)

The emotion in this poem has great immediacy. One wonders whether some of Fletcher's feeling concerning his own father's death (Giles Fletcher the elder and Irby both died in 1610) has gone into it. The poem is hauntingly musical, and the lines are given a dirge-like 'dying fall' by the use of feminine rhymes.

Phineas Fletcher's shorter poems, especially those appearing in *A Fathers Testament*, are more Metaphysical than Spenserian in character. Some of them resemble Herbert's both in matter and form, but without being dully imitative. In some, he comes near to greatness: in the poem beginning,

Vast Ocean of light, whose rayes surround
The Universe, who know'st nor ebb, nor shore,
(*Works*, II, 322)

or in,

See, I am black as night,
See I am darkness: dark as hell.
Lord thou more fair than light;
Heav'ns Sun thy Shadow: can Sunns dwell
With Shades? 'twixt light, and darkness what commerce?
(*ibid.*, 326)

Thus despite his obvious and very real Spenserian and mediaeval affinities, Phineas Fletcher resists any easy labelling. On the whole, I

think he was of his time. In the early seventeenth century to follow
Du Bartas was not much less up-to-date than to follow Donne. In
complimentary verses Fletcher is praised three times as the 'ingenious'
author of *The Purple Island*, and ingenuity – *argutezza* – was, as we
know, the aim of much seventeenth-century verse, especially of the
kind designated 'baroque'. There is a strong strain of the baroque in
Phineas Fletcher's work, but before examining this, something more
must be said of Giles.

Christs Victorie, and Triumph is, formally, a very fluid work, almost
druidical in its capacity to flow from one literary form into another.
Thus although there are Spenserian echoes throughout, the second book
is the only one extensively to adopt Spenser's method. Elsewhere,
method and manner suggest other influences, some, though not all,
identical with those cited as ancestors to *Paradise Regained* in Miss
Barbara Lewalski's *Milton's Brief Epic* (1966). As he himself indicates in
his preface, Fletcher's poem is in the tradition of Christian epic
inaugurated by Juvencus, in his fourth-century *Historia Evangelica*,
and by Sedulius, in his fifth-century *Paschalis Carminis*. A revival of
interest in these and similar writers in Italy in the early sixteenth century
coincided with, or led to, the production of new Christian epics in the
Virgilian manner, the most celebrated being Sannazaro's *De Partu
Virginis* and Vida's *Christiad*. Tillyard says of Fletcher that he 'is quite
untouched by the classicising trend of epic in Europe. He writes as if
Vida's *Christiad* . . . had never been written,'[9] but this is not so. The
epic elements in the poem tend to be foreshortened, but they are there.
The title itself has a heroic ring to it, and occasionally Christ is spoken
of as if he were a martial hero:

> Here let my Lord hang up his conquering launce,
> And bloody armour with late slaughter warme . . .
>
> (*C.V.T.*, IV, 30)

There are also such features as the opening announcement of theme
(in Virgil's manner), the invocation, the retinue of Virgilian personifications attending on Justice, and the epic similes. Above all, however,
Fletcher's poem is to be related, especially in its third book, where its
subject is the Passion, to a form of Christian poetry distinct from,
although possibly developing out of, the Christian epic. I refer to the

[9] Tillyard, *op. cit.*, 371.

G

poetry of *Tears*, a popular counter-Reformation form, of which the earliest example appears to be Tansillo's *Le Lagrime di S. Pietro* (1560, enlarged version 1585). While this type of poem is, as Southwell's 'St. Peters Complaint' especially makes clear, a religious counterpart to the secular 'complaint', it also exists in close relationship to the cult of the penitent, particularly that of the Magdalen, found in counter-Reformation art. It tells the story of the Passion, but does so lyrically and dramatically, and from the point of view of the particular speaker. It employs an excited emotional rhetoric, with stress on such figures as apostrophe, exclamation, rhetorical question, antithesis, paradox, and pun. Writers on the Passion from the Church fathers onwards, and including Sedulius and Vida, had tended to employ such rhetoric, but the 'Tears' poets carried the tendency much further by making the rhetoric predominate and by dissolving narrative, very largely, into declamation.

Christs Victorie, and Triumph as a whole has a somewhat discontinuous structure. It is, in fact, four separate poems (each with its own title), very loosely related to each other. Each poem pursues a different method from the rest: the first presents a mediaeval debate or psychomachia; the second is a Spenserian allegory; the third meditates on the Passion in the manner of the 'Tears' literature; the fourth is a sustained Christian-Platonic beatific vision. The dramatic immediacy of the third book especially seems a perfect illustration of Professor Martz's thesis concerning the effect of the Ignatian meditation on literature. The book covers all the events of the Passion and Crucifixion, but does so, not in narrative fashion, but through apostrophe and comment, presenting the action as if it were taking place here and now:

> See drouzie Peter, see whear Judas wakes,
> Whear Judas kisses him whom Peter flies:
> O kisse more deadly then the sting of snakes!
>
> (*C.V.T.*, III, 26)

> It was but now they gathered blooming May,
> And of his armes disrob'd the branching tree,
> To strowe with boughs, and blossomes all thy way,
> And now, the branchlesse truncke a crosse for thee,
> And May, dismai'd, thy coronet must be . . .
>
> (III, 33)

See whear the author of all life is dying: . . .

> Loe how his armes are stretch't abroad to grace thee,
> And, as they open stand, call to embrace thee,
> Why stai'st thou then my soule; ô flie, flie thither hast thee.

(III, 34)

Protestant or not, a poet who writes like this has had some contact with the literature of the counter-Reformation.

The baroque character of Giles Fletcher's verse has long been acknowledged, and he is often seen as, in English, a bridge between Southwell and Crashaw. From the frequency with which they are quoted, however, one receives the impression that this baroque character rests upon a few stanzas alone, those in which Christ's beauty is described in extravagantly voluptuous terms (*C.V.T.*, II, 11–13). Here the resemblance to Tansillo and the poetry of the counter-Reformation is clear, as it is also in another stanza on the same subject:

> One of ten thousand soules I am, and more,
> That of his eyes, and their sweete wounds complaine,
> Sweete are the wounds of love, never so sore,
> Ah might he often slaie mee so againe.
> He never lives, that thus is never slaine.
> > What boots it watch? those eyes, for all my art,
> > Mine owne eyes looking on, have stole my heart,
> > In them Love bends his bowe, and dips his burning dart.

(II, 9)

This may seem to look forward to Crashaw's hymn to St. Theresa, but it also looks back, most decidedly, to Southwell and Tansillo.[10]

---

[10] Southwell's St. Peter 'complains' of Christ's eyes in a lengthy passage ('Saint Peters Complaint', 325 *sq.*), in which the eyes are described as, amongst other things, 'You graceful quivers of loves dearest darts', 'These blasing comets, lightning flames of love'. Tansillo is still closer to Fletcher:

> Ma gli archi, che nel core gli aventaro
>   Le saette più acute, e più mortali;
>   Fur gli occhi del Signor, quando il miraro:
>   Gli occhi fur gli archi, e i guardi fur gli strali,
>   Che del cor non contenti, sen passaro
> Fin dentro a l'alma, e vi fer piaghe tali,
> Che bisognò, mentre che visse poi,
> Ungerle col licor de gli occhi suoi.
> > (*Le Lagrime Di S. Pietro* (Venetia, 1592), sig. A7ᵛ).

On a more general view, what critics have in mind when they describe Fletcher as baroque is his combination of Italianate sensuousness with a 'witty' use of rhetorical figures. One of the best of recent attempts at re-defining the literary baroque is that made by Professor Frank Warnke (who would differentiate Fletcher as 'high baroque'). Professor Warnke describes the difference between the baroque, or, as he would have it, high baroque, and Metaphysical styles as one, partly, between 'a taste for contrast and antithesis' and 'a leaning toward paradox and synthesis'.[11] Fletcher, however, is addicted to both antithesis and paradox. But the figure most characteristic of him, since it is embodied not only in the style but in the very structure of the poem, is *antimetabole*, defined by the Elizabethan, John Hoskyns, in his *Directions for Speech and Style* as 'a sentence inversed or turned back', as in 'If any for love of honour or honour of love.' Antimetabole, which is both a figure of words and a figure of thought, could be regarded as a kind of half-way house between antithesis and paradox. Antithesis is involved in the contrasting pattern, yet the parts of the antithesis are not simply set side by side, but, by being brought together at the centre, are combined in a circular shape which is a kind of synthesis, though one in which the elements 'maintain their separate and warning identity' and do not 'enter into a solid union',[12] their union consisting simply of their having been brought within a single compass. (The criss-cross implied by the other name for this figure, *chiasmus*, defines the nature of the union.) The figure appears (with some permissible syntactical variation and combined with antithesis) in the opening stanza of the poem:

The birth of him that no beginning knewe,
        A   B
Yet gives beginning to all that are borne,
        B   A
And how the Infinite farre greater grewe
                        A   B

Cf. also Valvasone, *Le Lagrime di Santa Maria Maddalena* (1587), sig. V8ʳ:
        I'sento l'arco, e le saette ardenti,
        Che da i tuoi sguardi in questo petto aventi.

[11] Frank J. Warnke, *European Metaphysical Poetry* (New Haven and London, 1961), 20.
[12] I borrow the phrases quoted from James Smith's well-known essay 'On Metaphysical Poetry', *Determinations* (1934), 36.

By growing lesse, . . .
   B   A

How worthily he died, that died unworthily . . .
    A   B   B   A

The pattern thus established (A B B A) is repeated in the poem's
structure, which disposes its four books in the order Heaven Earth
Earth Heaven. This pattern of relationships is the poem's theme.
Through it Fletcher expresses his awareness of the distance between
earth and heaven, but also of the traffic between and temporary union
of them brought about by the Incarnation. His opening statement of
his purpose makes this plain. He intends to show

> how the rising Morne,
> That shot from heav'n, did backe to heaven retourne,   (I, 1)

but also

> How God, and Man did both embrace each other,
> Met in one person, heav'n, and earth did kiss.   (I, 2)

And he does show it, visually, by the presentation and arrangement of
his material. During the debate between Justice and Mercy, for instance,
we are constantly made to see Heaven and Earth, placed in relationship
with each other. The eyes of both protagonists are bent downwards,
those of Justice in anger, to survey the whole breadth of earth and the
wickedness of man, and to commend God for flinging 'the worlds rude
dunghill . . . farthest from the skies'; those of Mercy in pity, to see
Repentance 'In a darke valley, drowned with her owne tears', and to
rejoice that God has now joined himself to man for man's salvation.
The book ends, after Mercy's speech, with the lines

> So downe shee let her eyelids fall, to shine
> Upon the rivers of bright Palestine,
> Whose woods drop honie, and her rivers skip with wine.

It is the signal for the transition to the next book, for the closing of the
scene in Heaven and the opening of that on Earth, but it also brings the
entire action into perspective. In the next two books the action is
centred on Earth; Heaven is now in Earth, God in Man. (Christ at his

death is described as 'this heav'nly earth'.) Our attention accordingly is
focused on Earth, and the mystery of the union is brought home to us
by the poet's own excited commentary. In the fourth Book the double
vision and movement are re-established, but the movement is now in
the opposite direction, from Earth to Heaven. Fletcher deals briefly with
the Resurrection and so reaches the Ascension, which is the climax of
the poem. As Christ ('the sparkling Earth') is borne upwards on the
wings of angels, we see, paralleling the episode in the first book, in
which Justice and Mercy look down, the disciples now looking up:

> The rest, that yet amazed stood belowe,
> With eyes cast up, as greedie to be fed,
> And hands upheld ...   (*C.V.T.*, IV, 14)

In the amazing triumph that follows, Earth is not forgotten, for not
only do we see those saints in Heaven who even 'In earthly bodies
carried heavenly mindes'; we also see Christ 'looking downe on his
weake Militants', those saints still 'in this lower field dispacing wide'.
In this way not only is the separation (yet potential union) of Earth and
Heaven maintained, but the triumph itself is brought into the present
day.

Such a vision as this may be described as 'baroque' in the sense that it
expresses the sort of astonishment, or sense of 'the marvellous', that
Marino demanded in his famous statement,

> È del poeta il fin la meraviglia ...
> Chi non sa fa stupir, vada alla striglia.

The wonder before which Fletcher stands stupefied is the *rapprochement*
of Heaven and Earth, God and Man:

> Wonder doeth call me up to see, O no,
> I cannot see, and therefore sinke in woonder,
> The man, that shines as bright as God, not so,
> For God he is himselfe, that close lies under
> That man ...   (II, 6)

What he sees most clearly and expresses most fully is the polarity of the
relationship, but that perception and expression are complicated,

crossed, so to speak (as in a chiasmus), by his sense of wonder at the paradox which he is aware of but cannot fully grasp.

To describe Fletcher's work thus, however, is to see it only in terms of the *literary* baroque. Actually the most strikingly baroque part of Fletcher is his visual imagination. Many of the pictorial and descriptive effects he achieves vividly recall the work of baroque artists, of Bernini, Rubens, Gentileschi, and others. Pangloretta's fountain, for instance, with its roof of painted clouds, its 'gaping mermaides' and 'Lions mouths' is a thoroughly baroque achievement: we have surely seen it somewhere, in some Italian square? Or again there is the 'globe of winged Angels' that in Fletcher's description of the Ascension 'burst' from Heaven to catch Christ swiftly up on 'their spotted feathers'. These angels have appeared elsewhere in the poem: dancing round the canopy of Mercy ('And little Angels, holding hands, daunc't all around'); bearing Mercy into the breast of Christ (II, 2); tempting him (false angels, these) to presumption:

> A flight of little Angels, that did wait
> Upon their glittering wings, to latch him strait;   (II, 37)

bearing him food after the Temptation ('A heavenly volic of light Angels flew'). It is a precise visual detail, and if it seems familiar, its familiarity comes surely from our having seen similar 'globes' in baroque paintings and frescos. (Fletcher's emphasis on the littleness of the angels perhaps increases the familiarity by suggesting also the *putti* of the secular baroque.) And not only the angels, the whole of Fletcher's portrayal of the Ascension is like a baroque painting. The suddenness and swiftness of the angels, the amazement of the spectators, their gestures, the very inclusion of spectators in the picture, all these are characteristic of baroque Assumptions and Ecstasies.

And after the Ascension comes the apocalyptic conclusion. The description of the triumph of Christ and the joys of the New Jerusalem with which the poem ends is one of the most sustained passages of poetic rapture to be found anywhere, and it is, most of it, magnificent. Fletcher's material is traditional; his figures and images can be found in the Bible, in the church Fathers, in hymns of Paradise like that of St. Peter Damiani, and in devotional works of Fletcher's own day. Fletcher's realisation of it, however, is his own, and is comparable with nothing so much as with the work of some great baroque artist, with, for example, the Gesù ceiling of Giovan Battista Gaulli at Rome. The ioyous dynamism and energy which in the first book had seen Christ 'shooting' from heaven to earth and had presented the Nativity as a happy affair of carolling angels, dancing stars, and 'young John, glad child' leaping in the womb, now reappear and seize the occasion. Christ 'leaps' from Earth 'to climbe his Angells wings'; the angels themselves 'spring' nimbly to the stars. Even the 'everlasting doors' are bidden to 'toss' up their heads, as if merely to lift them were too sober a gesture. After this, all is excited rush and movement:

> Out leap the antique Patriarchs, all in hast,
> To see the pow'rs of Hell in triumph lead,
> And with small starres a garland interchast
> Of olive leaves they bore, to crowne his head,
> That was before with thornes degloried,
>   After them flewe the Prophets, brightly stol'd
>   In shining lawne, and wimpled manifold,
> Striking their yvorie harpes, strung all in chords of gold.

> To which the Saints victorious carolls sung,
> Ten thousand Saints at once, that with the sound,
> The hollow vaults of heav'n for triumph rung:
> The Cherubins their clamours did confound
> With all the rest, and clapt their wings around:
>   Down from their thrones the Dominations flowe,
>   And at his feet their crownes, and scepters throwe,
> And all the princely Soules fell on their faces lowe.

> Nor can the Martyrs wounds them stay behind,
> But out they rush among the heav'nly crowd,
> Seeking their heav'n out of their heav'n to find,
> Sounding their silver trumpets out so loude,
> That the shrill noise broke through the starrie cloude,
>   And all the virgin Soules, in pure araie,
>   Came dauncing forth, and making joyeous plaie;
> So him they lead along into the courts of day.   (IV, 17–19)

Both the riotous confusion here and the sheer brilliance recall the baroque ceiling.

To return now to Phineas Fletcher. He too, though less completely and consistently than Giles, is a baroque writer. Rather surprisingly, his descriptions in *The Purple Island* of Penitence and of the sorrowing Eclecta are more suggestive of the 'weeping Maries' of the counter-Reformation than is Giles's picture of Repentance (*C.V.T.*, I, 64–9), though Giles does place his figure 'in a darke valley' and show her feeding a river with her tears. In each instance, however, the reminders of the Magdalen, markedly absent from Spenser's portrayal of the penitent (*F.Q.*, I, x, 27), which we might have expected them to follow, are significant as a further indication of the artistic sympathies of the writer. Of Penitence, Phineas Fletcher tells us, her 'cloudie dropping eyes were ever raining . . . yet was it angels wine, which in her eyes was masht' (*P.I.*, IX, 27, 28). And he sees Eclecta as 'Limming true sorrow in sad silent art':

> Whose swoln eyes, pickled up in brinie tears,
> Crystalline rocks, corall the lid appeares,
> Compast about with tides of grief and feares; . . .

> While her fair hands, and watrie shining eyes
> Were upward bent upon the mourning skies,
> Which seem'd with cloudie brow her grief to sympathize.
>
> (XII, 43–45)

Although there are resemblances here to the representations of Penitence in the emblem books – for example, to the penitent Anima of the *Pia Desideria* of the Jesuit, Herman Hugo, (Antwerp, 1624) – the feeling expressed seems to take them out of the emblem category into the wider 'Tears' tradition. Phineas Fletcher may well have been as much acquainted with the literature of the counter-Reformation (which made the Magdalen's tears a frequent theme) as Giles was, even though he does not adopt its manner to the same extent.

Where, however, he appears most baroque is in his liking for gaudy effects and brilliant colour (seen even in his choice of title for his *magnum opus*). These effects at times suggest the baroque plastic arts; his description of Eclecta, for instance,

> Her amber hair, like to the sunnie ray,
> With gold enamels fair the silver white,   (*P.I.*, XII, 85)

exactly reproduces the colour-effects achieved in some Bernini interiors. But normally we are reminded, rather, of Marino, especially of his secular poems. Both Fletcher and Marino when writing of the natural world or of women, like to turn them into jewels and precious metals. As a way of seeing woman, this seems obsessional with Fletcher. His women frequently have silver brows or cheeks. (Note, too, Eclecta's 'coral' eyelids.) Erythre, with

> Her golden hair, her silver forehead high,
> Her teeth of solid, eyes of liquid pearl,   (X, 41)

seems more an idol than a creature of flesh and blood, and in the 'Hymen' for his cousins' wedding we are in fact assured,

> Their bodies are but Temples, built for state,
> To shrine the Graces in their silver plate.
>
> (*Works*, II, 224)

The most astonishing example, however, is the description of Venus in *Brittain's Ida*, where

> Her chin, like to a stone in gold inchased,
> Seem'd a faire jewell wrought with cunning hand,
> And being double, doubly her face graced.   (III, 8)

(As an ideal of feminine beauty, this perhaps has something in common also with the florid and ample female figures of Rubens.) A phrase like 'you snowie fires', addressed by Fletcher to his 'nymphs', also sounds Marinistic. Quite probably Fletcher studied Marino directly, although the resemblances between them might be accounted for by a shared taste and sensibility, and by an admiration for the same models, such as Tasso (who likes brilliant colour effects).

Neither 'baroque' nor 'Spenserian', used separately, is sufficient to describe the Fletchers. We need both terms together, and need to see the implications of each as enlarging yet modifying those of the other. Their baroque qualities qualify their mediaevalism and take them firmly into their own century. Their Spenserian sensuousness works along with their baroque tendencies, but the moral temper that they share with Spenser, the sheer human sympathy and compassion seen in their prose works, in *Elisa*, and in many moving passages in *Christs Victorie, and Triumph*, save them ultimately though not at all times from the charges of 'religious emotionalism', of 'facile religiosity', often levelled against the baroque artist. Both are better poets than has yet been acknowledged. Of Giles Fletcher in particular we may say, as he himself quotes St. Basil as saying of Nazianzen (*C.V.T.*, 'To the Reader'), that he

by imitating the singing Angels in heav'n, himselfe became, though before his time, an earthly Angel.

The Spenserians and Milton;
Conclusion

he five followers of Spenser under discussion in the present study were all minor poets, poets capable, it is true, of producing very distinguished work on occasion, but incapable of rising permanently above the second rank. Spenser had, however, one 'poetical son' who possessed a genius equal to, indeed surpassing, that of his 'original'. This was, of course, Milton. The subject of Milton's relationship to Spenser is too large and too complex to consider here, but we may observe that it is clearly, in many respects, a different kind of relationship from that of the Spenserians. Milton's possession of genius makes it so. Passages of Spenserian imitation such as the Spenserians give us do not occur in his verse. He neither sought to be, nor has ever been considered, a second Colin Clout, a Spenser re-born. There is something ridiculous in the very notion. All that Milton sought to be was himself. His values, literary and human, were, many of them, the same as Spenser's, and where, as in *Comus*, he could learn from Spenser and be aided in the realisation of his own insights and designs, Spenser's 'influence' is clear. But it is a matter of learning and assimilating, not of imitating. Milton's 'Spenserianism' is a good deal less obvious than that of the Spenserians proper, though it is also a good deal more complete, in the sense that he is the truest successor to what is most sage and serious, as well as to what is most creative, in Spenser.

But that Milton has a direct, as well as a collateral, relationship with the Spenserians themselves has long been recognised. His earliest verse shows decidedly more signs of their influence than it does of Spenser's, and his knowledge of them, certainly of the Fletchers, remained a permanent possession with him, contributing something even to *Paradise Lost* and *Paradise Regained*. It is something of a feather in the cap of the Spenserians that we can think of Milton as in a sense 'one of them', and that not by virtue only of his affinities with Spenser, but also by virtue of his affinities with them, considered independently of Spenser. For the 'Spenserian' as I have portrayed him here is something of a hybrid, liege-man to Spenser, and yet a free-man too; Clarion, the butterfly of *Muiopotmos*, in poet's form. (Keats, choosing lines from that poem as motto for *Endymion*, showed that he recognised the type.) Milton, naturally throughout his life of their party (since it was Spenser's too) in his devotion to the Muse, his sense of the importance and the divinely inspired nature of the poet's office, his awareness of his place in a tradition going back to Orpheus and the other 'old poets', also, for a time at least, is linked with them in a more personal and intimate alliance, as, so to speak, their comrade and companion. I am not thinking now principally of his 'borrowings' from them, though these are valuable as evidence. Most of these borrowings are well known, and I shall not repeat them. What I think I discern in Milton is something more diffused (and therefore harder to establish) than that. Milton is a Spenserian in his early poems, it seems to me, in a larger sense than is implied simply by his being a borrower from them. He is 'one of them' because he has caught their tone, because he shares their aims and enthusiasms, and has made their programme his. As a young poet he writes in the fresh, personal manner they so often employ, exuberantly expressive of his delight in 'mirth and youth, and warm desire' and in the joys of friendship. It is possibly a Spenserian rather than an especially Ovidian or Horatian voice we hear in some of the familiar Latin Elegies, especially in the First, where Milton praises the beauty he finds among London women:

> Gloria Virginibus debetur prima Britannis,
>   Extera sat tibi sit fœmina posse sequi,   (71–2)

in terms similar to those used many times by Browne and Wither in reference to the 'nymphs of Thame'. In these poems he writes enthusiastically also both of his enjoyment of poetry and of his own poetic ambitions, of his search for a theme,

> Such where the deep transported mind may soare
> Above the wheeling poles, and at Heav'ns dore
> Look in . . .
>   ('At a Vacation Exercise', 33–5)

Such confidences and aspirations can, as we have seen, be matched in the Spenserians. So can the search itself, in the particular form it takes, which, as he tells us in the 'Epitaphium Damonis' and elsewhere, was for 'a truly British strain'. Twice – in the epitaph, and indirectly in 'At a Vacation Exercise' – Milton associates the search with the English rivers. It is as if he were seeking his own equivalent for *Poly-Olbion* (and, possibly, *Britannia's Pastorals*) as well as for *The Faerie Queene*. And when in 'Mansus' he writes of the Druids and their praise of heroes, his preoccupations seem even closer to Drayton's. Even in 'Lycidas', the allusions to Mona and Deva and the Druids, though made appropriate by the 'sad occasion dear', are another reminder of Drayton, and of Browne. Milton's mind, in his early verse, occupies the same places as theirs, pursues the same topics and interests.

This is clearest of all in his pastoral. In 'L'Allegro' and 'Il Penseroso' and in some of the songs in *Comus* even the metre resembles theirs, recalling Wither's 'darling measure' and the River-God's songs in *Britannia's Pastorals*. More important, the gaiety and homeliness of the pastoral scenes in 'L'Allegro' seem in direct line of descent from theirs. H. E. Cory notes this, commenting,

L'Allegro . . . is the kinsman of Willy and Perigot, of Drayton's Batte and Gorbo, Browne's Willy and Roget, and Wither's Philarete.[1]

L'Allegro himself, however, is not a shepherd, though he moves among shepherds. The kinship, in so far as it comes through character, not setting, lies in his 'youthfull jollity', in the fact that he is a 'youthfull Poet', singing of the joys of the countryside, of conviviality, and of poetry. In *Comus* too the freshness and detail of the pastoral background – the constant reminder of 'chewing flocks', of 'labour'd Oxe' and 'swink't hedger' and of 'all the fleecy wealth That doth enrich these Downs' – almost certainly owes something to the Spenserians' example. Would this recreation of pastoral Britain have been quite so rich and authentic, one wonders, had not Britannia first had her Pastorals?

Similarly in 'Lycidas', quite apart from the precise literary echoes of the Fletchers, we have what could be regarded, in part, as a pastoral on 'Fletcherian' lines. The link is Cambridge: this is a poem commemorating a Cambridge friendship, as so many of Phineas Fletcher's poems – not only *The Purple Island* and the *Piscatory Eclogs*, but the

Cory, *op. cit.*, 353.

lyrics too – had done. The opening description of the shepherds' upbringing, when they 'fed the same flock, by fountain, shade, and rill', follows the convention Fletcher had employed: they could be the same fountains. Perhaps too the fertilising presence in Milton's mind of Fletcher's verse accounts, in part, for the presence in the poem both of 'Camus, reverend Sire', and of 'The Pilot of the Galilean Lake'. The 'watery' reference may, at any rate, be associated with Fletcher's use of the fisherman, along with the shepherd, as symbol for the priest.

When, moreover, the young Milton turns to the writing of religious verse, the Fletchers, as is well known, provide one of his chief models. The Nativity Hymn is itself a Christ's victory and triumph in brief. It gives, however, only three lines to the Passion. The unfinished poem in which Milton attempted to treat of that theme was, it seems, to have been a poem of the same type as Fletcher's. The allusions to Christ as 'most perfect Heroe', to 'Cremona's Trump' (i.e. Vida's Christiad), and to the author's tears and 'plaining vers', and the 'pensive trance, and anguish, and ecstatick fit' which he at least endeavours to achieve, make that plain. The stanza form approximates to those used by the Fletchers almost throughout their work, and is in fact identical with that of Phineas Fletcher's Elisa. Milton's use of an alexandrine for the last line of the stanza (here, and in the Nativity Hymn) must be seen as due to the Fletchers', rather than to Spenser's, example.

We may find, then, a Spenserian 'type' in the young Milton. We may also find his experience of particular works of the Spenserians shadowed in his own poems. Thus his reading of Browne's Pastorals seems to have been of the unconsciously creative kind. Milton's own copy of the poem, annotated by himself, has survived. The annotations are simply glosses, not critical comments. No principle seems to be discoverable in them, although it is worth observing that Milton notes no less than five passages descriptive of morning, three of night, and one of noon. (Some of his descriptions are, however, inaccurate; he writes 'morning', when what Browne is writing about is 'noonstead', or even night.) One of the passages on morning is that which I earlier (pp. 151–2) compared with 'L'Allegro', and other passages follow the same pattern, evoking the hour through description of the shepherd's or countryman's activities. Possibly these passages impressed Milton sufficiently to have contributed something, unconsciously, to the structure and content of 'L'Allegro', with which they certainly have much in common. Milton also notes the 'fairies Description' in Book I,

song 2 (sig. E4^r), which employs similar material to 'L'Allegro' (101–6).
(With 'She was pincht, and pull'd she sed', compare, in Browne, the
Fairy Queen's command to her elves 'To pinch those Maids that had
not swept their shelves'.) Unconscious recollections of the *Pastorals*
may also be, in fact I think almost undoubtedly are, embedded in
Comus. Like the Lady, Browne's first and chief heroine, Marina,
wanders alone, tracing (in her case literally) 'huge Forests, and un-
harbour'd Heaths Infamous Hills, and sandy perilous wildes', and at
the beginning of her wanderings has to defend not indeed her chastity,
but her constancy, in argument, and does so with a firmness comparable
with that of the Lady. Milton's first annotation, moreover, is made in
reference to the River God's speech at the beginning of the second
song of the Pastorals, Book I. Marina, having tried to commit suicide,
has been taken unconscious by the God out of the river, where he now
contemplates her beauty. At first, he sounds a little like Comus:

> This face, this haire, this hand so pure
> Were not ordain'd for nothing sure.
> Nor was it meant so sweet a breath
> Should be expos'd by such a death;
> But rather in some lovers brest
> Be given up . . .   (*B.P.*, I, sig. D3^r)

Then, as he wonders whether it has been a case of attempted murder,
he becomes more like the Elder Brother:

> No savage Beast can be so cruell
> To rob the earth of such a Iewell.
> Rather the stately Unicorne
> Would in his brest enraged scorne,
> That Maides committed to his charge
> By any beast in forrest large
> Should so be wronged. *Satyres* rude
> Durst not attempt, or ere intrude
> With such a minde the flowry balkes
> Where harmelesse virgines have their walkes.   (sig. D3^v)

Later, having decided to make her his own, he strikes his 'ruling wand'
upon his brook, to summon 'the watry Nymph' his sister, and together

they sing to awaken Marina from her sleep. Handed over to the Nymph's care, Marina thanks the God:

> may first
> (Quoth *Marine*) Swaines give Lambs to thee;
> And may thy floud have scignorie
> Of all flouds else; and to thy fame
> Meete greater Springs, yet keepe thy name.
> May never *Evet*, nor the *Toade*,
> Within thy Bankes make their abode! . . .
>
> But on thy Margent still let dwell
> Those flowres which have the sweetest smell.
> And let the dust upon thy strand
> Become like *Tagus* golden sand.   (sig. E2ᵛ–E3ʳ)

This reminds the reader of *Comus* of the Attendant Spirit's speech of thanks to Sabrina, and it seems likely that Milton's reading of Browne was at least one of the ingredients that went to the making of that episode.

Just occasionally too, Milton seems (like Keats later) to be unconsciously echoing phrases or cadences of Browne. When Comus's victims are said 'To roule with pleasure in a sensual stie', do they do so, I wonder, because Browne had written 'And wallowing lie within a sensuall sinke' (*B.P.*, I, sig. G1ʳ)? Or, when the Attendant Spirit calls himself to order with the words 'But to my task', is it an echo of Browne's

> But to the cause. *Great Goddesse* understand
> In *Mona* Ile thrust from the *Brittish* land . . .
>   (*B.P.*, II, sig. P4ʳ)

as the old shepherd puts Thetis 'in the picture' (as the Spirit does us) before a similar rescue-operation? Browne's phrase 'the brodred Vale', coupled as it is with an allusion to the 'sweet *Nightingale*', (*B.P.*, II, sig. G2ʳ), is also worth noting, in view of the Lady's

> By the violet imbroider'd vale
> Where the love-lorn Nightingale . . .

And it is just possible that Browne's fine line, 'Deckt with the riches of th'unsounded deepe'(*B.P.*, II, sig. B2ᵛ), is haunting Comus's answer to the Lady at 732–6. Certainly it harmonises well with it, both in thought and expression.

Milton's use of septasyllabics in the Attendant Spirit's epilogue may be an indication that Wither's praise of *Faire-Virtue* was in his mind here. Certainly the last lines of *Comus*, with their praise of virtue and their advice to her lovers:

> She can teach ye how to clime
> Higher then the Spheary chime,

are closer to Wither than to any other writer I can think of. Wither's poem did after all set out to show 'Virtue in her shape how lovely', and Milton may well have found it attractive. In some of his other works, Wither has the appearance of being a far-from-mute inglorious Milton, even a kind of parody of him. 'If ever an English poet . . . deemed himself a prophet . . . it was Milton,' wrote H. J. C. Grierson.[2] But this overlooks Wither. The similarity of their attitudes on this matter is indeed striking. 'But when God commands to take the trumpet and blow a dolorous or a jarring blast, it lies not in man's will what he shall say or what he shall conceal,' Milton writes. This is precisely Wither's justification of his outspokenness in *Britain's Re-membrancer* and elsewhere:

> Thy God hath toucht thy *Tongue*, and tipt thy Pen;
> And, therefore, feare not thou the face of men,
> Lest he destroy thee, . . .   (*B.R.*, p. 313)

and again,

> Take heed, therefore, that nothing thou refuse
> To utter, which he prompts unto thy *Muse*.   (p. 314)

Many of the criticisms his Muse is prompted to utter would have had all Milton's approval: of the lewdly-pampered luxury of the court; of 'dumb dogs' among the clergy; of shepherds who both fleece their sheep and leave them hungry. Where Wither differs from Milton,

[2] H. J. C. Grierson, *Milton and Wordsworth* (1937), 26.

however, as Mr. Allan Pritchard has finely argued, is in his failure to recognise, first, that in writing that claims to be poetry as well as prophecy, human art must be added to divine inspiration; and, secondly, that for religious and political polemics, prose is a more suitable medium than verse.[3] Too often Wither tries to achieve a sublimity like that of *Paradise Lost* (and believes that he has achieved it) with material more suited to the *Animadversions* or *Eikonoklastes*. On the other hand, he has one *prose* work where comparison with Milton is possible, and is damaging to neither. This is *The Schollers Purgatory* (1624), in which Wither states his case against the Stationers in his quarrel with them over the patent relating to his *Hymnes*. Wither writes here with a cogency and vigour and moral clarity approaching Milton's. As a personal apologia, it recalls some of the autobiographical passages of Milton's prose, especially when (for once) Wither insists on the *care* he took in the preparation of his *Hymnes:*

> I did not leape on a suddaine, or irreverently into this employment; but haveing consumed almost ye yeares of an Apprentisship, in studies of this kinde, I entred therinto conscionably and in the feare of God.   (*S.Purg*, p. 44–5)

His declarations of his trust in God, which owe much to the Psalmist (Wither is seeing himself as a second David), have a Miltonic ring too:

> He that hath showne me troubles will (as he hath often done) now also deliver me,   (p. 96)

and like Milton, he can be exalted and racy by turns:

> Yea, I vowe, all their great threats are but so many handfulls of dust cast into the wind; and all the mischeefe the whole body of their forces is yet able to bring about, cannot breake me of so much sleepe as one flea.   (p. 111)

In defending his translation of the Canticles he employs a similar argument to that Milton uses in the *Areopagitica*: 'sensuall men', he agrees, have abused the Canticles, but if we are *all* to be deprived because of this,

> the use of most thinges should be taken away; for, many men abuse their liberty in that which is most lawfull.   (p. 64)

---

[3] Allan Pritchard, *op. cit.*, 226.

This identity of view was not permanent, however; in *Haleluiah*, only three years before *Areopagitica*, Wither appears ready to carry the practice of licensing to the absurd lengths later ridiculed by Milton. 'It may soon be discovered,' he writes, 'that as well *Censores Canticum* as *Librorum* will be necessary in these times.'

Wither lacks the self-discipline and the governing intelligence to be finally comparable with Milton. Nevertheless, they share the same *ethos*, and their work touches in several areas.

But the longest-lasting of all Milton's Spenserian alliances was that with the Fletchers. There is nothing to suggest that he ever repudiated his early attraction to them, ever came to see their work as mere 'abominable fustian' or its equivalent. On the contrary, it continued to occupy a place in his imagination, becoming part of the store of literary experience upon which he drew when he created *Paradise Lost* and *Paradise Regained*. In the Satan of *Locustae* and *The Apollyonists* (one of the most dignified and heroic portrayals of the character before Milton's and certainly much nearer to the Satan of *Paradise Lost* than is the Satan of Milton's own 'In quintum Novembris'), Milton could have found most of the qualities – hatred, pride, envy, courage, defiance – that appear in his own Satan. The several 'great consults' that take place in Phineas Fletcher's poem also anticipate his – those of *Paradise Regained* as well as of *Paradise Lost*. The tone of these 'consults', as conveyed in the speeches of Abaddon or Equivocus as well as of Lucifer, is the tone of Milton's – forceful, sardonic, and (again) defiant. If we did not know their respective dates, we should probably accuse Fletcher of writing Miltonic pastiche:

> But me, oh never let me, Spirits, forget
> That glorious day, when I your standard bore,
> And scorning in the second place to sit,
> With you assaulted heaven, his yoke forswore.   (*Ap.*, I, 31)

>   . . . his fiery eye,
> Much swol'ne with pride, but more with rage, and hate . . .
>   (I, 18)
>   . . . a dusky cloud
> Hangs on his brow; his eyes fierce lightnings shroud . . .   (IV, 6)

Fletcher's Virgilian aspirations are here worth recalling: they, and the fact that he is paraphrasing a poem of his own written originally in Latin, make his verse at times syntactically similar to Milton's.

Phineas Fletcher is also remembered for having given Milton the germ of his idea for the allegory of Sin and Death. 'The Porter to th'infernall gate is Sin,' writes Fletcher,

> A shapelesse shape, a foule deformed thing,
> Nor nothing, nor a substance.   (I, 10)

Milton keeps the idea of a 'shape', but transfers most of its shapelessness to his other shadowy figure, Death, (not in Fletcher). His Sin, like Fletcher's,

> seem'd Woman to the waste, and fair,
> But ended foul.   (P.L., II, 650–1)

Yet the foulness does not take the same form. Milton's Sin ends as a serpent; of Fletcher's we are told that her 'back parts' were horrible, though the exact nature of the horror is left vague. Fletcher is following Spenser's Duessa, Milton, Spenser's Error. Milton is emphasising sheer ugliness, and kinship with evil; Fletcher, deceit. Thus while Fletcher's creation, though interesting, remains within the bounds of allegory, Milton's exceeds those bounds and acquires an independent, supernatural existence. It is an interesting example of the transmuting imagination of genius in action, working upon inferior material and reshaping it to its own ends.

It was not only their Spenserian allegory that Milton found congenial in the Fletchers. The baroque qualitites in his own work suggest another kind of response – an enthusiastic response to the apocalyptic elements in them both, to the lurid violence of Phineas and to the sparkling transcendence of Giles. Verbal echoes (for example, the 'christall doores' of Christs Victorie, and Triumph, IV, 15, recalled in Paradise Regained) suggest that Milton's imagination has responded especially to the starry, the heavenly parts of Giles's poem – not surprisingly, since they are the best parts of it. Christs Victorie, and Triumph is recalled not only in the Nativity hymn, in such figures as 'the meek-eyd Peace ... With Turtle wing the amorous clouds dividing'; not only in the scenes between tempter and tempted in the Wilderness; but also wherever 'globes' of angels appear, in the 'Globe of circular light' of the Nativity hymn (stanza XI), in the 'Globe of fierie Seraphim' who surround Satan (*P.L.*, II, 512), and above all in the 'fiery Globe Of Angels on full sail of wing', who at the end of *Paradise Regained* carry the Saviour through the air to a 'flowry valley' where 'a table of Celestial Food' awaits him.

Drayton is the only one of the Spenserians to leave, apparently, no particular stamp upon the work of Milton. And yet the sympathies between him and Milton are perhaps the profoundest of all. For, standing between Milton and Spenser, below them and yet of their company, Drayton shares their vision, large, comprehensive, rapturous and sane, of the poet's nature and the poet's function in society. 'These abilities . . . are the inspired gift of God rarely bestowed . . . and are of power beside the office of a pulpit to inbreed and cherish in a great people the seeds of virtue and public civility.' That is Milton's faith, as it is Spenser's and Drayton's. Drayton gave more attention to 'Warrs, hitherto the onely Argument Heroic deem'd' than Milton did, but he too learnt 'the better fortitude Of Patience', if not of heroic martyrdom, and learnt it as an ageing poet in an alien society, with difficulties, if not with dangers, encompassed round.

All the Spenserians somewhere in their verse address God directly, invoking His aid, or that of the Holy Spirit, or the Heavenly Muse. In this they are Bartasian. Milton wrote in the same tradition. Drayton's address at the beginning of *Noahs Floud* may be taken as typical:

> Eternall and all-working God, which wast
> Before the world, whose frame by thee was cast, . . .
>
> My mighty Maker, O doe thou infuse
> Such life and spirit into my labouring Muse,
> That I may sing (what but from *Noah* thou hid'st)
> The greatest thing that ever yet thou didst
> Since the Creation; that the world may see
> The Muse is heavenly, and deriv'd from thee.
> O let thy glorious Angell which since kept
> That gorgeous *Eden*, where once *Adam* slept;
> When tempting *Eve* was taken from his side,
> Let him great God not onely be my guide,
> But with his fiery Faucheon still be nie,
> To keepe affliction farre from me, that I
> With a free soule thy wondrous workes may show . . .

Milton developed far beyond the Spenserians, but among his English contemporaries, their work provided the soil out of which he grew.

The great want of the Spenserian poets, made all the more obvious through their imitation of Spenser, is creative power. This keeps them in the rank of minor poets, even though they are all capable of writing so well on occasion as to make the distinction between 'major' and 'minor', if not meaningless, at least temporarily irrelevant. In following Spenser, there is much that they cannot do, and much that they do not try to do. Thus although they imitate his moral allegory (Browne and the Fletchers especially), they cannot animate their moral figures as Spenser animates his. They have considerable pictorial powers: Phineas Fletcher's figures in *The Purple Island* especially are well-drawn, clear, and vivid. But they remain static, iconographic, having, at most, the kind of life represented in Spenser by the Seven Deadly Sins or the procession of the Seasons. Browne's Spenser-derived personages are more free-ranging, but have no vitality. Giles Fletcher has more of Spenser's ability to convey moral meanings by the use of detail that is both evocative and significant, as is seen in his portrayals of Justice and Mercy, for example. But nowhere in these writers do we find the psychological sympathies and insights that humanise the allegories of Spenser. 'The heart of a phantom is beating!' may be the astonished response to many of Spenser's figures. It never could be to those of his followers.

Their (perhaps instinctive) choice of passages for imitation tends on the whole to de-humanise Spenser, the Spenser of *The Faerie Queene* at any rate. Their primary allegiance is to Colin – to the pastoral poet, but also simply to the poet as he appears in his poems, rather than to the poems themselves. This devotion is founded partly on 'human interest': they enjoy receiving Colin's confidences concerning his experiences in love and art, and they reproduce such confidences in their own work. For *The Shepheardes Calender* they feel delighted affection, for *The Faerie Queene* perhaps rather awed admiration. Probably they know instinctively that the latter is beyond their powers of reproduction; that its secret is one that will never be given up. At any rate, they never get near the heart of it. They imitate certain outstanding passages – Despair, Acrasia, Belphœbe – in a kind of craving to have them again. Their choice tends to reduce Spenser's individuality, either by making him appear more Ovidian that he is, and hence closer to Marlowe and the other Elizabethans (this is the effect particularly of *Brittain's Ida*), or by giving undue prominence to one mediaeval strain in him through the artificial isolation of the elements of psychomachia, as in Browne's allegory of Truth and Riot, or generally in *The Purple Island*. Spenser's mediaeval world as a world – the chivalric background and action that connect him with Malory – they reject completely. Even Drayton, who must have had most sympathy with it, creates in his own verse a historic Middle Ages, a world of affairs, not of romantic adventures. The knights of *The Purple Island* are merely fighters, not questing knights (they are at a siege). They are not part of the world they live in, as are Spenser's personages: the island so elaborately described in the first part of the poem is never ranged over in action. And all the Spenserians are alike in their neglect of Spenser's first heroine, Una. Hidden more, perhaps, by her nun's habit than by her veil, her demure beauty passes them by, and with it both the radiance of Spenser's vision and the depth of his human sympathies.

Yet, as I have tried to show, the Spenserians cannot be valued or understood solely in terms of their relationship to Spenser. Spenser was to them a source of inspiration and a model. Their most direct and obvious imitations of him were probably always more satisfying to themselves than to the reader, although contemporaries seem to have admired them for their imitative skill itself. More significant, and to us more valid, are those parts of their work where they have borrowed from Spenser, not the substance, but the mode; have learned his method and then proceeded to practise it in their own way. This is the case with, for example, Drayton's wonderful description of the interior of Mortimer's Tower (*Barons Warres*, VI): this, though without Spenser's inspiration it would perhaps never have come into being, is by no means a replica of Spenser's work. To a lesser extent, this is true also of Phineas Fletcher's allegorical figures in *The Apollyonists*: 'Error, a crooked swaine' may have a Spenserian pedigree, but he exists in his own right. Above all, this applies to the Spenserians' pastoral, where they do not merely reproduce Spenser's work, but develop creative hints and suggestions inherent in it. The Spenserians can never be explained *without* reference to Spenser. Although they had other models – Sidney, Marlowe and, above all, Du Bartas – he remains the most important formative influence upon them. His value for them, over and above what they learned from him consisted simply in being *there*: he was patron saint, guardian angel, to them, the element in which they moved, a standard of reference, a perpetual fountain or *Bonfont*, as he himself names the poet in *The Faerie Queene*, Book V. He enfranchises them as poets, makes them denizens of his kingdom, and they accordingly may be seen to 'hail and climb, golden in the heydays of his eyes' (to misappropriate Dylan Thomas). In that hailing and climbing they find out new games for themselves. Derivative, conventional, imitative as they are, the Spenserians paradoxically have a freshness of appeal that comes from their readiness to explore and experiment. They are not great poets, yet to know their work is to feel very close to one section of seventeenth-century literary life and at the same time to breathe a fresh air that brings with it suggestions of new developments to come.

Index